The ONE YEAR® BOOK OF DAILY WISDOM

365 meditations on Bible wisdom
you need to manage the demands of each day

TYNDALE HOUSE PUBLISHERS, INC.
CAROL STREAM, ILLINOIS

Visit Tyndale's exciting Web site at www.tyndale.com

TYNDALE and Tyndale's quill logo are registered trademarks of Tyndale House Publishers, Inc.

One Year is a registered trademark of Tyndale House Publishers, Inc.

The One Year Book of Daily Wisdom

Designed by Beth Sparkman

Published in 2002 as The One Year Book of Proverbs by Tyndale House Publishers, Inc., under ISBN 0-8423-5607-X.

The One Year Book of Daily Wisdom first published in 2006.

ISBN-13: 978-1-4143-1496-9
ISBN-10: 1-4143-1496-5

Printed in the United States of America

12 11 10 09 08 07 06
 7   6   5   4   3   2   1

INTRODUCTION

Welcome to *The One Year Book of Daily Wisdom*.

The book of Proverbs is one of the more difficult books in the Bible to read. It includes no stories and few explanations. It lacks flow. In fact, the proverbs weren't collected for reading, but for savoring.

In the book of Proverbs, God provides us with a training ground for biblical meditation. Most verses in Proverbs can stand alone. They are bite-sized portions of deep wisdom. Individual proverbs allow us to wrap our minds around a single profound idea and explore it through meditation. That is crucial. If we don't move beyond reading, Proverbs will never accomplish the mind-shaping and life-changing effect God intended it to have on us.

So, what is biblical meditation?

Years ago, Billy Graham and others promoted a wonderful idea for developing systematic Bible reading. As part of a larger plan of study, Mr. Graham pointed to the happy coincidence between the thirty-one chapters of Proverbs and the number of days in a month. He revealed a personal practice of reading each day the chapter of Proverbs that corresponded to that particular day of the month. Thousands have discovered the wisdom of that approach. It creates a familiarity with the book of Proverbs that leads to meditation and application.

Biblical meditation begins when the Scriptures have taken residence in our minds. We can meditate on what we have just read, but we can meditate more productively if we have read a passage enough times that we have memorized it. If you have meditated just once on a passage of God's Word, you have only begun to delve into the depths you will eventually discover if you persist. Meditation improves with repeated exposure!

The One Year Book of Daily Wisdom allows you to practice this discipline. It assumes that you will read the chapter of Proverbs for the day. Then, each day, a single proverb will be lifted for closer examination.

As a way of broadening the scope of your thinking, and as an occasional change of pace, we have included some proverbs spoken by Jesus and others in Scripture that deserve our special attention. They are a way of learning and meditating on proverbial sayings that can be found throughout the Bible.

The principle of *repetition* in meditation will be illustrated by one reading per month that will focus on Mark 12:29-31: "Jesus replied, 'The most important commandment is this: "Listen, O Israel! The LORD our God is the one and only LORD. And you must love the LORD your God with all your heart, all your soul, all your mind, and all your strength." The second is equally important: "Love your neighbor as yourself." No other commandment is greater than these.'" Twelve visits throughout the year to these same verses will not exhaust the wealth of spiritual riches in what could be called "The Greatest Proverb."

If *The One Year Book of Daily Wisdom* has the desired effect, you will have an increased sense of confidence as you meditate on God's Word. And if God's Word has its desired effect on you, as a result your life will be transformed. May you discover the truth of Psalm 1:2 and become a person whose life demonstrates the components of joyful living: "But they delight in the law of the LORD, meditating on it day and night."

How to get the most out of *The One Year Book of Daily Wisdom:*

If you skipped the Introduction, go back and read it!

Keep this book with your Bible, so you can read the chapter of Proverbs for the day. You should know that the quoted proverbs in *The One Year Book of Daily Wisdom* come from the New Living Translation of the Bible.

Keep a notebook with this book so you can record insights that come as you meditate on individual proverbs throughout the year.

Note in your Bible individual proverbs that have struck you on particular days. Some have found it helpful to put the date in the margin next to the proverb and two or three words to jog their memories about the personal significance of that proverb.

Don't beat yourself up if you miss a day of reading occasionally. Don't try to catch up; just pick up at the current day's reading. Persistence will develop into a habit.

JANUARY 1

How would a wiser version of you look and act differently? The book of Proverbs promises to provide wisdom. The first six verses list at least fifteen aspects of wise living that can be gained through a continuous exposure to the book. Today's highlight verse aims at three areas of instruction: discipline, successful lives, and actions characterized as right, just, and fair.

The three areas of instruction have to do primarily with outward behavior. Discipline involves positive habits that demonstrate self-control. Successful lives covers those situations in which we work with others, making sure our participation promotes goodness. Wisdom also learns to manage the fine balance between right, just, and fair actions.

We must be instructed into wisdom. It does not come naturally. That is why the quality of our wisdom will always depend on the source of our wisdom. If God has instructed us, our wisdom will be genuine.

A WORD FOR TODAY
Practice right, just, and fair actions today.

Dear Lord, help me to recognize that you are the ultimate source of all wisdom and that I can count on you to instruct me.

Read
Proverbs 1

WISDOM
IN ACTION
Their purpose is to teach people to live disciplined and successful lives, to help them do what is right, just, and fair.
Proverbs 1:3

JANUARY 2

**Read
Proverbs 2**

🦅

WISE HERITAGE

*My child, listen
to what I say,
and treasure
my commands.
Tune your ears to
wisdom, and
concentrate on
understanding.*
Proverbs 2:1-2

Kids mimic. One of the unavoidable realities of raising children involves seeing ourselves in their actions. They pick up words, tones, and habits from us. What parents haven't experienced the shock of hearing a familiar expression or seeing a certain mannerism from their children only to realize that the children are mimicking them!

Unfortunately, children don't always choose the most flattering characteristics to mimic. We want them to do as we say, not as we do. They will tend to do what we do rather than what we say, and at the worst possible times. They have an uncanny way of publicizing our contradictions by imitating what we want to hide.

We live wisely before our children when what we do matches what we say. If our doing and our saying are the same and good, it doesn't matter which one they mimic. When we are inconsistent, forcing our children to choose whether to imitate our words or our actions, we do them a great disservice. We can't really expect them to treasure what we don't think is valuable enough to demonstrate by our lives.

A WORD FOR TODAY
Walk what you talk.

*Dear Lord, help me to be an example of consistency
before others so that even my failures become good
lessons for them as I depend on you for forgiveness.*

JANUARY 3

What connection can we find between loyalty and kindness that would cause them to be the subject of Solomon's solemn thought? They are qualities that require both internal (heart) and external (necklace) evidence in order to be true. Loyalty and kindness may be faked—for a while. The context indicates that Solomon was thinking of character traits that create a solid relationship between a person and God as well as between that person and others. The very next proverb says, "Then you will find favor with both God and people, and you will earn a good reputation" (Proverbs 3:4). A good way to remember the principle of this proverb relies on a version of an old saying: "When it comes to loyalty and kindness, you may be able to fool people part of the time, but you will fool God none of the time."

The phrase "Never let loyalty and kindness leave you" also deserves attention. Neither kindness nor loyalty fits as an automatic or permanent trait. They are hard won and easily lost. Both require continual practice with people and before God.

A WORD FOR TODAY
Keep a promise.

Dear Lord, help me see the opportunities you offer me to keep loyalty and kindness fresh in my life today.

**Read
Proverbs 3**

MORE THAN
SKIN DEEP
*Never let loyalty
and kindness leave
you! Tie them
around your neck
as a reminder. Write
them deep within
your heart.*
Proverbs 3:3

JANUARY 4

Read
Proverbs 4

WISDOM R & D
Get wisdom; develop
good judgment.
Don't forget my
words or turn
away from them.
Don't turn your
back on wisdom,
for she will
protect you. Love
her, and she will
guard you.
Proverbs 4:5-6

Businesses that want to survive and succeed must invest in research and development. Money, personnel, and time make up that investment. A company unwilling to improve on even good products will · quickly find that others will eagerly step in to profit from making better versions of the same things.

Daily life tests wisdom. Yesterday's insight may help face the first of today's problems but fall short on the second. Every day allows us to apply what we have already learned and to engage in fresh research and development for tomorrow. We "get wisdom" and "develop good judgment" as we acknowledge our lack of wisdom and our poor judgments. Part of each day's investment will involve the mistakes and errors that lead to wisdom. That wisdom grows as we remember and don't turn away from God's words. We love wisdom when we realize she always has more to teach us.

A WORD FOR TODAY
Invest in wisdom.

Dear Lord, help me to love your Word today as I seek
to practice wisdom.

JANUARY 5

Appearances offer tempting deceptions. Whether they come in the form of a thin coating of ice on a deep pond or an enticing cover on a book, what we see often doesn't turn out to be what we get. The first few steps may seem secure enough and the first pages may seem harmless, but the end results chill the body and soul. The writer of this proverb understood that character counts more than appearance.

Proverbs offers truth without subtlety. The sweetest kiss can't make up for a dark heart. Sweetness and smoothness tend to be temporary—poisons and swords cause permanent damage. The poison of immorality leaves relationships ruined and trust severed. Those who cannot see beyond their momentary needs and wants will discover the painful consequences of their shortsighted decisions.

A WORD FOR TODAY
Think beyond appearance.

Dear Lord, help me to think twice about your truth rather than looking twice at temptation.

Read
Proverbs 5

THIN ICE!
The lips of an immoral woman are as sweet as honey, and her mouth is smoother than oil. But in the end she is as bitter as poison, as dangerous as a double-edged sword.
Proverbs 5:3-4

JANUARY 6

HANDCUFFS

*My child, if you
have put up security
for a friend's debt or
agreed to guarantee
the debt of a
stranger—if you
have trapped
yourself by your
agreement and are
caught by what you
said—follow my
advice and save
yourself, for you
have placed yourself
at your friend's
mercy. Now swallow
your pride; go and
beg to have your
name erased.*

Proverbs 6:1-3

Scams, disappointments, and financial ruin often begin with misplaced trust. What does the requirement of a cosigner or guarantor indicate right away? It tells you that someone who handles money for a living doesn't consider the primary signer fully able or willing to pay the debt. They need a third person to share the risk—and if you sign on the dotted line, then you are putting yourself at risk. If the person for whom you cosign a debt defaults on the loan, then you become responsible for that person's debt. Have you anticipated what it will take to pay the debt yourself? The proverb recognizes how easy it is to fall into these commitments. Better to avoid them—at all costs!

In other words, if you would hesitate or be unable to give or loan this "friend" the money, then why would you want to place yourself in a position of being responsible for the debt by cosigning? A genuine friendship represents too valuable an item ever to be equated with money or real estate. Those who trade on your friendship do not have your best interest in mind.

A WORD FOR TODAY
Consider before committing.

*Dear Lord, if a friend has a genuine need, give me
wisdom to help him/her find a responsible way to
meet that need.*

JANUARY 7

The decision to follow Jesus may begin as a simple choice, but following the Lord daily will not be easy. He never said it would be. In fact, Jesus' statements often show us how far we have to go. For example, we seldom succeed in loving our neighbors, which Jesus took as the expected starting point from which to love our enemies. We ask, "Lord, how can I call them enemies and love them?" To which God answers, "Now you get my point!"

Forget about differentiating between neighbors and enemies. Simply start next door. Who lives there? How well do you know them? What are their needs? What specific action could you take (have them over for a meal, help them with a project, pray for them, return with gratitude something you've borrowed and kept for too long, etc.) that would be an expression of love for them? Carry out that action in the next several days.

A WORD FOR TODAY
Love doesn't discriminate.

Dear Lord, help me love my neighbor _____
in some specific way this week.

Read
Proverbs 7

UNHEALTHY DISCRIMINA-TION
You have heard the law that says, "Love your neighbor" and hate your enemy. But I say, love your enemies! Pray for those who persecute you!
Matthew 5:43-44

JANUARY 8

Read
Proverbs 8

🖙

CRYSTAL CLEAR

My words are plain to anyone with understanding, clear to those with knowledge.

Proverbs 8:9

First, to whose "words" does this proverb refer? This chapter is one of the few in Proverbs dedicated entirely to one specific theme. Wisdom speaks throughout the chapter. She states the case for her own trustworthiness.

This particular proverb offers two healthy perspectives on wisdom. It states that wisdom belongs to people who have already gained wisdom (understanding). The more wisdom they gain, the more wisdom seems plain—the plain truth. Wisdom also grows in those with knowledge, those who can make the logical connections between what they know and how they should act.

This could be called the before-and-after experience of wisdom. Knowledge leads to wisdom, which leads to greater understanding. As understanding grows, further wisdom stands out in plain sight. A passion for wisdom leads to wisdom, which in turn leads to even more wisdom.

Wisdom advertises results. She challenges people to take her up on her promise.

A WORD FOR TODAY
Wisdom grows.

Dear Lord, fill me with that unquenchable thirst to know you, the source of all wisdom.

JANUARY 9

This is just the kind of parable that provokes a meditation question: Why seven columns? Do they represent seven principles, or seven characteristics of wisdom? Throughout history there have been numerous and ingenious efforts to identify each of the seven columns. Though interesting, the explanations haven't been persuasive.

The proverb itself offers few clues. Other proverbs that mention numbers usually do so to introduce a list. See, for example, Proverbs 6:16-19; 30:15-16, 18-19, 21-23. The verses that immediately follow 9:1 include other actions that Wisdom has set into motion: She prepared a great banquet (v. 2), and she sent servants to invite and broadcast the same invitation over the city (v. 3). Clearly, the writer was using figurative language.

The tone of this proverb conveys the idea that Wisdom is an expansive host. Her house is spacious and complete. The only thing she lacks is enough guests to take advantage of her invitation. How often have you visited Wisdom's house?

A WORD FOR TODAY
Live in Wisdom's house.

Dear Lord, allow me to make good use of the wisdom you have already provided to me, and keep me alert for more.

Read
Proverbs 9

UNDER CON-
STRUCTION
Wisdom has built her house; she has carved its seven columns.
Proverbs 9:1

JANUARY 10

BIODEGRADABLE REPUTATION

We have happy memories of the godly, but the name of a wicked person rots away.
Proverbs 10:7

The people in Old Testament times had a high regard for the value of a person's name. Names carried with them special significance. In a culture of verbal agreements, where a promise carried the weight of a binding contract, a person's name represented his character.

Certain names remind us of people long dead who have left an indelible mark on history, or on us. Other names receive mention only when they serve to illustrate a negative lesson. The first group seems to grow in value over the years, but the second seems to fade, or as the text says, "rots away." The application of this proverb becomes a pointed question about life: What will the mention of our names bring to people's minds after we have died?

A WORD FOR TODAY
Leave a godly legacy.

Dear Lord, thank you for the people who give me happy memories. Allow me to keep their example in mind as I live my life.

JANUARY 11

We tend to think of God as a reactor rather than a responder. Because God is good, he reacts to anything that disturbs his normal pattern. However, this view of God seriously diminishes our capacity to appreciate God's divine delight over good.

We know God delights because we know he delights in his own work. After each day's worth of the creation masterpieces, God didn't summarize his effort with the resounding declaration, "This is normal!" No, God's delight must have reverberated through every fiber of his expanding creation when he thundered, "This is good!" Six times in the first chapter of Genesis we are told that God saw his creation as good. By the end of the sixth day, God concluded that his work was excellent in every way (Genesis 1:31). God responds to good with delight.

God desires to delight in us. He does this partly, this proverb tells us, when we practice honesty. The test of honesty comes when we are tempted to think what we do doesn't matter because no one is watching. But we *always* have an audience. Does God delight in what we do?

A WORD FOR TODAY
Offer God delight each day.

Dear Lord, help me live this day with a constant recognition that you enjoy the good in my life even more than I do.

**Read
Proverbs 11**

GOD DELIGHTS
The LORD detests the use of dishonest scales, but he delights in accurate weights.
Proverbs 11:1

JANUARY 12

THANKS!
I NEEDED THAT

*To learn, you must
love discipline; it is
stupid to hate
correction.*
Proverbs 12:1

In one sense, this proverb describes two different types of people: those who learn, and those who refuse to learn. The first, the learners, understand and accept the necessity of discipline as part of the learning process. The second, the refusers, ignore and reject correction. The learners decide to love discipline; the refusers decide to hate anything and everything that might offer a good lesson. The learners grow in wisdom; the refusers sink into stupidity.

Both types of people may be dealing with the same experience, for discipline and correction often take the same form. For example, both the learners and those who refuse to learn can make the same mistake. When it is pointed out to the first, they appreciate the correction and adjust their actions. Meanwhile, the second resent the correction and often refuse to change their ways.

Love or hatred for discipline can be claimed anytime, but the proof comes when discipline occurs. How we respond demonstrates whether we have made the wise choice to learn or the wrong choice to remain foolish.

A WORD FOR TODAY
Learn tenaciously.

*Dear Lord, please remind me today that when I make
my next mistake I have also created a good opportunity
to learn. Help me love that!*

JANUARY 13

Adults who know how to practice loving discipline are grown-up versions of children who have been wisely trained. The cycle or process begins with an adult. Until discipline is offered, a child has no choice between acceptance and refusal. The earlier in life that loving discipline is offered, the greater a child's opportunity to develop wisdom.

Both the wise child and the mocker are the products of training. Mockery is a form of disrespect that must be confronted early in life. Someone who is young and a mocker has not benefited from early discipline. Perhaps the child's capacity to make fun of others was considered cute. Eventually that skill becomes an ingrained habit. Such a youth has become so accustomed to disrespecting others through mockery that he or she finds it almost impossible to listen.

Children aren't born wise. It takes loving and courageous discipline to teach them wisdom. When that isn't given, mockery and other natural evidences of sin take over. Wise parents seek help from God and his Word every step of this process.

A WORD FOR TODAY
Accept correction.

Dear Lord, forgive my own parents' failures and thank you for their successes. Help me to benefit from all the past by learning and applying wisdom.

Read
Proverbs 13

WELCOMED
DISCIPLINE
*A wise child
accepts a parent's
discipline; a mocker
refuses to listen
to correction.*
Proverbs 13:1

JANUARY 14

Read Proverbs 14

☞

BOTTOM LINE

Jesus replied, "The most important commandment is this: 'Listen, O Israel! The LORD our God is the one and only LORD. And you must love the LORD your God with all your heart, all your soul, all your mind, and all your strength.' The second is equally important: 'Love your neighbor as yourself.' No other commandment is greater than these."

Mark 12:29-31

What really matters? What's up? What's the bottom line? When all is said and done, what has to be said and done? The questions may sound different, but they all express in one way or another the common, deep-rooted desire in people to know that their lives mean something.

Jesus had an answer for the man who had asked him a question. It had two parts, or dimensions: the vertical (our love for God) and the horizontal (our love for people, including ourselves). Every other true rule for living falls under the summary that Jesus gave.

Because Mark 12:29-31 encapsulates this central proverb and key commandment, we will return to it in one reading each month. If Jesus said something was the most important statement of wisdom, we can expect to gain great benefit from giving it our repeated attention.

A WORD FOR TODAY

The greatest proverb—"Love God."

Dear Lord, teach me to consider important what you consider important. Keep me from distractions that focus my attention on what is not important.

The wisdom in this proverb can be found in the volume and the tone of our responses to anger. We know that some of the harshest, anger-provoking words can be spoken very quietly. Sometimes it takes a shouted "I love you!" to move an argument in a better direction. The tone, or character, of our responses—more than their volume—determines the outcome of a tense exchange.

Wise listeners pay attention to both words and tone. Sometimes a person's angry words and tone are justified. The gentleness of an answer doesn't necessarily eliminate the anger; it deflects it so that truth can be discovered. Meanwhile, harsh or thoughtless words not only create angry responses but often intensify anger that is already present.

Godly wisdom seeks to respond gently because it places a higher value on truth than on the particular wrapping of words and tone. Gentleness unwraps the feelings and expressions to find the truth.

A WORD FOR TODAY
Authentic power includes gentleness.

Dear Lord, help me learn to affect people for you by listening to both their words and their tone and by answering them gently.

Read
Proverbs 15

DEFLECTING ANGER

A gentle answer deflects anger, but harsh words make tempers flare.
Proverbs 15:1

JANUARY 16

**Read
Proverbs 16**

❧

BEYOND
PREPARATION
*We can make our
own plans, but
the LORD gives
the right answer.*
Proverbs 16:1

One of the exciting evidences of a personal relationship with God occurs when he supplies us with an
answer we know didn't originate with us. Preparation, or gathering our thoughts, puts us in the best
position to recognize God's answers. But preparation does not eliminate our need for God to supply
answers. The value of good preparation comes from
the way it disciplines our heart and mind to respond
to God's direction.

There are two challenges behind this proverb.
The first involves our willingness to do our best at
preparation. The second involves our willingness
to rely on God before, during, and after we have
prepared. The discipline of studying these proverbs
day by day represents significant preparation for
wise living. But the appropriate application of that
wisdom comes with God's help. We must not forget
the stunning truth that the wise collector of these
sayings failed in many ways to rely on God. Solomon
received many right answers, but he didn't put some
of them into practice. Gathering wisdom doesn't
automatically mean we are living wisely.

A WORD FOR TODAY
Thought precedes but doesn't replace trust.

*Dear Lord, please allow me to put into practice today
a wise insight you have supplied in your Word.*

JANUARY 17

Impurities cannot be removed from silver and gold until the costly metals have been melted. Heat causes the liquid state that allows the impurities to rise to the surface, where they can be skimmed off. When a precious metal has been purified, *tried* and *tested* are some of the terms used to describe it.

So, how does God test a heart? He melts it. He allows it to suffer unprovoked difficulties, as well as the consequences of poor decisions, in order to bring "heat" into our lives.

The smelting process provides an excellent illustration of the word *repentance*. Repentant people have a molten heart. Repentance brings the impurities of the heart to the surface where they can be confessed and burned away by forgiveness. At the same time, a molten heart can be re-formed. A repentant attitude describes people whose central motivations reach a state that allows God to continually reshape them so they will be useful for God's kingdom. Effective repentance eventually leads to humility. Genuine humility describes a person continually willing to be cleansed and reshaped by God.

A WORD FOR TODAY
Welcome the heat.

Dear Lord, I give you permission to melt down those parts of my heart that are hard, so that I can be more purely yours.

Read
Proverbs 17

BENEFICIAL
MELTDOWN
Fire tests the purity of silver and gold, but the LORD tests the heart.
Proverbs 17:3

JANUARY 18

Read
Proverbs 18

VERBAL
REFRESHMENT

Wise words are
like deep waters;
wisdom flows from
the wise like a
bubbling brook.
Proverbs 18:4

Did Jesus have this proverb in mind as he watched
the woman approach the well in Samaria (John 4:6)?
Perhaps. He told her that his words were life-giving
water (John 4:14). Did Jesus' conversation with the
woman at the well have the refreshing effect promised in this proverb? It certainly did.

What a transformation! The woman went from
being the town outcast to being an outspoken evan-
gelist. Her message? "Come and see a man who told
me everything I ever did! Could he possibly be the
Messiah?" (John 4:29). Jesus' words had shown her
that he really knew her and her needs. They also
conveyed his care and his ability to meet her needs.
She became a "bubbling brook" that drew others to
taste Jesus' life-giving water (John 4:39-42). We can
have the same effect on others as we experience
daily intimacy with Jesus.

A WORD FOR TODAY
Drink wisdom.

Dear Lord, I know that my words will not have a life-
giving and refreshing effect on others unless they come
from you. Please fill me with such words.

JANUARY 19

The comparison in this proverb may catch the reader by surprise. Why doesn't the second line read "rich and dishonest"? Good question! Although we might tend to jump to the conclusion that riches and poverty automatically sit at opposite ends of any spectrum, the truth resides in the fact that wealth and poverty can be the companions of any number of character traits. For everyone who is rich and dishonest, there is probably someone who is poor and dishonest.

This proverb points out that poverty and honesty are not inseparable. Someone who is poor and honest is wealthy by comparison to someone who is a fool and dishonest, for the latter does not appreciate the depth of his poverty. Dishonest fools, whether rich or poor, are good for little more than to serve as negative examples. Meanwhile, the poor who are honest offer some of the best examples of genuine wisdom to the world. They accomplish a lot with little, and often work their way right out of poverty.

A WORD FOR TODAY
Honesty is a priceless commodity.

Dear Lord, help me to see and be honest about areas of poverty in my life. I desire to experience how you supply where I lack. Thank you!

Read
Proverbs 19

WORSE THAN POVERTY
Better to be poor and honest than to be dishonest and a fool.
Proverbs 19:1

JANUARY 20

Read
Proverbs 20

PICKING FIGHTS OR PICKING YOUR FIGHTS

*Avoiding a fight is
a mark of honor;
only fools insist
on quarreling.*
Proverbs 20:3

This proverb does not deny the fact that conflict may be necessary. Rather, it challenges those who go out of their way to create conflict. It also turns upside down the typical attitude that honor is best defended by eagerness to fight. Honor doesn't "insist on quarreling" in order to prove itself.

The wise person pictured in this proverb learns to see a fight coming. Such a person knows that a fight may demonstrate who is stronger more often than it demonstrates who is right. Thus, fighting may not move the parties any closer to a resolution. Hostilities may bury the truth more deeply. It is better, and more honorable, to seek the truth before a fight breaks out.

Quarreling usually turns out to be an attempt to verbally defeat an opponent by superior volume, threat, or insult. Rarely does quarreling have to do with the truth. Therefore, those who readily resort to quarreling reveal their foolishness, even if those doing so happen to be ourselves!

A WORD FOR TODAY
The wise don't quarrel.

*Dear Lord, I admit I can be foolish and quarrelsome.
I need your help to recognize this temptation when it
appears in my life.*

JANUARY 21

Jesus never hesitated to add sobering warnings to shocking announcements. In the preceding verses, he had informed his disciples plainly of his approaching execution and resurrection. Because they couldn't imagine what he meant by describing his own death, they didn't even consider what he meant by his prediction to be raised the third day.

Quickly rejecting Peter's insistence that Jesus' outlook was unacceptable, the Lord turned his attention to the disciples with the challenge in today's proverb. Note that his audience (the disciples) probably assumed that they were already his followers, but his words questioned that assumption. Jesus noted four characteristics of genuine disciples: (1) a disciple desires to follow; (2) a disciple sets aside self-centered plans, expectations, and schedules; (3) a disciple accepts (takes up, shoulders) the burdens associated with following Christ; and (4) a disciple actually does *follow* Christ.

A WORD FOR TODAY
Actually follow Jesus today.

Dear Lord, point out to me anything on my schedule today that is nothing more than selfish ambition. Please give me courage to put that aside and follow you.

**Read
Proverbs 21**

PREPARING FOR THE JOURNEY
Jesus said to his disciples, "If any of you wants to be my follower, you must turn from your selfish ways, take up your cross, and follow me."
Matthew 16:24

JANUARY 22

Read
Proverbs 22

REPUTATION
APPRAISAL
Choose a good
reputation over
great riches; being
held in high esteem
is better than silver
or gold.
Proverbs 22:1

Today's proverb offers us one practical application of yesterday's wise saying. Jesus spoke of the dangers of selfish ambition and challenged his disciples to have a godly ambition that intentionally seeks to please God, even to the point of bearing a cross (Matthew 16:24).

Here, godly ambition makes the choice between a good reputation and great riches. Both can be pursued, but only one has lasting value. Only one will prove itself ours beyond this life. Riches will stay behind, no matter what we sacrificed to gain them. Why should we choose what we will have to leave behind when we can choose something of eternal value?

Godly ambition aims high. Godly ambition sets its sights on living the kind of life that will create a good reputation with God. If that can be accomplished, everything else will fall into place. Ultimately, this great purpose in life becomes possible when we realize that God will actually help us gain his high esteem.

A WORD FOR TODAY
Practice godly ambition.

Dear Lord, help me to intentionally seek to make choices that please you. I want to have a good reputation with you!

JANUARY 23

The writer advises us not to weary ourselves trying to get rich because those riches have a way of disappearing. Like birds that fly to the bird feeder and just as quickly are gone, so money has a way of disappearing with a whisper of wings.

Who has not deposited the paycheck in the bank, only to wonder—a day later—where it all went? Even a windfall of wealth has the wings of a bird. Or we get that pay raise, but immediately raise our standard of living so that we still never have enough money. It seems to fly away.

The focus of life should never be riches, for that is a desire that will never be satisfied. Who ever says, "I have enough money; I don't need any more"? But if we can learn contentment with what we have, we will not be wearying ourselves going after riches only to watch them fly away.

A WORD FOR TODAY
Money is a mirage.

Dear Lord, help me not to focus on the wrong priorities but to learn contentment in you.

Read
Proverbs 23

BANKRUPT
EFFORT
Don't wear yourself out trying to get rich. Be wise enough to know when to quit. In the blink of an eye wealth disappears, for it will sprout wings and fly away like an eagle.
Proverbs 23:4-5

JANUARY 24

Read
Proverbs 24

🥀

WISE
DISCRIMINATION
Don't envy evil
people or desire
their company.
Proverbs 24:1

Sometimes evil does seem to triumph over good. Sometimes bad people win. Sometimes good guys finish last. Sometimes the wicked prosper while the good wonder. The implication of this proverb is that evil people may indeed have what we desire.

Unfortunately, the word *discrimination* has been twisted to carry primarily negative connotations. But discrimination has to do with our capacity to judge or weigh people and situations before entrusting ourselves to them. We may discriminate for the wrong reasons, but that doesn't invalidate the importance of that ability. We don't want our children to discriminate against people because of skin color, but we certainly want their capacity to discriminate in full force when a drug pusher or a peddler of immorality approaches them. Wise discrimination sizes up people for the right reasons. Wise discrimination allows us to spot people of character and make a point to associate with them. And wise discrimination warns us when to be cautious of certain people and avoid their company.

A WORD FOR TODAY
Good bait often hides an evil hook.

Dear Lord, I know how easy it is to envy those I shouldn't. Help me to wisely discriminate where I rest my emotions and desires.

JANUARY 25

Timing is almost as important as truth when it comes to advice. Hindsight may have the reputation for perfect vision, but it arrives too late to prevent a disaster. Even the best advice, given at the wrong time, may not be recognized. Timely advice is a lovely package with contents that we really need.

Effective counsel arrives at the right time. It is neither so early that it is forgotten when needed nor too late to be useful. The timing of advice is as much the evidence of wisdom as the contents of advice. Anyone can say, "Be careful," after their friend has already stubbed his toe. Timely advice says, "The last time I traveled this path, there were some roots that tripped me up. Let's be careful." Both statements are good advice, but timing makes the second one lovely.

A WORD FOR TODAY
Accept God's timing.

Dear Lord, I know that learning your wisdom is my responsibility, but I want to consciously depend on you for timing when I share it with anyone else.

**Read
Proverbs 25**

PERFECT
DELIVERY
Timely advice is lovely, like golden apples in a silver basket.
Proverbs 25:11

JANUARY 26

Read
Proverbs 26

SEASONS

Honor is no more
associated with
fools than snow
with summer or
rain with harvest.

Proverbs 26:1

Fools, summer, and harvest represent the givens in this proverb. Each one comes with a set of characteristics or expectations. In summer, we expect heat; at the harvest, cool weather. Snows don't fit with summer, and rains make a mess out of harvest. Likewise, when it comes to fools, honor is always out of season.

So what are the traits that accompany fools? To use the terms of this proverb, dishonor summarizes a foolish profile. Dishonor describes people who don't take responsibility for their decisions ahead of time so they can make them carefully, nor do they take responsibility for their mistakes and failures once they occur. Whenever we find ourselves surrounded by thoughtless decisions and excessive blaming, we can safely assume that a crop of fools has sprouted. The last thing we expect to find is honor. And if we expect to be people of honor ourselves, we won't go with them.

A WORD FOR TODAY
Foolishness sown never reaps honor.

Dear Lord, I give you permission to expose the foolishness in my life. Help me be a person in season when it comes to honor.

JANUARY 27

James, the brother of Jesus, penned one of the finest comments on the truth of this passage: "Look here, you who say, 'Today or tomorrow we are going to a certain town and will stay there a year. We will do business there and make a profit.' How do you know what your life will be like tomorrow? Your life is like the morning fog—it's here a little while, then it's gone. What you ought to say is, 'If the Lord wants us to, we will live and do this or that.' Otherwise you are boasting about your own plans, and all such boasting is evil. Remember, it is sin to know what you ought to do and then not do it" (James 4:13-17).

According to James, we don't ignore tomorrow. But we don't take it for granted either. Because God holds the future, we make plans based on his overriding will and wisdom. We don't know what will happen tomorrow, but we know and trust someone who does!

A WORD FOR TODAY
Live for God today; trust him with tomorrow.

Dear Lord, it is easy to presume on tomorrow—even on the rest of today. Help me to treasure each moment as a gift from you.

Read
Proverbs 27

FUTILE
FORECAST
Don't brag about tomorrow, since you don't know what the day will bring.
Proverbs 27:1

JANUARY 28

Read
Proverbs 28

THE
BEGINNING OF
GOD'S
BLESSINGS

*God blesses those
who are poor
and realize their
need for him, for
the Kingdom
of Heaven
is theirs.*
Matthew 5:3

As a way of highlighting some of the key proverbial statements that Jesus made, we will focus once a month on the Beatitudes. Most of them are found in the opening verses of the Sermon on the Mount (Matthew 5–7). For the purposes of these reflections, beatitudes are promises given by Jesus that attach God's blessing to a specific action or attitude on our part.

The sequence of the Beatitudes in the Sermon on the Mount describes the process of transformation that people experience when they pass from darkness to light, death to life, and separation from God to union with God.

The first beatitude describes those at the starting point: people who *realize their need* for God. They have stopped wondering *if* they need God; they *know* they do. They freely and honestly admit their deep spiritual poverty. There is no clearer, more life-changing moment of truth than when we acknowledge before God our utter spiritual bankruptcy and accept his grace. God blesses that conviction with a gift—the Kingdom of Heaven!

A WORD FOR TODAY
We never grow beyond needing God.

Dear Lord, today I acknowledge my poverty of spirit in the following ways: _____. Thank you for the freedom to approach you with my needs.

JANUARY 29

This proverb offers a healthy alternative to the drab life too many Christians take for granted. We avoid sin's traps too seldom and rejoice too little over our occasional escapes. We give far too much attention to discovering how close to sinful living we can come without becoming trapped. Meanwhile, we don't give nearly enough attention to the ways of escape that God has pledged to provide when we are tempted (1 Corinthians 10:12-13).

When was the last time you understood the danger of sin so clearly that you shouted for joy because you escaped? Have you cheered over today's close calls? Until avoiding sin becomes at least as exciting and thrilling as temptation itself, we won't know we are making much real progress toward righteousness.

A WORD FOR TODAY
Be suspicious of temptations.

Dear Lord, remind me to be more expressive over the victories you help me win when I escape one of sin's traps.

Read Proverbs 29

CHEERS
Evil people are trapped by sin, but the righteous escape, shouting for joy.
Proverbs 29:6

JANUARY 30

Read
Proverbs 30

IMPRESSIVE PANORAMA

Who but God goes up to heaven and comes back down? Who holds the wind in his fists? Who wraps up the oceans in his cloak? Who has created the whole wide world? What is his name—and his son's name? Tell me if you know!
Proverbs 30:4

When people understand events clearly, we often say that they "see the big picture." Today's highlighted proverb makes the point that the clearest view of the "big picture" will always include God. The sequence of rhetorical questions helps us consider the awesome identity and capacity of God. Much like the litany of questions that God showered on Job (Job 38:1–41:34), these push us toward humble and silent worship.

Agur was feeling overwhelmed (Proverbs 30:1), insignificant (30:2), and limited (30:3). But when he turned away from his own smallness to contemplate God's greatness, an atmosphere of confidence filled the rest of the chapter. He began with a little picture, no bigger than himself, but he soon looked at the big picture and forgot that he was weary and worn out. God gave him a new and refreshing point of view.

A WORD FOR TODAY
God will always be greater than we can imagine.

Dear Lord, when I look at all you have made, I know it makes me feel smaller, but it also fills me with wonder over how great you are! I worship you.

JANUARY 31

This proverb states a strong biblical antidote to the prevailing "mind your own business" mentality that cripples righteous living today. Yes, there are situations in which we shouldn't meddle. Those who can speak or fend for themselves do not necessarily *want* our help. Yet most of us are aware of children and others who cannot speak for themselves but are suffering injustice while those who could help do nothing. The size of the problem does not excuse our silence.

Twice this proverb directs us to "speak up." The problem for most Christians is not that we *can't* see things that are wrong or that we *can't* speak up. The problem is that we *won't* speak up. Why? We're intimidated, ashamed, or simply disobedient. If we're unwilling even to speak up, it is practically certain that we will also be unwilling to "see that they get justice." A warning from James that we read several days ago applies here just as well: "Remember, it is sin to know what you ought to do and then not do it" (James 4:17).

A WORD FOR TODAY
Speak up for those who can't.

Dear Lord, I realize my heart needs to be opened more than my eyes do. Help me speak up for those who can't defend themselves.

Read Proverbs 31

A TIME FOR SPEAKING UP
Speak up for those who cannot speak for themselves; ensure justice for those being crushed. Yes, speak up for the poor and helpless, and see that they get justice.
Proverbs 31:8-9

FEBRUARY 1

**Read
Proverbs 1**

A GOOD
BEGINNING

*Fear of the LORD
is the foundation
of true knowledge,
but fools despise
wisdom and
discipline.*
Proverbs 1:7

The Bible makes it clear that God is sovereign. In other words, he has total and complete authority. We, his creations, should indeed "fear" him—for he has ultimate power. Yet we also know from the Bible that God is loving, merciful, and compassionate. So we are not afraid of God; instead, our "fear" should be reverence and awe that an all-powerful, sovereign God would care to reach out to us. When we fear the Lord, we are beginning to have knowledge about what really matters for our lives, which creates an attitude open to wisdom.

Those who would turn away at the possibility of having true wisdom are called "fools." Such people despise what matters most, and therefore their lives are spent focusing on all the wrong priorities. God promises to give wisdom to all who ask (James 1:5). Let us fear the Lord so that he can teach us and make us wise.

A WORD FOR TODAY
Discover true fear.

Today, Lord, may I seek wisdom from you, knowing that you are the ultimate source of all wisdom and knowledge.

FEBRUARY 2

Some things are worth searching for, waiting for, and working for. If we lost a hundred dollar bill, we would probably turn the house upside down trying to find it. We would retrace our steps until we remembered where we had put it. In adventure stories, there is often a hidden treasure that both the good guys and the bad guys are intently seeking—even to the point of death. Most of the time, they don't know what the treasure holds; they just know *something* is there and they want to be the first to find it.

It is with such passion that we should search for "insight" and "understanding." These are as valuable as hidden treasure. Life is a mystery; so much is unclear. Our sovereign God will not give us all the answers, but he does promise a certain amount of insight and understanding that will help us through. To find him is to find the greatest treasure of all.

A WORD FOR TODAY
Search for the source of wisdom.

Today, Lord, may I seek you and the insight and understanding you give as I deal with the difficult and confusing situations in my life.

Read Proverbs 2

TREASURE HUNTING
Cry out for insight, and ask for understanding. Search for them as you would for silver; seek them like hidden treasures.
Proverbs 2:3-4

FEBRUARY 3

Read
Proverbs 3

WITH ALL
YOUR HEART
Trust in the LORD
with all your heart;
do not depend on
your own
understanding.
Proverbs 3:5

How much do we trust God, really? Do we relegate him only to the huge crises in our life, not wanting to bother him with the mundane problems? Or do we do the opposite—relegating him to the little problems, while we work through the big decisions on our own? What keeps us from trusting God with all our heart in *all* our situations?

To trust God with all our heart means to turn everything over to him so that he can guide us and direct our paths (3:6). Of course, we can still work through our problems logically. We have been told in Proverbs to cry out for understanding (2:3), so we do need it, but ultimately we do not depend on that understanding. Instead, we depend on God. When we trust in him, we have the final authority— the one who sees the big picture—helping us to take the next step along the path of life.

A WORD FOR TODAY
Understand what "all" means.

Today, Lord, teach me how to trust in you with all
my heart.

FEBRUARY 4

Jesus certainly had a way of boiling things down to the basics. He was surrounded with people who were experts at finding loopholes and exceptions in the law. But they were skilled at the art of overlooking the obvious, as Jesus pointed out a number of times. His description of people straining out gnats while swallowing camels (Matthew 23:23-24) may strike us as hilarious until we gag on the truth that he is talking about people like us.

The mouthful of reality in Jesus' joke points out our tendency to see ourselves as the exception. We want others to treat us as we deserve to be treated, but we balk at treating them the same way. We know what we want others to do for us, but doing the same for them is too much trouble. They might not reciprocate. The principle in this proverb, of course, is the risk involved in following Jesus. Common sense might tell us to see how others treat us so we will then know how to treat them. Jesus rejects that approach. He tells those who want to be his disciples that they must actively pursue treating people as they themselves want to be treated.

A WORD FOR TODAY
What goes around does come around.

Today, Lord, remind me not to wait until others do for me; help me do for them first.

Read
Proverbs 4

RISKING
KINDNESS
Do to others whatever you would like them to do to you. This is the essence of all that is taught in the law and the prophets.
Matthew 7:12

**Read
Proverbs 5**

A CROOKED
PATH

*Her feet go down
to death; her steps
lead straight to
the grave. For she
cares nothing
about the path
to life. She
staggers down a
crooked trail and
doesn't realize it.*

Proverbs 5:5-6

The immoral woman is a person who has turned
from godly paths toward pleasure, passion, and lust.
How apt is this chapter for today, for we don't need
to go much farther than the local newsstand or a
few clicks on the Internet to find plenty of immoral
women and men. The Bible is clear that to follow
these people's ways is a path to death, footsteps to
destruction. And so many people are tempted onto
that path—some who should know better, many
who don't.

God created sex within the confines of marriage
to be intimate and beautiful. Satan knew what he
was doing when he made illicit sex so exciting. But
against the "no one gets hurt" thinking stand millions
of broken families, diseased bodies, and lonely people. Immorality is a path to death. Believers who
have been tempted onto the path need to consider
the consequences and turn around before it is too
late.

A WORD FOR TODAY
Immorality dulls awareness.

*Today, Lord, help me to be strong against temptation to
immorality. Help me to run from temptation, and guide
me in your paths.*

FEBRUARY 6

Who doesn't want to hit the snooze button when that blaring alarm wakes us out of our slumber? Fortunately, this proverb doesn't mean that using the snooze button every morning is going to send us onto the streets, homeless. Nor does it mean that a bit of rest from our labors will ruin us. Indeed, the Bible even talks about God resting from his labors (Genesis 2:2), and Jesus and his disciples went away to rest (Mark 6:31). These should not be considered the workaholic's life verses, for they are not meant that way.

These verses are talking about a habit of laziness. Lazy people always have an excuse for not being productive with the gifts and talents God has given them. Laziness will have its consequences, often leading to poverty and scarcity, as these verses predict.

God calls us to work, support ourselves and our families, and be productive for his kingdom. God has little use for lazy laborers other than graciously to transform them into productive ones.

A WORD FOR TODAY
Laziness lulls us into disaster.

Today, Lord, help me to work hard and well at the tasks you have placed before me.

**Read
Proverbs 6**

LAZY
LABORERS
A little extra sleep, a little more slumber, a little folding of the hands to rest—then poverty will pounce on you like a bandit; scarcity will attack you like an armed robber.
Proverbs 6:10-11

FEBRUARY 7

Read Proverbs 7

PRECIOUS OBEDIENCE

*Obey my commands
and live! Guard my
instructions as you
guard your own eyes.
Tie them on your
fingers as a
reminder. Write
them deep within
your heart.*
Proverbs 7:2-3

Many people look at the Bible as a long list of dos and don'ts. They think that God gives all kinds of laws in order to keep people from having any fun or pleasure in life. They might look at these verses and say, "See? All God wants is for people to *obey*!"

But they have it wrong. Yes, God does command obedience, but not because he is some tyrant who needs to have people be subject to his every whim. Instead, God requires obedience because he knows that obedience is best for *us*. Obedience to God's laws helps us to live life to all its fullness—protected from foolish mistakes and able to make wise choices. That's why the writer tells us to guard these teachings like precious possessions, tied on our fingers, written in our hearts so we can never forget.

A WORD FOR TODAY
Love precedes real obedience.

*Today, Lord, help me to remember your commands
so that I might truly live for you.*

FEBRUARY 8

Silver, gold, rubies—sounds like the standard fare of royalty. Who among us does not strive for a certain amount of wealth, comfort, and security? We may not have precious metals and jewels on our wish lists, but we all set goals and strive to achieve certain standards of success. While gold, silver, and jewels are fine in themselves, they should never be our ultimate goal, nor should they be obtained in wrongful ways. The writer says that we should choose instruction, knowledge, and wisdom far above anything else in this life.

The trappings of success are nothing without wisdom and understanding to go along with them. We all know very rich people who have acted foolishly in business or in their family lives. They may have it all, but they are the most unhappy and bitter people around. Ultimately, a person who has nothing but wisdom is by far the richest person of all.

A WORD FOR TODAY
We can't desire anything worth more than wisdom.

Today, Lord, show me where my priorities are wrong so that I will be striving for the right things in the right way.

**Read
Proverbs 8**

WISE
ACCOUNTING
Choose my instruction rather than silver, and knowledge rather than pure gold. For wisdom is far more valuable than rubies. Nothing you desire can compare with it.
Proverbs 8:10-11

FEBRUARY 9

Read
Proverbs 9

THE WIDEST INVITATION

*She has sent
her servants to
invite everyone
to come. She
calls out from
the heights
overlooking
the city.*
Proverbs 9:3

Wisdom does not hold exclusive parties. She is not seeking only the brightest, the best looking, or the most likely to succeed. She does not keep anyone who desires to come from taking part in her festivities. In other words, wisdom is available to anyone who asks for it!

In this picture of wisdom as a woman inviting people to her spacious home, we see a picture of the grace of our great and loving God. In the Garden of Eden, Eve thought that eating the fruit would make her wise (Genesis 3:6). She thought that God was keeping something from her, and so she disobeyed. She failed to realize that God had given her all that she needed to know. So she and Adam turned their backs on wisdom and welcomed the ultimate foolishness of sin. Although we all now exist under the curse of sin, God seeks to give us the wisdom that we need in order to have a relationship with him. What grace! Wisdom is calling. Have we answered?

A WORD FOR TODAY
Wisdom—an equal-opportunity life.

Today, Lord, may I respond to the invitation to find your wisdom.

FEBRUARY 10

Some people are very good liars. They can make up all kinds of stories and fabrications of events in order to keep themselves from being incriminated. What often happens, however, is that they can't keep all their lies straight.

By contrast, when we speak only the truth, we have only one story to remember, the true one— no trying to remember to whom we told what, or which lie we told in what way. In other words, as the verse says, with integrity we can walk safely. We stand on a solid foundation, the truth—even if that truth is difficult to have to tell. Being a liar, however, sends us on crooked paths where we slip and fall.

People of true integrity are difficult to stereo-type. Often they seem a bit unreal, because so much of what they do is clearly right. Their firm footing, however, makes them people we know we can trust. They show us that when we speak and live the truth, we walk with sure footsteps into and through every situation.

A WORD FOR TODAY
Integrity—a life that stands.

Today, Lord, may I be truthful and trustworthy; may I build a reputation for integrity so that I may walk safely.

**Read
Proverbs 10**

WORTHY
EXAMPLES
People with integrity walk safely, but those who follow crooked paths will slip and fall.
Proverbs 10:9

FEBRUARY 11

**Read
Proverbs 11**

FAMILIARITY

*Jesus replied, "The
most important
commandment is
this: 'Listen,
O Israel! The LORD
our God is the one
and only LORD. And
you must love the
LORD your God with
all your heart, all
your soul, all your
mind, and all your
strength.' The second
is equally important:
'Love your neighbor
as yourself.' No other
commandment is
greater than these."*
Mark 12:29-31

The man who asked Jesus the question that brought
this profound response received something as familiar as his own name. As a devout Jew, in accordance
with Deuteronomy 6:4-9, he had probably said
those very words as he left his home that morning.
He said them every day. They were a spiritual verbal
habit, as ingrained as wiping his feet before entering
the house. Now he heard them from Jesus as the
central commandment from God. He had no trouble agreeing with Jesus, and he said so (Mark
12:32). He knew the right answer when he heard it,
even though it was familiar.

Jesus' response to the man's agreement makes a
stunning point: "You are not far from the Kingdom
of God" (Mark 12:34). He was close because he
knew; now he just had to go and *do!* He wasn't in yet.
But Jesus let him know he definitely had the right
idea. We know Jesus' words silenced the crowd; we
don't know if the man entered the kingdom or settled for being close. His predicament invites us to
consider where we have settled: not far from the
kingdom of God, or in it?

A WORD FOR TODAY
The greatest proverb—"Love God."

*Lord, I affirm my trust in you as the one who declares
me a citizen of your kingdom by grace. Help me practice
the love life of the kingdom today.*

FEBRUARY 12

Proverbs has much to say about wives and husbands. This one offers a glimpse of the way spouses have a deep influence on one another. This has nothing to do with the perfection of the husband, for no husband can be perfect. Nor does it refer to a wife being no more than a doormat or a trophy on display. Instead, this verse is referring to a loving relationship in which both husband and wife honor each other. And it reveals the power a wife has in a relationship.

When a wife builds up and supports her husband, when she is faithful and loving, then she is like a crown on his head and she brings him joy. But when she hurts and shames him by her actions or words, she can ruin him. Husbands and wives need to work together to build a relationship in which they are "worthy" for each other. Then they will find great joy in their marriage.

A WORD FOR TODAY
Live your role.

Today, Lord, may I be a joy to my husband (wife), helping him (her) to be the best he (she) can be for you.

**Read
Proverbs 12**

HOME
TREASURE
A worthy wife is a crown for her husband, but a disgraceful woman is like cancer in his bones.
Proverbs 12:4

FEBRUARY 13

Read
Proverbs 13

SPEECH
CONTROL

*Those who control
their tongue will
have a long life;
opening your mouth
can ruin everything.*
Proverbs 13:3

In the New Testament, James wrote, "The tongue is a flame of fire. It is a whole world of wickedness, corrupting your entire body. It can set your whole life on fire" (James 3:6).

How true are these words! Who has not spoken words in a fit of anger, only to regret them immediately? The tongue can run away with us sometimes, and we say things that are better left unsaid. And once those words have escaped our lips, there is no way to get them back. They can indeed "ruin everything" —or at least cause devastating damage that may take many years to repair.

How much better for us to control our tongue, to think before we speak, to measure our words carefully. Then we will say what we mean in the best way possible. We will be clear, concise, and concerned for the welfare of the listener. And we will show self-control, for we will be in control of our tongue.

A WORD FOR TODAY
Longevity is tied to lingual control.

Today, Lord, may I think before I speak, learning from your Holy Spirit the self-control I need in order to control my tongue.

FEBRUARY 14

In Proverbs 12:4 we read how a woman can build up or destroy her husband by her actions and words; the same holds true for her household. Like it or not, the woman of the house—the wife and/or mom—has a huge influence over her family. She literally has the power to build or tear down her home with her own hands.

How does a wise woman "build" her home? Consider other proverbs to get a bigger picture. She cares for her husband and family (31:27); she has discretion (11:22); she builds up with her words and is not quarrelsome (19:13; 21:19); she is understanding (19:14); she is a great treasure (18:22). She is trustworthy, and so is capable of enriching her husband's and children's lives (31:10-12). The opposite characteristics would obviously "tear down" a woman's home. Women have great influence and the responsibility from God to live wisely.

A WORD FOR TODAY
Women are homebuilders.

Today, Lord, help me to take the steps needed to "build" my home into the place you want it to be.

Read
Proverbs 14

CONSTRUCTION SITE
A wise woman builds her home, but a foolish woman tears it down with her own hands.
Proverbs 14:1

FEBRUARY 15

Read
Proverbs 15

GOD'S
DELIGHT
The LORD detests
the sacrifice of the
wicked, but he
delights in the
prayers of the
upright.
Proverbs 15:8

The teaching in this verse occurs in various forms throughout Scripture (see 1 Samuel 15:22; Hosea 6:6; Micah 6:6-8; Matthew 12:7; Hebrews 10:8-9). The point is that God does not delight in people who go through the motions of faith without allowing it to make any difference in their hearts or minds. In Old Testament terms, it would be like bringing an animal to sacrifice only because the law required it, not in order to be cleansed from sin. In today's language it would be like attending church, and even serving there, without allowing God to penetrate one's heart and life. That is the "sacrifice of the wicked," and the Lord hates it.

God delights, however, in the prayers of his followers. He longs to hear from his people who are open and listening—seeking to grow and change in order to please him. We delight God when we, his children, come to him in prayer because we love and need him.

A WORD FOR TODAY
Godly prayer delights God.

Today, Lord, may I delight you by my devotion, my life, and my prayers.

FEBRUARY 16

People can justify anything. We human beings have an amazing capability to rationalize our actions and so remain "pure" in our own eyes. Many subscribe to the adage that "the end justifies the means," and they will explain away all manner of wrong behavior if they think it will bring them to the desired "end."

However, while we may be fooling everyone around us, we are not fooling God. He sees right through us, down to our basest desires and motivations. No matter how "pure" we may think we are, a God's-eye view will quickly show us otherwise.

If we have felt God's touch on our conscience regarding our motives in a particular situation, we need to ask forgiveness. Then we need to ask God to help us straighten out our thinking so that we are following his commands every step of the way. His Word provides a faithful mirror.

A WORD FOR TODAY
Be aware of God's awareness.

Today, Lord, examine my motives and show me how to act in accordance with your will.

Read
Proverbs 16

FAITHFUL
MIRROR
People may be pure in their own eyes, but the LORD examines their motives.
Proverbs 16:2

FEBRUARY 17

*Those who mock the
poor insult their
Maker; those who
rejoice at the
misfortune of others
will be punished.*
Proverbs 17:5

It is difficult to imagine the type of person who would mock the poor or rejoice at the misfortune of others. But in our own little ways, we may do just that without realizing it. Do we turn up our nose at the poorly dressed—and perhaps a bit fragrant—person at church who obviously has very little? Do we suppose that people with financial difficulties have probably caused their own problems and don't deserve our concern? Do we walk away, thanking God that we are not poor like they are?

God makes it clear that he created all people—rich and poor alike (22:2). The rich have nothing that God has not given them; therefore, they have no reason to be arrogant. Jesus told a parable about this very topic in Luke 16:19-31. We ought to be compassionate to those less fortunate, seeking God's wisdom for how we can help.

A WORD FOR TODAY
Realize the ultimate destination of every message you send.

Today, Lord, thank you for all the blessings you have given me. Show me how to be compassionate toward others.

FEBRUARY 18

Clearly, discipleship has little to do with how we feel and almost everything to do with how we obey Jesus Christ. In other words, since there is no feeling to which disciples are immune, it is possible to experience almost any feeling and remain a faithful disciple of Jesus. The central question for the disciple of Jesus is not "How do I feel right now?" but "Am I continuing to obey?"

Note that Jesus did not promise an "obey–feel good, obey–feel good" kind of instant-gratification cycle to his disciples. His standard of faithfulness covers those who "keep obeying." If there is a cycle in Jesus' proverb, it might be described in this way: Those who keep obeying find in their persistent obedience a deeper awareness of what is true, which leads in turn to a greater sense of freedom to continue to obey.

A WORD FOR TODAY
Knowing precedes obedience.

Lord, keep me aware throughout the day that I want to be an obedient disciple of yours for the long run of life.

**Read
Proverbs 18**

DISCIPLESHIP MARATHON
Jesus said to the people who believed in him, "You are truly my disciples if you remain faithful to my teachings."
John 8:31

FEBRUARY 19

**Read
Proverbs 19**

MISPLACED ANGER

*People ruin their
lives by their
own foolishness
and then are
angry at the LORD.*
Proverbs 19:3

Many people thumb their noses at God and his laws for living. They refuse to be hemmed in by his "restrictive" commands. Instead they decide to have sex before marriage, commit adultery, gamble, drink heavily, use drugs, lie, cheat, and steal. Then come the consequences from those actions—unplanned pregnancy and a total change in life plans, a ruined marriage and family, loss of jobs and finances, even jail. Though they have done all these things against God's laws, they get mad at God for their awful situation. What's wrong with this picture?

Certainly there are many times when people suffer for no known reason—for example, look at Job. However, if we are honest with ourselves, our suffering is usually caused by our own foolishness. God can still bring good out of it, but he will not erase the consequences. When we stop being angry at God, we can learn the lessons he has for us.

A WORD FOR TODAY
Anger at God is self-destructive.

Today, Lord, may I accept the consequences for my own actions, trusting that you can still work miracles in my life.

FEBRUARY 20

What better motivation exists for us to be people of integrity than that our children will be blessed for it! Parents who are godly, who live with integrity and truthfulness, are wonderful examples to their children. Granted, this does not always guarantee that children will turn out perfectly, but children will nevertheless receive a great blessing from having such parents.

So what does it mean to "walk with integrity"? It means that we "walk the talk." In other words, plenty of people *know* the right thing to do, but when the right time comes, they don't do it. They know they should tell the truth, for example, but if telling the truth will hurt, they opt for a lie instead. Children learn best from models they see and hear, but if they learn to bend the truth whenever needed, they set themselves up for problems in life. But if they learn to follow God and walk their faith, then they will have been greatly blessed.

A WORD FOR TODAY
Integrity makes a great inheritance.

Today, Lord, help me to walk with integrity so as to be a good example to others.

**Read
Proverbs 20**

A HERITAGE
OF BLESSINGS
*The godly walk
with integrity;
blessed are their
children who follow
them.*
Proverbs 20:7

FEBRUARY 21

Read
Proverbs 21

ROYAL
AQUEDUCT
*The king's heart is
like a stream of
water directed by the
LORD; he guides it
wherever he pleases.*
Proverbs 21:1

God rules his creation. Nothing is outside his authority—not even the leaders of the nations and kingdoms of this world. No person is placed in a position of power outside of God's will. This can be a great comfort when we see leaders take over in various places, especially leaders with whom we do not agree.

So what does this mean for the cruel tyrants of the world? It means that they too are under God's authority. Satan may author their evil acts, but their wrongdoing can occur only within the boundaries God sets. Why those boundaries are where they are for some nations is a question only God can answer. But we can rest assured that no power is in authority outside of God's plan. God always accomplishes his will, even through the most wicked leaders. God is always the final authority.

A WORD FOR TODAY
God is in charge.

Today, Lord, may I trust that you are the sovereign authority over all that happens in my nation. May I trust you, even as I work on your behalf.

FEBRUARY 22

In the minds of most people throughout history, riches have been the sign of God's blessing while poverty reveals God's curse. According to Solomon, however, the rich and poor are on equal footing before God because God made them both. The wealth of rich people cannot get them any closer to God than poor people can get. And the poor person's poverty is not a free ride to heaven. The thing that matters is the state of a person's heart. In fact, Jesus explained that it is actually harder for the rich to enter God's kingdom because they have a more difficult time understanding their need (Matthew 19:23).

Because God created both the rich and the poor, and because both have been infected by the curse of sinfulness on humanity, they both need the Savior. We are not to show favoritism either way but are to look on both the rich and poor as people whom Christ died to save.

A WORD FOR TODAY
Circumstances vary; God doesn't.

Today, Lord, give me sensitivity to all people, regardless of their status, so that I might be able to tell them about you.

Read
Proverbs 22

EQUAL VALUE
The rich and poor have this in common: The LORD made them both.
Proverbs 22:2

FEBRUARY 23

Read
Proverbs 23

INEVITABLE
JUDGE

Don't cheat your
neighbor by moving
the ancient
boundary markers;
don't take the land
of defenseless
orphans. For
their Redeemer is
strong; he himself
will bring their
charges against you.
Proverbs 23:10-11

The word *Redeemer* has two very distinct applications in this proverb. Within the culture of Israel, orphans and widows were the responsibility of their extended family, represented by the closest relative, who was called a "redeemer." An excellent example of how this worked can be seen in the book of Ruth.

From the perspective of God's purposes in composing Scripture, the Old Testament redeemers were built into the culture so that we could understand the role and wonder of the great Redeemer, Jesus. His life, death, and resurrection declare the divine strength behind God's plan.

Whatever the temporary successes of evil or injustice in this world, God has the final judgment. Whatever boundaries are violated or property or dignity stolen, God will make things right in his time.

A WORD FOR TODAY
God has the final word.

Today, Lord, help me be especially aware of those who
feel defenseless. Please guide my words and actions on
their behalf.

FEBRUARY 24

Substitute any number of words for "house" in this proverb, and you will get the idea of the writer's intent. Consider how we build our "home," our "life," our "business," our "church"; how we set our "goals"; make our "decisions." In others words, anything we build in this life should be based on a foundation of wisdom, good sense, and knowledge. We build wisely by understanding God's direction and guidance. We develop good sense when we use our mind and experiences to think through our options.

Through accumulated knowledge, God helps us take what we have learned about the particular situation or decision and avoid others' mistakes. When we make use of these God-given directions, we can build a home, life, or business that is valuable to all—but mostly to God, for it will then be able to accomplish his will in the world. When God is the master builder, we can be sure what we are building is part of eternity.

A WORD FOR TODAY
Working with God—the perfect business plan.

Today, Lord, as the architect of my life, take the plans I've tried to make and become my master builder.

**Read
Proverbs 24**

BUILDING
PLANS
A house is built by wisdom and becomes strong through good sense. Through knowledge its rooms are filled with all sorts of precious riches and valuables.
Proverbs 24:3-4

FEBRUARY 25

Read
Proverbs 25

❦

GODLY
SORROW
God blesses those
who mourn, for they
will be comforted.
Matthew 5:4

This second beatitude, like the first (January 28), concerns the internal remodeling of the soul of a disciple. Those who come to realize they are spiritually bankrupt (poor in spirit) must then move on to repentance (mourning)—a genuine, deep sadness over sin to the point of real change. Those who acknowledge they are lost in sin and take full responsibility for their condition will receive God's comfort.

Just as grieving over the loss of a loved one can take different forms and require varied amounts of time, so the spiritual mourning that God blesses may have an ongoing effect throughout a Christian's life. While it touches the whole person, it will not touch everyone the same way. For instance, we tend to equate mourning with tears. Unfortunately, most of us know people who shed tears of repentance but return immediately to the same sin. Others give amazing evidence of spiritual transformation without shedding a tear. Spiritual mourning is necessary but personal. As it occurs, God promises to bless in a comforting way.

A WORD FOR TODAY
Authentic repentance includes grief.

Today, Lord, give me one lesson or reminder that helps
me understand the importance of allowing the things
that break your heart to break my heart.

FEBRUARY 26

Proverbs is certainly not a book for the faint of heart or weak of stomach! It confronts adultery, sin, and folly in no uncertain terms and with vivid images. Here we have a graphic picture of the type of person who makes a mistake and then makes it again. This person, here called a "fool," has not learned from the foolish mistake and so is doomed to repeat it. This is as disgusting as the habit of a dog that goes back to its own vomit.

Everyone makes mistakes—even foolish ones. If we desire to be wise, our mistakes can become beneficial. Many times we have said things we now regret, spent money we should not have, acted in ways that now embarrass us, or faced severe consequences for a foolish mistake. But most of us learn from those mistakes and put those hard lessons to use so that we do not make those mistakes again. That is the path of wisdom.

A WORD FOR TODAY
Mistakes teach us or we repeat them.

Today, Lord, help me remember and learn from my past mistakes so that I don't have to repeat them.

**Read
Proverbs 26**

SICKENING
PICTURE
As a dog returns to its vomit, so a fool repeats his foolishness.
Proverbs 26:11

FEBRUARY 27

**Read
Proverbs 27**

WORTHWHILE
PRAISE

*Let someone else
praise you, not your
own mouth—
a stranger, not your
own lips.*
Proverbs 27:2

How simple, yet how profound! We all know people who, often to cover their insecurities, are quick to tell us all their accomplishments. Such people rarely receive words of praise from us, for we resist praising someone who is always praising himself or herself.

On the other hand, many people who certainly deserve praise humbly refuse to shower themselves with kudos. We are often surprised to discover the depth of such people, and the breadth of their accomplishments. We give praise so that others can know about them as well. What a joy it is to give well-deserved praise to someone who hasn't sought it!

We should strive to be humble people. When we don't draw attention to ourselves with self-centered praise, we allow others to do it for us. But even if no one notices our efforts or accomplishments, we know that God sees and is pleased with our hard work for him. Ultimately, his praise is the most important of all.

A WORD FOR TODAY
Humility accepts delayed praise.

Today, Lord, may I do your work patiently, not seeking praise but knowing that you are pleased.

FEBRUARY 28

Justice means righteousness, lawfulness, and moral rightness, the quality of being true or correct, the moral principle determining just conduct. So justice has a moral quality. It contains a concept of what is right and, therefore, must also have a concept of what is wrong. Only people who understand these concepts of right and wrong can understand and administer justice. By extension, only those who follow the Lord can understand justice. Why? Because they subscribe to the foundational laws of the one who created them.

Thus, as this proverb points out, evil people don't understand justice. Because they refuse to subscribe to justice's moral underpinnings given by God in his Word, they are left to discover their own truths. As a result, many conclude that there is no truth. Others conclude that everyone can have different truths. Both perspectives are hopelessly doomed. And as a building without a foundation will crumble, so justice can never be served without the foundation of right and wrong as given by God in his Word.

A WORD FOR TODAY
Justice is pointless without God.

Today, Lord, teach me the foundational truths about life that are given in your Word.

**Read
Proverbs 28**

AWARENESS
OF JUSTICE
Evil people don't understand justice, but those who follow the LORD understand completely.
Proverbs 28:5

MARCH 1

Read
Proverbs 1

🥀

LIFE'S PASSAGES

My child, listen
when your father
corrects you.
Don't neglect
your mother's
instruction.
Proverbs 1:8

Why should we listen to our parents? Especially as we grow older, we might think this proverb no longer applies to us. However, listening to our parents' teaching is a way of honoring them, and numerous passages in the Bible connect honoring our parents with living a long and blessed life (see the fifth commandment, Exodus 20:12). This naturally raises questions about how God connects longevity with parental honor.

When we honor our parents by listening to them, we gain wisdom to avoid the hard lessons our parents had to learn. Even more, we have an amazing chance to develop a positive view of aging. If we respect our parents, we are more likely to embrace our own process of aging as a blessing.

As your parents give you advice, put yourself in their position. When you are their age, would you rather be treated as a constant burden or respected as a blessing to the family?

A WORD FOR TODAY
Value parental wisdom.

Lord, you created the stages of life. Help me to respect my parents as I will want to be respected.

MARCH 2

How can someone become wise? Many people think that wisdom comes only through education or experience. But the truth is that wisdom is also a remarkable gift from God. That's right—it's a *gift*. God does not discriminate in bestowing wisdom on the young and the old, the scholar and the servant. In fact, God takes special joy in giving wisdom to those whom society considers unworthy.

On the other hand, God views the world's idea of wisdom as foolishness. Since God is the ultimate source of wisdom, those who try to become wise on their own will not succeed.

If you want wisdom, first seek the creator of wisdom. The Lord grants wisdom because he wants you to be confident of the hope that is within you. So continue to question and search out the answers! He waits patiently to offer you the meat of his Word. If you seek him, he will pour out understanding.

A WORD FOR TODAY
God created wisdom.

Lord, give me an understanding of who you are so that I may confidently stand for you.

Read Proverbs 2

TAKING WISDOM FOR GRANTED
The LORD grants wisdom! From his mouth come knowledge and understanding.
Proverbs 2:6

MARCH 3

**Read
Proverbs 3**

WISDOM IN
ACTION
*Don't be impressed
with your own
wisdom. Instead, fear
the LORD and turn
away from evil.*
Proverbs 3:7

If anyone could have been impressed with himself, it was Solomon. God made him the wisest man alive. Yet, despite Solomon's great wisdom, he still made many poor choices that eventually led him away from God.

Solomon's life illustrates a valuable lesson: Wisdom becomes useless if it is not applied. We can *know* what is right, but if we do not *do* what is right, our knowledge lacks value. Searching for wisdom does not put us on the wrong track, for we are told to search for it. However, the proverb points to something far beyond the search for wisdom. It tells us to fear the Lord and obey him. Fearing the Lord means giving God a proper place in our life. When we respect God in humility, we are more likely to turn from evil to obedience.

A WORD FOR TODAY
Fear of the Lord tempers wisdom.

Lord, help me not only to know your path, but also to walk that path in obedience.

MARCH 4

God commanded us to love. It would have been easier if God had just said, "Run a mile each day," or given us some other physical task. Then we wouldn't have to think about it. We could create a routine of basic action. But God speaks of love as an action that requires our whole selves.

Why must we love God? In the divine plan for those creatures called human, loving God is as essential as breathing is to physical life. We must breathe. We can make ourselves unable to breathe, or we can refuse to breathe—but not without consequences. We *must* love God because the alternative, though possible, is unthinkable and unbearable. How tragic that many choose to give "lip service" rather than "lung service" to this basic law of spiritual life. Take a deep breath and ask yourself what specific opportunities you will have today to demonstrate your love for God.

A WORD FOR TODAY
The greatest proverb—"Love God."

Lord, teach me to love you with my whole being and share this love with others.

**Read
Proverbs 4**

WHOLE LOVE
Jesus replied, "The most important commandment is this: 'Listen, O Israel! The LORD our God is the one and only LORD. And you must love the LORD your God with all your heart, all your soul, all your mind, and all your strength.' The second is equally important: 'Love your neighbor as yourself.' No other commandment is greater than these."
Mark 12:29-31

MARCH 5

**Read
Proverbs 5**

STAY AWAY!
*Stay away from [an
immoral woman]!
Don't go near the
door of her house!*
Proverbs 5:8

"DANGER! Bridge out ahead!" This proverb screams out like a yellow warning sign along the side of the road. And that's what it is supposed to be—a two-part warning about temptation.

The first part of the proverb gives us directions about sin that seeks us. It tells us to stay away! Just look at Joseph in Genesis 39. He ran away when Potiphar's wife propositioned him to have an affair with her. If you find yourself in a similar situation, don't try to be brave. Just get out of there!

The second part shows us what to do when we are tempted to seek out sin. Don't go near it! Translated into today's society, this verse might suggest driving a different route home from work to avoid passing an adult bookstore.

You can't control the actions of other people, but you can ask God to help you control your own behavior.

A WORD FOR TODAY
Wisdom knows when to stay away.

Lord, give me the strength to run away from sin. Help me to stay on your path day by day.

MARCH 6

Hate is a strong word. In fact, it almost seems out of character for God to hate. Isn't he supposed to be a God of love? We might use the word *hate* lightly when we speak, but the thought of God's hatred conveys a very frightening concept. This view of God helps us think more seriously about his response to our actions.

Notice the things that God hates—pride, dishonesty, and impurity. Interestingly, each phrase connects these sins with a part of the body. Now, our physical bodies are not bad in themselves. God created us in his image to perform great acts. Our bodies are his masterpiece. Yet, the greatest gifts of a human can become the most evil when they are twisted for evil purposes.

Each day you have an opportunity to use your body for good deeds or for wickedness. Choose today to honor God with your body. Avoid corrupting yourself with the things God hates.

A WORD FOR TODAY
Imitate God's hatred.

Lord, I am fearfully and wonderfully made! Help me to use each part of my body to uplift others.

**Read
Proverbs 6**

WHAT
GOD HATES
*There are six things
the LORD hates—
no, seven things he
detests: haughty
eyes, a lying tongue,
hands that kill the
innocent, a heart
that plots evil, feet
that race to do
wrong, a false
witness who pours
out lies, a person
who sows discord in
a family.*
Proverbs 6:16-19

MARCH 7

**Read
Proverbs 7**

🍃

A SISTER'S WISDOM

*Love wisdom like a
sister; make insight
a beloved member
of your family. Let
them protect
you from an
affair with an
immoral woman,
from listening to the
flattery of a
promiscuous woman.*
Proverbs 7:4-5

Whether biological or spiritual, our sisters and other family members remain in a unique position in our lives. When we are blinded by our temptations, they can step in and say, "Open your eyes. You don't want that." While often painful, our family's honesty may help us to wake up. This honesty directly confronts the seductive lies of our temptations.

In this same way, wisdom acts as a sister, guarding us from our temptations. Wisdom and insight lose their effectiveness, however, when we stubbornly refuse to listen. Notice the wording: We must "*let them* protect" us. To overcome temptation, we must first be willing to listen. Wisdom, like our family members, often reveals to us that which we are unable to see. When we are willing to listen, God's wisdom will guide us along the correct path.

A WORD FOR TODAY
Wisdom and insight can be your siblings.

Lord, help me to open my ears to your wisdom, so that I may open my eyes to temptation.

Wisdom, good judgment, knowledge, and discernment all apparently live in the same neighborhood. For the purposes of meditation and practice, these terms may be used interchangeably. Within this proverb, though, wisdom clearly takes the chief position. The other three terms seem to indicate aspects or components of wisdom. Good judgment has to do with decision making. Knowledge has to do with gathering and organizing facts. Discernment describes a capacity for understanding people or events in subtle ways.

Those who seek wisdom from God will find along the way that they are also discovering and growing in good judgment, knowledge, and discernment. Your commitment not only to read Proverbs daily but also to concentrate on a single proverb for meditation means that you are spending time every day in wisdom's neighborhood. Good things will come out of that time investment.

Read
Proverbs 8

WISDOM'S
PARTNERS
I, Wisdom, live together with good judgment. I know where to discover knowledge and discernment.
Proverbs 8:12

A WORD FOR TODAY
Wisdom knows the way.

Lord, please continue to lead me into wisdom and the good companions that come with her. Guide me to use wisdom in your service.

MARCH 9

**Read
Proverbs 9**

A SPECIAL
INVITATION
*"Come in with me,"
she urges the
simple. To those
who lack good
judgment, she
says, "Come, eat
my food, and
drink the wine
I have mixed."*
Proverbs 9:4-5

An invitation has arrived in the mail. The whole town has been invited to a huge banquet! We excitedly rush to get dressed in our best clothes. At the last minute, we call our best friend or loved one to check on the time. To our dismay, he tells us he is too busy—he isn't going to the banquet!

In this same way, God has prepared a banquet for each one of us. If we choose to go, God offers us food unlike any other—his wisdom. And God's wisdom nourishes us completely. However, some of us never take the time to reply to his generous invitation.

Don't let any other pursuit in your life cause you to ignore the invitation of wisdom God has for you. All that God requires is a response.

A WORD FOR TODAY
Listen to Wisdom's invitation.

Lord, I desire your wisdom. Help me follow your will and make good choices today.

The world's way of promoting peace differs remarkably from God's way. We would rather let everyone do as they please—just "wink" and mind our own business when we see others sin. This sort of practice, however, does not work. As humans, our life is unavoidably tied to and affected by those around us.

On the other hand, God's way of promoting peace begins when we hold his truth as of utmost importance. This means we have the responsibility to bring back, gently but sternly, those who stray from the truth.

The process of confronting others might be uncomfortable, but peace does not appear when all our problems disappear. We will always have struggles! Peace comes when problems and sin within relationships are dealt with correctly and humbly.

A WORD FOR TODAY
Peace requires honesty.

Lord, help me to stand boldly when others seek to compromise your truth.

Read
Proverbs 10

PROMOTING
PEACE
People who wink at wrong cause trouble, but a bold reproof promotes peace.
Proverbs 10:10

MARCH 11

Read
Proverbs 11

SLAVERY TO SALARY

*No one can serve
two masters. For you
will hate one and
love the other; you
will be devoted
to one and despise
the other. You
cannot serve both
God and money.*
Matthew 6:24

How do we serve money? Workaholism, bondage to debt, living above our means, the "I have to have it" attitude—these are all signs that point to a faulty system of priorities. These behaviors enslave us to money because they consume all our thoughts and time.

Jesus asked some hard questions of the people who desired to follow him. Jesus told one wealthy man to give all his possessions away before becoming a follower (Matthew 19:21-22). Sadly, the man ended up walking away. Jesus knew the man loved money more than he loved God.

If we want the Lord to be first in our life, we first must examine our attitudes. Are we working and living for money or for God?

A WORD FOR TODAY
Money is a harsh slave master.

Father, help me to examine my perspective. May my life be dedicated to you and not to making money.

MARCH 12

This proverb compares the lives of two types of people: those who have no foundation, and those who choose God as their foundation. What kind of foundation have you chosen for your life? How clearly have you communicated it to your family? If we choose to live our lives without God or neglect to pass down our faith to our children, we deprive them of a firm foundation. After we are gone, they will have nothing upon which to stand.

On the other hand, by developing godliness in our own lives, we benefit not only ourselves but also the generations that come after us. Today's proverb demonstrates this truth by describing the godly through their children. When we pass on a heritage of faith, we create a firm foundation for our kids' lives. Then, when we are no longer with them, they will have the grounding to continue to grow and rely on God.

A WORD FOR TODAY
Godliness is both taught and caught.

Lord, help me to grow in godliness so I may pass your truth on to my children.

Read
Proverbs 12

A FIRM
FOUNDATION
The wicked die and disappear, but the family of the godly stands firm.
Proverbs 12:7

MARCH 13

Read
Proverbs 13

TRUE SUCCESS
Godliness guards
the path of the
blameless, but
the evil are misled
by sin.
Proverbs 13:6

What describes godly living? We develop godliness when we seek to make choices in accordance with God's will. These good decisions help us live successful lives. This is true even when the good results do not occur obviously or immediately.

Sometimes it may seem that poor choices will actually prosper us more than godly ones. Isn't it easier to cheat and steal than it is to work hard?

While these choices may tempt us with their short-term benefits, they set in motion a series of events that eventually will destroy us. For instance, people who step on others to get to the top will find that they have no support when they finally get there.

When we choose to make honest decisions and follow God's will for us, he will lead us into true success. The success wrought through godliness completely surpasses any temporary accomplishment gained through dishonesty. That's what God calls a "whole-life" kind of success, and it lasts for eternity.

A WORD FOR TODAY
Godliness produces real success.

Today, Lord, show me how to make godly decisions
in my work and at home with my family.

MARCH 14

Wouldn't it be great to see into the future? To have the ability to bypass future mistakes? In a way, Christians have this ability. God has given us a precious gift—the gift of "sight."

This sight is not like the false sight of fortune-tellers or magicians. It is the spiritual ability to see *who* is in the future, instead of merely *what* is in the future. So, we no longer blindly grope around in this life as those who are lost. Christ is our future and our hope.

Just as a successful marathon runner knows the location of the finish line before setting goals for the race, we identify Christ as our finish line. This great knowledge allows us to set daily goals for wise living. In the end, each day of our lives may be lived victoriously if we remember our final outcome. The Christian's race is already won through Christ's victory on the cross. And when we cross the finish line of life, we will be in Christ's presence.

A WORD FOR TODAY
Wisdom offers foresight.

Lord, help me to look ahead to you so that I may live victoriously.

Read
Proverbs 14

VICTORIOUS
FORESIGHT
The prudent understand where they are going, but fools deceive themselves.
Proverbs 14:8

MARCH 15

Read
Proverbs 15

MATTERS OF THE HEART

Even Death and Destruction hold no secrets from the LORD. How much more does he know the human heart!
Proverbs 15:11

We humans have a knack for forgetting the true knowledge of God. Just look at Adam after he sinned. He thought he could hide from God! Like Adam, we often hide what we truly feel in our hearts. Perhaps we think we are too evil, or that we've let God down. In the midst of our trials, we hide from God. We forget that God knows us down to our deepest motives!

This thought can be very frightening. It can also be extremely comforting. God knows us as we are right now—and he *wants* us as we are right now. So unlike any other relationship, we can let down our guard with God.

We can forget about trying to conquer that one temptation before coming to God. We can forget about dressing up and putting on a good face. God knows what's in our hearts, and nothing we feel is too terrible for him to handle.

A WORD FOR TODAY
God knows you.

Lord, give me the courage to come to you honestly, so that I may be healed.

MARCH 16

If we are serious about our work, we probably have specific vocational goals already laid out. Perhaps we want to expand our industry, or advance to a certain position by a particular date. It's easy to get into a mode where we rarely think about work and God simultaneously. *Anyway,* we might think, w*hat business does God have in my business?*

Note the proverb's progression: Our plans will succeed *after* we commit our work to the Lord. Committing our work to God does not imply that we can't make a profit. It means that God wants to be Lord over every part of our lives, including our daily work. It also means that God desires to be pleased with the way we do our work because we are doing it for him.

There's no task too mundane or ordinary for God. He will bless us if we seek his guidance in our work. His power does not stop when we begin our workday.

A WORD FOR TODAY
God is willing to supervise.

Lord, help me to have balance in my daily life as I work my hardest yet trust you for success.

Read
Proverbs 16

GOD'S
BUSINESS
Commit your actions to the LORD, and your plans will succeed.
Proverbs 16:3

MARCH 17

Read
Proverbs 17

THE POWER
OF WORDS
*Eloquent words
are not fitting for
a fool; even less
are lies fitting for
a ruler.*
Proverbs 17:7

Have you ever been drawn into watching an infomercial on TV? After what seems like a few minutes, you realize you've just spent an hour hearing about a kitchen utensil. This illustrates the power of persuasive words. These words catch our attention. They cause us to believe.

Now this might not be harmful if we're listening to just infomercials. However, some of the most eloquent and powerful speakers (Adolf Hitler, for example) have been able to convince people to believe atrocious things.

As Christians, we need to guard against mistaking powerful, persuasive words for the truth. Moreover, we also need to be careful not to mistake eloquent speech for wisdom. Throughout the Bible God used people with poor speaking ability, such as Moses and the apostle Paul, to spread his Word. In the end, a person's character, not position, should be used to judge the value of his or her words.

A WORD FOR TODAY
Wisdom outlasts eloquence.

Lord Jesus, help me to distinguish between persuasive lies and your truth.

MARCH 18

Jesus used childlikeness to describe people who are real citizens of the Kingdom of Heaven. This proverb begins with the act of repentance ("turn from your sins") and then describes a process with the word "become." In fact, the word "become" is used twice to indicate that this is an ongoing experience of learning and growing.

So what did Jesus find so compelling about childlikeness? He specifically mentioned humility. How are children humble? They exhibit a trusting curiosity. They are full of questions for which they really want answers. Their questions don't hide an unwillingness to believe. They want to learn! As a child trusts a loving parent, so a citizen in the Kingdom of Heaven deeply trusts the heavenly Father.

From the moment we turn from our sins, we begin the lifelong learning experience of growing in deep trust of our heavenly Father.

A WORD FOR TODAY
Kingdom childlikeness involves humility.

Lord, becoming like a trusting little child in your presence will develop a humility that pleases you. Help me become more childlike.

**Read
Proverbs 18**

WISE
CHILDLIKENESS
[Jesus] said, "I tell you the truth, unless you turn from your sins and become like little children, you will never get into the Kingdom of Heaven. So anyone who becomes as humble as this little child is the greatest in the Kingdom of Heaven."
Matthew 18:3-4

MARCH 19

**Read
Proverbs 19**

TO FESTER
OR FORGIVE
*Sensible people
control their temper;
they earn respect
by overlooking
wrongs.*
Proverbs 19:11

Anger is an emotion that double-crosses us when we least expect it. When we are angry with someone, we often think that our anger is hurting that person. We fume and rage internally, but gradually the bitterness begins to eat away at our own spirits. In the end, our anger actually hurts us!

So how can we control our temper? Controlling temper does not entail stuffing our emotions deep inside to fester. Instead, the proverb couples restraint with the action of overlooking wrongs. Instead of festering, we are given a tool to lessen our anger when it begins.

At the point when we start to get angry, we can make a *choice* to overlook wrongs. In other words, we can choose to release our anger through forgiveness. We will never have control over other people's actions, but we do have control over our own. If we must express anger, it should be done early rather than late, with a calm sense of self-control and restraint. That itself is a mark of spiritual maturity.

A WORD FOR TODAY
Wisdom holds anger's reins.

Lord, give me a forgiving spirit so that I will be able to let go of my anger toward others.

MARCH 20

How often do we see the evil around us and pray for God's justice? We wonder, *Why does God allow all this evil to go on!* This kind of thinking leads to two of the most common double standards: (1) judging others more harshly than we judge ourselves, and (2) believing God should judge *others* but remain lenient with *us*.

The Lord despises double standards because they elevate one person at the expense of others. These man-made standards also lack the mercy of God.

In our cry for fairness, we should not forget the frightening consequences of justice. As sinners, God could justly destroy each one of us today for missing the mark of perfection. When we remember that God's patience and mercy block his judgment toward us, we will be more likely to show others patience and mercy.

A WORD FOR TODAY
Wisdom weighs by a single standard.

Today, Lord, give me the strength to replace judgment with mercy.

Read
Proverbs 20

GOD'S
MEASURE
False weights and unequal measures— the LORD detests double standards of every kind.
Proverbs 20:10

MARCH 21

Read
Proverbs 21

SECRET
MOTIVES
People may be right
in their own eyes,
but the LORD
examines their
heart.
Proverbs 21:2

At first glance, this proverb seems to be contradicting itself. How can our heads tell us one thing while our hearts tell God another? Yet exactly that often happens. We can talk ourselves into believing that we are acting correctly because we can rationalize our behavior. Our feelings (heart), however, often show the reality no matter what we say.

Perhaps outwardly we do nothing wrong, but the proverb reveals that God is more concerned about our secret motives. For example, by tithing each week we act in obedience. Yet if we tithe with bitter resentment in our hearts, we might fool our neighbors, but we will not fool God.

So even "good" deeds lose their value if we lack the right heart. Ultimately, our motives should be to please God. Our actions become worthless if we seek to please only ourselves or to impress others.

A WORD FOR TODAY
God sees what we excuse and ignore.

Lord, examine my heart and remove any unclean
motives.

MARCH 22

Interestingly, this proverb *expects* that dangerous situations will arise in our lives. If these situations are indeed inevitable, then we should plan a course of action. For some people, taking action means devising endless preventive measures. Still others feel that taking precautions implies that they are not living in faith. Neither of these solutions displays a balanced trust in God.

We must examine where our confidence lies. Are we really trusting in God? Trusting does not mean that we should purposely step into pitfalls. If we see ourselves heading for danger, we can take precautions to avoid the situation. We lack faith when we feel that we alone possess the strength to conquer any temptation. Humbly anticipating our weaknesses will allow us to bypass harsh consequences.

A WORD FOR TODAY
Wisdom prepares.

Lord, help me to live wisely by knowing my weaknesses and anticipating dangerous situations.

**Read
Proverbs 22**

ANTICIPATING
DANGER

A prudent person foresees danger and takes precautions. The simpleton goes blindly on and suffers the consequences.
Proverbs 22:3

**Read
Proverbs 23**

TUNING IN
TO GOD

*Commit yourself to
instruction; listen
carefully to words
of knowledge.*
Proverbs 23:12

Have you ever used walkie-talkies to communicate with friends? If you have, then you know that both people have to tune in to the same frequency, otherwise they can't hear each other. This is a great picture of how communication works between God and us.

We must tune in if we want to hear God's instructions. Listening to God becomes difficult if we're too busy doing our own thing. So how can we tune in to God? First, the proverb tells us to commit ourselves to instruction. This could mean setting a spiritual goal and then relying on God to help us accomplish that goal.

Once we've made a commitment, then it's time to listen carefully. This means focusing our lives on hearing God's instruction. Our continued attention to the book of Proverbs will accomplish a significant amount of careful listening in our lives.

A WORD FOR TODAY
Listen carefully to wisdom.

Today, Lord, help me to attune my heart to your instruction.

MARCH 24

Muscular strength usually comes to mind when we hear words like *power* and *might*. Through self-discipline, this kind of strength may be achieved, but it has real limits. Although physical exercise is a good habit, the proverb stresses the importance of exercising the mind. Building our bodies provides us with endurance in a battle or competition. Nevertheless, neglecting strategy only allows an opponent with more cunning to defeat us.

The verse following this proverb aptly refers to victory during war. As Christians, we are warriors in an ongoing spiritual war. If we think we are strong enough alone, without the guidance of others, we will surely falter. By gaining God's wisdom and direction, we will be able to overcome challenges that appear too great for us.

A WORD FOR TODAY
Wisdom overcomes physical power.

Today, Lord, help me to take time to grow in wisdom and strength through your Word.

**Read
Proverbs 24**

TRUE
STRENGTH
The wise are mightier than the strong, and those with knowledge grow stronger and stronger.
Proverbs 24:5

MARCH 25

Read
Proverbs 25

MEEKNESS
*God blesses those
who are humble, for
they will inherit the
whole earth.*
Matthew 5:5

Older translations of this beatitude have often used the word *meek* to name the character trait Jesus had in mind. In Matthew 11:29, Jesus used almost the identical term to describe himself: "Take my yoke upon you. Let me teach you, because I am humble and gentle at heart, and you will find rest for your souls."

If *meekness* is an unfamiliar term to us, perhaps *humble* and *gentle* are a little too familiar. They don't capture the underlying fierceness that seems to hide within meekness. A meek person is not a weak person. A meek person is a person of immense character and, often, physical strength. What makes a person meek is the fact that, although he or she could exert power or overwhelming ability at any time, he or she actively chooses not to do so.

In order to meditate on meekness, picture the largest, strongest man that you know carrying his little daughter in his arms. Spiritual meekness depends on God's strength and power, choosing not to rely on obvious personal strength.

A WORD FOR TODAY
Meekness is the opposite of weakness.

Lord, to the degree that I can turn away from self-reliance and independence, grow me into a meek person. Teach me about being humble and gentle.

MARCH 26

Throughout history, people have made huge blunders by believing what they thought to be the right answer. Just look at the thousands of years that people believed the earth was flat. It didn't matter how much they believed they were right; they were still wrong!

For this reason, we should always be willing to examine what we hear, and especially what we believe. The people of Berea understood this principle (Acts 17:10-12). They made sure everything Paul preached to them could be found in the Scriptures. We would be wise to follow their example.

If we think we are too smart to make a mistake, we inevitably will do just that! We must continue to humbly scrutinize our beliefs against the Word of God. God will honor us more for admitting when we are wrong than for claiming that we know everything.

A WORD FOR TODAY
Wisdom doesn't boast.

Lord, give me the humility to inspect my beliefs and continue to search for your truth.

**Read
Proverbs 26**

HUMBLE
WISDOM
*There is more hope
for fools than for
people who think
they are wise.*
Proverbs 26:12

MARCH 27

Read
Proverbs 27

TAKE A
LOAD OFF
A stone is heavy
and sand is weighty,
but the resentment
caused by a fool is
even heavier.
Proverbs 27:3

When someone hurts or annoys us, our immediate reaction is to focus on the offense. In our resentment, the focal point remains on the other person, not us. The proverb reverses this progression. It chooses not to detail the fool's specific actions, but instead to describe the effects of resentment in our own lives.

Resentment, or bitterness, weighs us down. Once we've chosen to resent someone's actions, consuming anger becomes our only alternative. Ironically, we often feel we're teaching our opposition a lesson or hurting them in our bitterness. The opposite is true. We end up oppressing only ourselves.

When we're angry, forgiveness might seem like condoning bad behavior. However, forgiveness really means letting go of our own bitterness—essentially, taking a load off. From this beginning, God's hand can begin to mend the relationship.

A WORD FOR TODAY
Offenses are heavy loads to carry.

Lord, when I am tempted to hold on to my resentment,
help me to release it in forgiveness.

MARCH 28

Each of us has probably raised, known, or been a teenager who befriended certain people just to spite his or her parents. As parents, what kinds of emotions do we feel when this happens? Shame? Anger? Worry?

Parenting allows us to uniquely understand God's role as our heavenly Father. When we ourselves seek out "wild friends," we bring shame to God. And just like our response at our children's disobedience, God's anger builds when we intentionally sin against him.

As members of God's family, we represent him wherever we go. Many times our example will be one of the only pictures of God others will see. As Christians we have the opportunity to reinforce Christ's reputation or undermine it. Obeying God's law not only builds up God's family but also brings glory to God himself.

A WORD FOR TODAY
The wise keep good company.

Today, Lord, give me ways to show others your love through my obedience.

**Read
Proverbs 28**

GOD'S REPRE-
SENTATIVES
Young people who obey the law are wise; those with wild friends bring shame to their parents.
Proverbs 28:7

MARCH 29

🍂

DISCIPLINED WISDOM

To discipline a child produces wisdom, but a mother is disgraced by an undisciplined child.

Proverbs 29:15

In today's world, the lines between discipline and abuse have grown exceedingly blurry. Many parents, frightened to be labeled as abusers, have abandoned disciplining their children altogether. The message of the Bible offers us a different alternative.

A good model of discipline arises from Hebrews 12:6, which states, "The Lord disciplines those he loves." Thus, love and wisdom are integrally tied to God's discipline. God allows us to face some of the consequences of our sins. Through this painful process we begin to judge between good and evil on our own.

Likewise, we should discipline our children because we love them and want them to succeed. Success comes through self-discipline. If we truly desire our children to be self-disciplined adults, we must lovingly discipline them as children. Later they will be wise enough to avoid serious mistakes by first pondering the consequences of their actions on their own.

A WORD FOR TODAY
Parental discipline begins with self-discipline.

Lord, give me the strength to discipline my children in love and to accept your discipline myself.

MARCH 30

The truth of God's Word usually becomes painfully obvious as soon as we cease to follow it. When our plans crumble, we realize that God's Word does, in fact, show us the good way. In this aspect, our very lives prove the truth of God's Word.

But what about telling others about God's truth? Confrontation and debate still spark fear in the minds of many believers. We fear that we will be trapped if we step up to defend our faith in God. Ironically, the proverb reveals that it is *God* who defends *us*. He is our shield of protection.

If every word of God is true, he has said some pretty amazing things. For instance, Jesus said, "I will never leave you, nor forsake you." When we are faced with disbelief and cynicism, God remains with us to give us the right words and the courage to speak them.

A WORD FOR TODAY
God doesn't need our defense; we need his.

Today, Lord, help me to rely on you as my Shield and Defender.

Read Proverbs 30

THE BEST DEFENSE
Every word of God proves true. He is a shield to all who come to him for protection.
Proverbs 30:5

MARCH 31

ESTABLISHING VIRTUE

Who can find a virtuous and capable wife? She is more precious than rubies. Her husband can trust her, and she will greatly enrich his life. She brings him good, not harm, all the days of her life.
Proverbs 31:10-12

From this proverb, we see the qualities of a virtuous woman: strong, trustworthy, and supportive of her husband. Next, we may reasonably ask, "How did she acquire these virtues?" Wives who take after this model spend time developing their relationship with God. Virtue flows naturally from their lives as a result of this personal time in prayer and God's Word.

Accordingly, we gain insight into the health of our marriages by examining the level of intimacy we share with God. Strength and trust must first be developed with God before they can be fully demonstrated with our spouses.

Many times, when our relationship with our spouse begins to falter, we have really wavered in our dedication to God. We then fight an uphill battle to save our marriage. By first valuing our relationship with God, we acquire tools to maintain our relationship with our spouse.

A WORD FOR TODAY
A virtuous wife——the ultimate companion.

Today, Lord, may my devotion to my spouse reflect my devotion to you.

APRIL 1

The Bible seems to speak of forgiveness in at least two different ways. In an ultimate sense, forgiveness refers to God's eternal pardon of all our sins when we look to Christ as the only one who can make us right with God (John 5:24; Romans 8:1; Ephesians 1:7). No actions on our part can make this happen. This is the mystery of grace—God's undeserved favor to sinful men (Ephesians 2:8-9). Theologians call this "justification." Fully forgiven, we enter into relationship with a holy God.

Another kind of forgiveness mentioned in the Bible is the ongoing cleansing we need in order to maintain daily intimacy with God (1 John 1:9). It is this second kind of forgiveness that Jesus speaks of in the verses above. If we refuse to show mercy to those who have wronged us, we distance ourselves from God and will cease to experience and appreciate his wonderful love.

As you come to God to receive mercy for daily wrongs, ask yourself, "Have I forgiven all those who have wronged me?"

A WORD FOR TODAY
Forgiveness begins at home.

Today, Lord, remind me of the shocking way in which you canceled my debt of sin, and let that undeserved mercy move me to treat others with similar mercy.

Read
Proverbs 1

VESSELS
OF MERCY
If you forgive those who sin against you, your heavenly Father will forgive you. But if you refuse to forgive others, your Father will not forgive your sins.
Matthew 6:14-15

APRIL 2

Read
Proverbs 2

GOD'S
TREASURE
CHEST

He grants a
treasure of
common sense to
the honest. He is
a shield to those
who walk with
integrity.
Proverbs 2:7

"Treasure." What a "rich" word! It makes most folks daydream about pirates, dragons, or genies. Lost in thought, we imagine all we might do if we found a chest full of priceless gems and precious metals.

God offers treasure of a different kind. It is the richness of "common sense." This kind of rare wisdom is not about IQ or intellect; no, it's actually a moral matter of the heart. The idea here is "skill in living"—a treasure enjoyed only by the godly, by those who take God seriously in their daily lives. But not only that. Look closer at today's proverb. Those who live consistent, morally upright lives receive another priceless benefit: They are protected. Almighty God acts as their shield.

The insight to know how to live in a perverse and confusing world *and* protection as you live for God—can you think of a more valuable find than this?

A WORD FOR TODAY
Wisdom is treasure.

Today, Lord, increase my hunger for the "common sense"
that only you can give. Teach me how to walk with
integrity.

APRIL 3

"Get all you can, can all you get, and sit on the can." In many ways this quip *is* an accurate picture of modern materialism. We in the West seek to accumulate wealth and to use it largely for ourselves. How easy it is to forget that all we have is *from* God . . . and should be used *for* him (Colossians 1:16).

By giving the first and best portion of their harvest back to God, the ancient Israelites acknowledged his goodness and their dependence (Deuteronomy 26). Such humble gratitude served as a continual reminder that God is the source of all material blessings. In exchange for this honor, God promised to continue to provide abundantly for the needs of his people.

Of course, both Scripture and experience provide us with exceptions to this "piety guarantees prosperity" rule. Sometimes generous people *don't* reap a big financial return. But, as Jesus assured us, there is always great blessing and joy in giving (Acts 20:35).

A WORD FOR TODAY
Giving honors God.

Today, Lord, I want to keep in mind that everything I have is from you. Help me learn to hold my possessions loosely. Make me a godly giver.

Read
Proverbs 3

ETERNAL INVESTMENT
Honor the LORD with your wealth and with the best part of everything you produce. Then he will fill your barns with grain, and your vats will overflow with good wine.
Proverbs 3:9-10

APRIL 4

Read
Proverbs 4

GO FOR IT!

*Getting wisdom is
the wisest thing you
can do! And
whatever else you do,
develop good
judgment.*
Proverbs 4:7

We go to great lengths to "get" things. Some will arise early and drive all over town to find bargains and "get" great deals at garage or estate sales. Others work long hours to "get" a promotion or a big contract. Still others sweat and strain day after day to "get" in shape. More often than not, these determined efforts pay off.

According to today's proverb, the wisest thing we can do is to "get" wisdom. And "get" this: The implication of this verse is that such wisdom is available not just to the smartest person or to the lucky person who "gets" all the breaks, but to the person who decides to go for it. In other words, a wise life begins with the decision, "I will do whatever it takes to 'get' godly insight." You "get" wisdom when you make the choice to pursue it above all else.

A WORD FOR TODAY
Get it!

*Today, Lord, show me where my priorities are wrong.
Bring wise people into my life so I can have role models
to follow.*

APRIL 5

Regret is our anguished wishing to be able to turn back the clock and undo foolish choices . . . and the haunting realization that we cannot. Few things in life are more devastating than a heart filled with bitter remorse.

In Proverbs 5 it is the adulterer who groans in anguish. Following the sweet, short-term pleasures of illicit sex, the foolish person is left to wallow in the bitter, long-term consequences of his or her sin—including disease. What a timeless passage! Talk to anyone who has lost spouse, family, reputation, health, and/or spiritual vitality because of sexual misconduct, and you'll find a person overflowing with regret. Contrast this with the wise person who lives a disciplined life and submits to God's ways rather than his/her own passions.

"If only I had not . . ." is a sad statement made all the more tragic by the realization that we brought the nightmare upon ourselves.

A WORD FOR TODAY
Seed determines harvest.

Today, Lord, I pray for the grace to avoid sexual sin. Father, keep me pure, for your glory and for my own health.

Read Proverbs 5

THE MORNING AFTER

In the end you will groan in anguish when disease consumes your body. You will say, "How I hated discipline! If only I had not ignored all the warnings!"
Proverbs 5:11-12

APRIL 6

**Read
Proverbs 6**

THE SINFUL SEVEN

*There are six things
the LORD hates—
no, seven things he
detests:
haughty eyes, a
lying tongue, hands
that kill the
innocent, a heart
that plots evil, feet
that race to do
wrong, a false
witness who pours
out lies, a person
who sows discord in
a family.*
Proverbs 6:16-19

Our culture has a list for everything—the worst-dressed celebrities, the safest cars, the best places to live, the highest-paid athletes, the top colleges. Lists are always informative, often fascinating, and occasionally disturbing.

The Bible also has its share of lists. The Ten Commandments (Exodus 20) and the Beatitudes of Christ (Matthew 5:1-12) are the most famous. And then there's the lesser-known list of things God hates in Proverbs 6.

It is not intended to be an exhaustive list, but it is intended to give us pause. The primary idea is to show that people of corrupt character naturally live in a way that dishonors God. They live for self, giving little or no thought to their Creator and his standards. Check your own attitudes, thoughts, speech, and actions. Are you engaged in a lifestyle that the Lord says he detests?

A WORD FOR TODAY
Don't harbor attitudes God hates.

*Today, Lord, I want to do what you love—the things
that please you, not the things that you hate. Make
me self-aware, vigilant, and desirous of doing good.*

APRIL 7

The mantra on Madison Avenue is, and seemingly always has been, "Sex sells." Take any product—makeup, milk, even mufflers—and showcase it with gorgeous models in sensual settings. The formula works like a charm. Like moths to the flame, we are foolishly attracted. Hey, this isn't rocket science—seductive things are meant to seduce!

In Proverbs 7, Solomon tells the sad story of a young man who encounters a seductive woman. She is attractive, alluring, and dressed (literally) to kill. This temptress is the epitome of style and fashion. She has "the look."

Because this man is "naive"—he lacks the wisdom to look beyond the surface or see beyond the moment—he ends up as willing prey in the trap of this adulterous woman—"like a stag caught in a trap . . . like a bird flying into a snare." And our fate is likely the same whenever we become enamored with eroticism.

A WORD FOR TODAY
Don't be surprised by temptation.

Today, Lord, I need to be careful about the images I see and dwell upon. Grant me the wisdom to see beneath the surface and beyond the moment.

Read
Proverbs 7

DRESSED
TO KILL
The woman approached him, seductively dressed and sly of heart.
Proverbs 7:10

APRIL 8

Read
Proverbs 8

BOILING IT DOWN

Jesus replied, "The most important commandment is this: 'Listen, O Israel! The LORD our God is the one and only LORD. And you must love the LORD your God with all your heart, all your soul, all your mind, and all your strength.' The second is equally important: 'Love your neighbor as yourself.' No other commandment is greater than these."

Mark 12:29-31

"Boil it down for me, Jesus," the Jewish scribe essentially asked. "Of all the laws on the books, which one should I focus on?" In so many words, this is the great dilemma of the ages: What is the point of life? Is there a succinct philosophy or worldview that spells out why we are here and how we are to live?

Not only did Jesus summarize over six hundred Jewish laws in a handful of short sentences, he also revealed the only way to a rich existence full of meaning and purpose.

Life is all about relationships, Jesus stated. Knowing God (and loving him with all that we are, in all that we do) is foremost. Hand in hand with this is our God-given responsibility to care for others and to look out for their interests (Philippians 2:3-4). When our passion and purpose in life is to please the living God and bless others, then (and only then) we will find the simplicity, freedom, and joy that eludes most people.

A WORD FOR TODAY
The greatest proverb—"Love God."

Today, Lord, I want to love more fully. Ignite within me a passion for you and a compassion for others.

APRIL 9

One of the first lessons every lifeguard learns is that it is extremely dangerous to try to save a struggling, thrashing person in danger of drowning. Such a person, desperate and unable to think clearly, often lashes out and pulls the would-be rescuer under as well.

In many ways, this is a good example of today's proverb. A wise, discerning person notices someone making foolish, perhaps even dangerous, choices. The wise person moves in to warn of danger. Instead of quietly and humbly taking this verbal rope (and being pulled to safety), the endangered one lashes back with angry, even personal, insults. He is unteachable and—barring a miraculous change— unreachable.

We can pray for the stubborn and foolish, but in truth, we really can't help them until they are willing to quit fighting and listen to what God says.

A WORD FOR TODAY
Count the cost before you rebuke.

Today, Lord, grant me the wisdom to hear the truth in any criticism I receive, and please show me when I need to try to intervene in the lives of others.

**Read
Proverbs 9**

THE TEST
OF CRITICISM
*Anyone who rebukes
a mocker will get an
insult in return.
Anyone who corrects
the wicked will get
hurt.*
Proverbs 9:7

**Read
Proverbs 10**

TROUBLEMAKER
OR
PEACEMAKER?

*Hatred stirs up
quarrels, but love
makes up for all
offenses.*
Proverbs 10:12

Some people don't just wake up on the wrong side of the bed, it almost seems they were born there! Mad at the world, they pick fights, agitate, and cause problems—as a way of life.

In stark contrast are those who live by love. They make it their goal to create an atmosphere where confession, confrontation, forgiveness, and contentment lead to peace. The Hebrew verb translated "makes up for" doesn't mean "conceals." It means "forgives." The idea is that love has no desire to rub someone's nose in his or her mistakes (1 Corinthians 13:5; James 5:20). The goal of love is to resolve offenses and problems. Once love makes up for an issue, it's over!

When conflicts arise, do you keep them stirred up or do you work toward resolution? God always knows our true intentions. We need his supernatural help in order to succeed at loving and forgiving.

A WORD FOR TODAY
Learn how love makes up for all offenses.

Today, Lord, I want to be an instrument of peace and healing. Keep me from bitterness, and enable me to forgive and to love.

APRIL 11

In his classic book *Mere Christianity*, C. S. Lewis wrote extensively about pride. He called it "the great sin," noting that it was through pride that the devil became the devil! As long as we are prideful, he argued, always looking down on everything and everyone, we cannot see the God who is above us.

In today's proverb, the word for pride comes from a Hebrew verb meaning "to boil up." The picture is of a kind of "bubbling arrogance" that seeks to dominate others and promote self. Note the result of this kind of mind-set and lifestyle: Those with inflated egos will soon be deflated!

God's way is the way of wisdom, which goes hand-in-hand with humility. This is the quiet, modest, trusting approach to life (Micah 6:8). The humble person does not "boil up" with a great need to be first or gain acclaim. A humble person is not threatened by the success of others.

A WORD FOR TODAY
Give pride the benefit of the doubt.

Today, Lord, free me from that strong urge to promote myself, to be noticed, to receive acclaim, and to be arrogant toward others. Teach me how to humble myself so that you can exalt me at the proper time.

Read
Proverbs 11

FULL OF SELF?
Pride leads to disgrace, but with humility comes wisdom.
Proverbs 11:2

APRIL 12

Read
Proverbs 12

❦

GET RICH
QUICK?
*A hard worker has
plenty of food, but
a person who
chases fantasies
has no sense.*
Proverbs 12:11

Item 1: Billions of dollars are spent each year on legalized gambling, even though it has been proven that one is more likely to get hit by lightning than to ever hit the jackpot.

Item 2: Exercise and diet products that promise big results in exchange for minimal effort are flying off the shelves.

Item 3: Over the last ten years, more people than ever have poured more money than ever into get-rich-quick schemes.

What's going on? The answer is simple: People want "something for nothing" (or, more accurately, "lots for very little"). Forget the notion of long-term discipline and slow, steady progress. Nothing less than instant, spectacular results will do.

God's Word offers an opposing view. We are urged to reject the frantic pursuit of get-rich-quick fantasies. The true secret of success (financial, physical, or spiritual) is hard work spread out over a long time. Diligent effort, not wishful thinking, is the way to prosperity.

A WORD FOR TODAY
Work is really the shorter route to riches.

Today, Lord, keep me from believing the lie that I can prosper without hard work. Help me to be diligent and to think long term, not short term.

APRIL 13

At Great-Grandma's hundredth birthday celebration, someone inevitably asks, "How did you do it? What's the secret to such a long life?" The answer will no doubt surprise you. Centenarians have been known to credit their longevity to everything from strawberry ice cream to daily naps to crossword puzzles!

Today's proverb addresses this question. In the ancient Near East, "light" symbolized physical life. For example, without the light of a campfire at night, a traveler was susceptible to danger, even death.

The point is that a wise, godly person will tend to have a long life. He or she will "walk in the light" (Isaiah 2:5; John 12:35)—keeping God's rules that provide for safety. Foolish, sinful people, on the other hand, tend to die early. They dwell in a kind of moral darkness that is fraught with traps and life-threatening trouble.

A WORD FOR TODAY
Godliness brings joy and light to life.

Today, Lord, help me remember that my life is in your hands. Help me avoid sinful attitudes and actions that put me at risk spiritually, emotionally, and physically.

Read
Proverbs 13

THE SECRET
OF LONG LIFE
The life of the godly is full of light and joy, but the light of the wicked will be snuffed out.
Proverbs 13:9

APRIL 14

**Read
Proverbs 14**

🍃

MAKING AMENDS

*Fools make fun
of guilt, but the
godly acknowledge
it and seek
reconciliation.*
Proverbs 14:9

The story is told of a deathbed visit paid to *Walden* author Henry David Thoreau by a Christian aunt. When she inquired if he had made his peace with God, he is reported to have said, "Why, I didn't know we had ever quarreled."

This is the mind-set of the skeptic or the cynic— or what Proverbs routinely calls the "fool." The concepts of guilt and repentance are laughable. The thought of needing to make amends with God or others is a joke.

Contrast this strong-willed arrogance with the response of the godly person. He or she owns up to wrong actions and hurt inflicted. More than that, the upright person seeks to make restitution, to set things right. Reconciliation (literally "good will" with God and people) is his or her primary goal.

This one pithy proverb explains how the humble find favor with God and people and why the proud never will.

A WORD FOR TODAY
Guilt is serious business.

Today, Lord, I want to experience the blessing of right relationships with you and others. Show me what I need to do to make this a reality in my life.

APRIL 15

In the current "climate of tolerance," it is taboo to call into question the behavior of others. When someone dares violate this unwritten cultural rule, even irreligious people (who seldom think of Jesus and certainly have no desire to follow him) are quick to paraphrase the words of Christ: "Who are *you* to judge? Let him who is without sin cast the first stone!"

This kind of noble-sounding rhetoric is not only foolish, it is also a distortion of what Christ meant. Today's "New Testament proverb" is primarily a call to examine ourselves *before* we criticize others. Jesus recognized how easy it is to be hypocritical, to spot the flaws of our neighbors even as we are blind to our own faults.

The biblical standard is to take a hard look at ourselves first (Psalm 26:2; 1 Corinthians 11:28). Only then are we in a position to lovingly help others see where they are off track (Galatians 6:1; 1 Thessalonians 5:14).

A WORD FOR TODAY
Expect to be judged the way you judge.

Today, Lord, I want to honor you by not being harsh with others. I want to be treated with mercy, so help me to treat others accordingly.

Read
Proverbs 15

THE CRITIC'S CORNER
Do not judge others, and you will not be judged. For you will be treated as you treat others. The standard you use in judging is the standard by which you will be judged.
Matthew 7:1-2

APRIL 16

Read
Proverbs 16

❦

THE ROOT
OF SIN

*The LORD detests
the proud; they will
surely be punished.*
Proverbs 16:5

Our human tendency is to assess sin superficially.
We look at external behavior and rank it. For example, "white" lies are often viewed as "no big deal";
stealing is regarded as a pretty major sin; and, well,
if you *really* want to offend God, engage in some
kind of sexual perversion—like pedophilia.

The Bible takes a deeper view of sin. God looks at
the human heart and says that the root of *all* disobedience—from unkindness to mass murder—is the
sin of pride. It's not surprising, then, to read in
Proverbs 16 that God *detests* pride.

Pride is that powerful yearning inside each of us
that says, "I will do things *my way*." Pride has no
regard for God's glory. It has no interest in exalting
his name. Pride rejects God's will for "what *I* want."
But in the end it reaps punishment, not freedom.

A WORD FOR TODAY
Pride leads to judgment.

*Today, Lord, show me where I stubbornly refuse to bow
my will to yours. Give me the grace I need to humble
myself before you.*

APRIL 17

Two teens get into trouble. One's brush with the law scares him straight. The other is in and out of court—and in and out of jail—for the rest of his life. How do we account for this difference? According to the book of Proverbs, the first kid is wise; the second is a fool.

A wise person carefully and quickly heeds words of warning. He or she realizes that a rebuke, while sometimes embarrassing, is actually a gift. Coming from an older, wiser saint, the discerning soul receives constructive criticism, knowing it can prevent much trouble and regret.

Meanwhile, fools are impervious to discipline. Not even excessive physical punishment can change the ways of the hardheaded and hard-hearted. They are stubborn and, barring a sudden change, headed for even bigger trouble.

We would do well to consider how *we* respond when corrected.

A WORD FOR TODAY
Learn to discriminate between foolishness and wisdom.

Today, Lord, I want to make progress in the area of being open to rebukes based on truth and offered in love. Make me teachable.

**Read
Proverbs 17**

SCARED
STRAIGHT
*A single rebuke does
more for a person of
understanding than
a hundred lashes on
the back of a fool.*
Proverbs 17:10

APRIL 18

Read
Proverbs 18

🌰

GRAPEVINE
GOURMET?
Rumors are dainty
morsels that sink
deep into one's
heart.
Proverbs 18:8

When it comes to food, what's your weakness? What scrumptious dish do you find almost impossible to resist? What delicious dessert causes you to salivate?

In the proverb for today, gossip is pictured as a mouthwatering morsel. It sure is a fitting image. Rumors tempt us like a sizzling entrée. Like addictive snack food, we can't seem to get enough. We crave more juicy details.

Dieters like to say, "A moment on the lips, forever on the hips." What seems so good in the short term ends up causing long-term pain. According to our verse, a similar phenomenon takes place with gossip. Once we indulge, we find rumors hard to forget. They sink deep into our hearts.

The best course of action? Any dieter can tell you: Don't give in to the temptation! If you never take that first bite, you won't have to worry about the second or the third.

A WORD FOR TODAY
Develop a rumor allergy.

Today, Lord, I want to develop an aversion to gossip. When rumors are being spread, help me to turn a deaf ear and not participate.

APRIL 19

Some wise guy has noted that marriage is the only institution on earth where everybody on the outside wants in, and everybody on the inside wants out! It's a humorous quip with a kick. Why *do* so many put so much hope in marriage? Why *do* so many couples have such great struggle?

In Old Testament times, marriages were typically arranged by the parents. This provided for simplicity in courtship, but it did not guarantee marital happiness. According to today's proverb, while passing along the family fortune may have been a somewhat "foolproof" transaction, good matchmaking necessitated the Lord's help and favor.

The same principle is still true. We need God's help to *find* the right mate. We need the grace of God to *be* a godly mate. If you're happily married, thank the Lord. If your marriage needs help, call on the Lord. Any and all good in your life ultimately comes from him (James 1:17).

A WORD FOR TODAY
Marriage is always a work in progress.

Today, Lord, I want to make a conscious effort to remember that every good gift in my life is from you—that goes for marriage, too.

**Read
Proverbs 19**

A GIFT
FROM HEAVEN
*Fathers can give
their sons an
inheritance of
houses and wealth,
but only the LORD
can give an
understanding wife.*
Proverbs 19:14

APRIL 20

Read
Proverbs 20

CREDIT WHERE
CREDIT'S DUE

*Ears to hear and
eyes to see—both
are gifts from the
LORD.*
Proverbs 20:12

This proverb can be interpreted in a couple of ways. Taken at face value, it seems to be saying that we ought to be grateful for our physical senses of hearing and sight. These auditory and optical capabilities are, indeed, a wonderful blessing.

On the other hand, since the Hebrew verb "to hear" is sometimes translated as "to obey," and since "to see" often means "to understand" elsewhere in the Bible, this verse may mean that *spiritual* insight and obedience are a gift from God (Ephesians 2:8-10).

Whichever interpretation you prefer—that this verse speaks of physical perception or that it refers to spiritual awareness and understanding—don't lose sight of the deeper truth. *God* is the source of all that we have. Thank *him* for his marvelous, undeserved blessings! And use his blessings for his glory!

A WORD FOR TODAY
It makes sense to use your senses!

Today, Lord, I want to give credit where credit is due. I want to praise you for blessing me with ears to hear and eyes to see. Help me use these to bring you praise.

APRIL 21

Consider the words of seventeen-year-old Heather: "When my folks were splitting up, they *showered* me with stuff, but what I really wanted and needed most was them. I would gladly trade all the gifts—even my car—to be close to them."

Giving gifts to alleviate guilt is a common practice—and not just among divorcing parents. Often, people who know they're not living as they should try to "make it up" to God through various religious gestures. In ancient times, this usually meant the sacrifice of a few extra animals. Now, it generally involves more time devoted to religious functions or a little something extra in the offering plate.

The Bible is clear. God cannot be "bought off." He isn't impressed by our "pseudo-devotion." To ignore God Monday through Saturday and then expect him to be satisfied with a few extra bucks or a couple of hours of ritual on Sunday morning is the height of hypocrisy. God doesn't want your stuff. He wants you—doing his will.

A WORD FOR TODAY
God can't be bought off.

Today, Lord, you desire my genuine obedience, not my slick attempts at appearing holy. Keep me from the insidious sin of hypocrisy.

Read
Proverbs 21

BRIBING GOD?
The LORD is more pleased when we do what is right and just than when we offer him sacrifices.
Proverbs 21:3

APRIL 22

*God blesses those
who hunger and
thirst for justice,
for they will be
satisfied.*
Matthew 5:6

What are people in our culture hungry for? If the infomercials we watch on TV are any indication, people crave rich food and buff bodies (how's that for a contradiction?). Our culture also seems to be thirsty for wealth, personal peace, and escapist entertainment. The problem is that such pursuits provide only temporary satisfaction. Then what?

In the Sermon on the Mount, Jesus urged his followers to "hunger and thirst for justice." Since this Greek verb is sometimes translated "righteousness," the point seems to be that we should long for things to be made "right." Our number one pursuit should be for a right relationship with God. Our continual prayer should be for the "rightness" of heaven to come down and fill the whole earth (Matthew 6:9-10).

When such eternal quests are our true longings, we can be assured that God will satisfy us—both now and in the life to come.

A WORD FOR TODAY
Develop a justice appetite.

*Today, Lord, I want to pursue you with greater passion.
Stir my heart. Create within me a deeper desire for the
things of heaven than for the stuff of earth.*

APRIL 23

Not so long ago, kids who got out of line got spanked. Parents administered this kind of physical discipline routinely, and most school principals also wielded a "board of education" to teach disobedient children important character lessons. No longer. Spank a kid today, even your own, and you may end up in court . . . or worse.

Obviously, we need to protect kids from child abuse, but is it wise to go to the opposite extreme? Not according to Proverbs. Today's verse encourages parents to exercise appropriate measures (even physical discipline) to correct defiant children. The goal is not merely outer conformity to a set of rules, but helping kids develop the kind of inner character and moral boundaries that will save them from potentially disastrous choices later in life.

By not correcting inappropriate behavior, we give our children the wrong idea that there are no consequences to wrong choices. Perhaps this is the ultimate child abuse.

Read Proverbs 23

TRUE CHILD ABUSE
Don't fail to discipline your children. They won't die if you spank them. Physical discipline may well save them from death.
Proverbs 23:13-14

A WORD FOR TODAY
Discipline communicates love.

Today, Lord, I am reminded that your truth is often at odds with the prevailing "wisdom" of culture. Give me the courage to do what is right, not just what is popular.

APRIL 24

Read
Proverbs 24

DON'T QUIT!
*If you fail under
pressure, your
strength is too
small.*
Proverbs 24:10

Pouting. Stomping. Yelling. Screaming. Crying. Worrying. Dissolving. Escaping. Enduring. Isn't it fascinating to watch the various ways people respond to adversity?

According to the Bible, trials are both normal and helpful. They enable us to *develop* godly character (Romans 5:3-4; James 1:2-4). Not only this, but the everyday pressures of stress, problems, and setbacks also *reveal* what we're really made of.

Proverbs 24:5 suggests that it is wisdom that gives strength. Therefore, the implication of today's proverb is that if we easily wilt when trouble comes, we must not be very wise.

What about you? Are you quick to wave the white flag when problems block your way? Do you quit at the first signs of stress? Don't run from adversity! Refuse to succumb to a lifestyle of whining and complaining. Remember that God is using tough situations to make you like Christ (Romans 8:29). Then call upon God's infinite power and wisdom (Ephesians 1:19-20).

A WORD FOR TODAY
Pressure brings out the worst and the best.

*Today, Lord, grant me the wisdom to see your hand
in my trials. I want to be strong. I want to persevere.
Sustain me today with the confidence that you are
in control.*

APRIL 25

Dinner at the best Italian restaurant in town: $100. Tickets to an award-winning play: $160. Fifteen minutes of constructive criticism expressed in love: Priceless.

If we were to copy a popular ad campaign of a major credit card, *that's* how we might paraphrase Solomon's wise counsel regarding confrontation.

Human nature tends to recoil from any and all criticism (even when it is valid). Rationalizing, justifying, and blaming are our natural reactions. And yet as believers in Christ, we have a *new nature* (2 Corinthians 5:17). The indwelling Spirit of God gives us the ability to respond in *supernatural* ways (Galatians 5:22-23). Consequently, we can, if we will, come to see criticism as an instrument of good in our life.

No one enjoys having his or her flaws pointed out. But the next time you are confronted, resist the urge to defend yourself and lash back. Listen. Think. Pray. Through hard, tough words, God may be offering you a priceless gift.

A WORD FOR TODAY
Accept criticism; the good kind will help you.

Today, Lord, I want to be humble enough to hear the truth about myself and wise enough to fix—with your help—whatever is not right in my life.

**Read
Proverbs 25**

PRICELESS!
To one who listens, valid criticism is like a gold earring or other gold jewelry.
Proverbs 25:12

APRIL 26

Read
Proverbs 26

DON'T
MEDDLE!
*Interfering in
someone else's
argument is as
foolish as yanking
a dog's ears.*
Proverbs 26:17

Most dogs will put up with a lot. (How else do you think they earned the title of "man's best friend"?) But few canines will let you yank their ears. Try that stunt, and even an unusually sweet Lab or golden retriever may snap.

This is the surprising analogy used to warn us against meddling in the quarrels of others. By inviting ourselves into conflicts that don't involve us, we may end up becoming the target of both angry parties. It's noble to want to help, to want to be a peacemaker (Matthew 5:9), but when tempers are flaring and pride is out of control, little good can be accomplished.

The wiser course of action is to sit back, watch, listen, pray, and wait for the passions to subside. Then, *if* we are invited to help resolve the problem, or *if* we are in a position where it is our duty to intervene, we can gently and carefully weigh in.

A WORD FOR TODAY
Stay out of an argument's crossfire.

Today, Lord, I want to be a peacemaker, but I do not want to be unwise. Give me the discernment to know if and when I should intervene.

APRIL 27

An old Jewish fable tells of two men, one *greedy* and the other *jealous*. A certain king offered to give them anything they asked for, but *twice as much* to him who asked *last*. The *greedy* man refused to ask first, because he wanted the double portion. The *jealous* man likewise refused to make the first request because he could not bear the thought of his neighbor receiving more than himself. Finally, the jealous man broke the impasse, requesting that *one* of his eyes should be taken out, in order that his neighbor might lose both.

Such is the nature of jealousy. It cheers for the ruin of others, and given the chance, will take an active role in bringing about their downfall. It was because of jealousy that Cain murdered Abel, that Joseph's brothers sold him into slavery, that the Jews had Christ crucified.

Unlike anger and wrath, which typically erupt and then pass, jealousy lurks long-term in the shadows of the human heart, ravaging souls and wrecking lives.

A WORD FOR TODAY
Reject jealousy.

Today, Lord, I ask you to keep me free from jealousy. Help me rejoice when others experience success and prosperity.

**Read
Proverbs 27**

CANCER OF
THE SOUL
Anger is cruel, and wrath is like a flood, but jealousy is even more dangerous.
Proverbs 27:4

APRIL 28

Read
Proverbs 28

FUTILE
PRAYING

*God detests the
prayers of a person
who ignores the law.*
Proverbs 28:9

Spiritual schizophrenia (also known as religious hypocrisy) is a common malady among Christians. The symptoms are easy to see: talking like a follower of Christ one moment and living like an unbeliever the next; "pious" participation in worship, prayer, or Bible reading immediately followed by lifestyle choices that do not honor or even acknowledge the existence of a holy God. Those who embrace this kind of "Jekyll and Hyde" lifestyle are often quite successful at fooling other people, but God is *never* fooled.

This is the point of today's highlighted proverb. Those who have no intention of obeying God's Word might as well keep their prayers to themselves. God is not swayed by the religious endeavors of blatant hypocrites (Psalm 66:18; Proverbs 15:8; Isaiah 59:2). In fact, we are told here that God detests such a person's phony prayers! If we want God to hear us, we must first be willing to hear from (obey) him.

A WORD FOR TODAY
Pure prayer doesn't rise from a polluted well.

Today, Lord, I want to live a consistent, God-honoring life. Show me blind spots in my life where I'm not practicing what I say I believe.

APRIL 29

When you get miffed, ticked, or steamed, are you more likely to (a) flip your lid; (b) fly off the handle; (c) hit the ceiling; or (d) blow either a fuse, a gasket, or your top?

Truth is, *lots* of things can happen when we get too hot under the collar, and most of them are not good. Uncontrolled anger causes more grief and regret than just about any other emotion.

The apostle James, under the inspiration of the Holy Spirit, offered this wise checklist for those moments when we feel our blood starting to boil. First, make an extra effort to listen (especially to what God might be trying to say to you in the situation). Second, bite your tongue (careless words will only aggravate a tense situation). Third, don't let your emotions cause you to sin (see Ephesians 4:26).

We should never ignore or deny angry feelings, but we should not let them control us either.

A WORD FOR TODAY
Accelerate listening; put the brakes on anger.

Today, Lord, I want to honor you in those frustrating, angry moments of life. Keep me from reacting sinfully. Help me respond graciously.

Read
Proverbs 29

IS IT BAD
TO GET MAD?
Understand this, my dear brothers and sisters: You must all be quick to listen, slow to speak, and slow to get angry. Human anger does not produce the righteousness God desires.
James 1:19-20

APRIL 30

Read
Proverbs 30

☙

NO EDITING
NEEDED

Do not add to
[God's] words, or
he may rebuke you
and expose you as
a liar.
Proverbs 30:6

What does it mean to "add to God's words"? Religious cults do it when they put other writings on a par with the Bible. Churches do it when they emphasize man-made traditions as much as or more than they do the teachings of Scripture. Individuals do it when they discard the clear pronouncements of the Word in favor of popular ideas or personal desires.

Today's passage warns against any kind of "editing" of God's Word. Because God delivered his revelation to the world without error, we do not need to tamper with Scripture. In fact, it is dangerous and foolish to attempt to add human speculation to divine revelation. Attempting to alter or amend the Word of God is, in effect, to question God's wisdom, his goodness, or his judgment. And according to this passage, any such arrogance will lead to a divine rebuke and the humiliation of being exposed as one who has knowingly obscured the truth.

A WORD FOR TODAY
Take God's Word straight.

Today, Lord, I want to treat your Word (and nothing else) as my ultimate authority and guide. Keep me from the great sin of adding to your words.

MAY 1

We have some wonderful opportunities to observe the marvels of God's creation in those educational shows about animals on television. It is interesting to learn how some animals give birth to their babies and then, almost immediately, the babies are off on their own. On the other hand, many animal parents have their young for a few years; they teach them how to hunt and how to stay away from predators—in essence, how to survive.

If God provided such training even in much of the animal kingdom, how important it is for people! God created human families so that parents could train their children. Human parents also give their children "survival" skills—but they do much more by giving spiritual, moral, and emotional training. When parents are a good influence, the children who listen will learn valuable lessons that will straighten and smooth their own road in life. Such parents are giving a great gift to their children—crowning them with grace and adorning them with honor.

**Read
Proverbs 1**

THE BEST
ADORNING
*What you learn
from [your parents]
will crown you with
grace and be a chain
of honor around
your neck.*
Proverbs 1:9

A WORD FOR TODAY
Value your parents' training.

*Lord, help me to be the parent you want me to be. May
I give my children the kind of instruction that will
crown them with grace and adorn them with honor.*

MAY 2

Read
Proverbs 2

ON GUARD

He guards the paths
of the just and
protects those
who are faithful
to him.
Proverbs 2:8

The Bible tells us that God is not only perfectly loving, merciful, and compassionate but also perfectly just: "The LORD our God was right to do all of these things" (Daniel 9:14). Because God is perfectly just, we can trust that everything he does is right and fair—whether we perceive it that way now or not. We know that whatever happens to us in this life has already passed through his hands—even perceived injustice. God promises to protect those who are faithful to him.

The world is full of injustice and corruption. While we watch injustice occur, we may wonder where God is. Yet the Bible assures us that he is guarding the paths of justice. In the end, the one who is perfectly just will punish all evil and reward his faithful children.

A WORD FOR TODAY
God rewards faithfulness.

Lord, help me to trust in your justice. Help me to know that ultimately you will make all things right, bring perfect justice to the world, and reward those who have remained faithful to you.

MAY 3

An undisciplined child is not a pretty sight. We have all seen a child who kicks and screams and behaves rudely. Children need discipline because their natural bent is toward sin and selfishness. Parents have to train their children to behave correctly. Sometimes this involves discipline, but that discipline is meant in love. Wise parents delight in their children and discipline them, knowing that such training will crown their children with grace and honor (1:9).

Like a loving earthly father, God also disciplines his children. Our natural bent, like all children, is toward sin and selfishness. Because God delights in us, he wants to teach us to live rightly for him. So when we feel the sting of God's discipline on our lives, we must not ignore it or be discouraged. Like obedient children, we must learn the lesson God has for us. God disciplines those he loves; if we are being disciplined, we know we are loved.

A WORD FOR TODAY
God loves through discipline.

Lord, let me remember that your discipline in my life happens because you love me. Show me what you are trying to teach me.

**Read
Proverbs 3**

BECAUSE
HE LOVES
My child, don't reject the LORD's discipline, and don't be upset when he corrects you. For the LORD corrects those he loves, just as a father corrects a child in whom he delights.
Proverbs 3:11-12

MAY 4

**Read
Proverbs 4**

OFF AND
RUNNING

*When you walk, you
won't be held back;
when you run, you
won't stumble.*

Proverbs 4:12

The picture of running through life seems to be an especially apt one for our culture. We run from this activity to that job to this responsibility to that commitment. Lots of that running, however, doesn't seem to be so wise. We may do way too much running, only to find ourselves stumbling, unable to fulfill our commitments as well as we would like because we're over-committed, tired, or burned out.

There's no doubt that we will continue to "run" at a certain pace, for life is very busy for most people. To be able to run through life guided by wisdom means knowing your own best pace and allowing for only the amount of activity that can be done realistically and well. Wisdom means seeking God's guidance so we know when to say yes and when to say no. Then we will do all things well, and we won't "stumble" along the way.

A WORD FOR TODAY
Wisdom avoids hurts and hurdles.

Lord, as I run through my activities, teach me how to be guided by wisdom. Show me when to say yes and when to say no.

MAY 5

How many teachers have read this verse with great satisfaction? They knew that the knowledge they were imparting to their students was essential to their lives, but how many students simply didn't care? And how many of those same students, faced with difficult challenges that demanded those lessons or skills later in life, would then lament, "Oh, why didn't I listen to my teachers?"

The context of this verse is specifically the teaching about immorality. The student (the son) who does not listen will find himself facing utter ruin. He will then lament that he should have heeded the instruction of his teacher (his father) who had been exactly right about the perils of immorality.

In any situation, we would be wise to listen and learn from our teachers. And as teachers, especially of our own children, we would be wise to help them to understand the ultimate value of the lessons we try to impart.

A WORD FOR TODAY
Regrets are late lessons.

Lord, help me to respectfully learn from those you have sent to teach me. Also, help me to teach those you have given me as students with enthusiasm and urgency so that they will understand the value of the lessons I give.

Read Proverbs 5

LISTEN AND LEARN
Oh, why didn't I listen to my teachers? Why didn't I pay attention to my instructors?
Proverbs 5:13

MAY 6

Read
Proverbs 6

🍎

MORE THAN
A TITLE

*Not everyone who
calls out to me,
"Lord! Lord!" will
enter the Kingdom
of Heaven. Only
those who actually
do the will of my
Father in heaven
will enter.*
Matthew 7:21

Jesus had just finished talking about how we can
know a person by his or her "fruit" (Matthew 7:20).
In other words, people can say whatever they want,
but inevitably their actions (their "fruit") will reveal
who they really are and what they really believe.
Therefore, Jesus knew that many people would
attempt to "sound religious" by saying the right
words and even referring to Jesus as "Lord." They
may attend church and "look" right. They may even
be able to fool a lot of people for a lot of the time.

Jesus made clear, however, that looking or sound-
ing religious will not get anyone into the Kingdom
of Heaven. The only thing that matters is obedience
to God the Father. That obedience refers to accepting Jesus' sacrifice on our behalf and allowing him
to save us. What matters is not what we *say* about
Jesus, but what we *do* about him.

A WORD FOR TODAY
Mix obedience with your faith.

*Lord, let me strengthen my personal relationship with
you. I want to obey your command to believe in the Son
you sent to die for me. I want to bear fruit for you
because I am your child.*

MAY 7

Temptation is easy to find. Most of us don't really have to try very hard to put ourselves in a situation where we are tempted to do wrong: the recovering alcoholic and the bar, the gambler and the casino, the sex addict and the newsstand or the Internet—even the dieter and the nearest cookie jar!

In this passage, the temptress seduces the young, foolish man. She knows what she wants, and she stands brazenly "in the streets and markets, soliciting at every corner." Temptation is brazen, for Satan desires to lure us to commit sin. He wants to see us fail, be embarrassed, ruin our witness for Christ, or fall back into addiction. To do so, he will solicit in every corner of our lives.

How do we stay out of his traps? We follow wise teachings, guard them, and write them deep in our hearts (7:1-3), so we can say "No!" to the brazen solicitations of temptation.

A WORD FOR TODAY
Beware of temptation ambushes.

Lord, help me to stand firm in the face of this temptation that is trying to lure me into sin. Give me words from your Word to help me say no to temptation.

**Read
Proverbs 7**

"NO SOLICITORS"
She is often in the streets and markets, soliciting at every corner.
Proverbs 7:12

MAY 8

Read
Proverbs 8

FEAR THE LORD, HATE EVIL

All who fear the
LORD will hate evil.
Therefore, I hate
pride and arrogance,
corruption and
perverse speech.
Proverbs 8:13

In this verse, Wisdom is the speaker (see 8:12), calling out for people to listen. Wisdom knows that fear of the Lord and evil are mutually exclusive. One cannot "fear the Lord" and enjoy any form of evil. In fact, God's people should "hate evil" in all its forms. Some of the forms of evil are outlined here: pride, arrogance, corruption, and perverse speech. These should be hated by people who love the Lord and desire wisdom.

Pride and *arrogance* refer to attitudes of superiority that usually result in offensive displays of haughtiness. These have no place among God's people who are called to be humble (1 Peter 5:6). *Corruption* is moral depravity, dishonesty, perversion. A corrupt person is debased in character. In contrast, God's people are to live above reproach (1 Peter 2:12). *Perverse speech* leads people astray and is improper. Believers' words should always be good and helpful (Ephesians 4:29).

A WORD FOR TODAY
Exercise hatred toward evil.

Lord, teach me how to live to fear you and to hate evil.
May I develop humility, may I live above reproach, and
may my words be helpful to all to whom I speak.

MAY 9

Why shouldn't we rebuke a mocker? Because a mocker hears without listening. A mocker pays attention only to mimic, ridicule, and humiliate. Even a mild rebuke will be returned as mockery, while an effective rebuke will simply be met with hatred.

Wise people don't enjoy being told they're wrong, but they understand that a truthful rebuke reflects love. So, where a mocker hears only more fodder for ridicule, a wise person hears an expression of love.

When we have people in our lives who are willing to rebuke us when necessary, we should be thankful. We should also be courageous enough to rebuke someone we love if we realize that he or she needs it. A rebuke given with love will help the other person. Hopefully, he or she will understand our motivation of love. And perhaps we will recognize that several of the rebukes we have received were actually expressions of love.

A WORD FOR TODAY
Rebukes complement wisdom.

Lord, help me rebuke lovingly. Help me also to hear the love in the rebukes of others.

Read
Proverbs 9

COURAGEOUS,
CONSTRUC-
TIVE CRITICISM
Don't bother correcting mockers; they will only hate you. But correct the wise, and they will love you.
Proverbs 9:8

MAY 10

Wise people treasure knowledge, but the babbling of a fool invites disaster.
Proverbs 10:14

Proverbs constantly seeks to help us understand the differences between wisdom and foolishness, and calls us to be people of wisdom. Wise people have certain characteristics; foolish people have certain contrasting characteristics. Knowing these characteristics gives us a mirror into our own lives. These also help us be discerning about the people with whom we choose to associate.

This proverb tells us that people who are wise "treasure" (or value and store up) knowledge. Wise people are constantly learning—from their own mistakes, others' mistakes, from the world around them, from God's Word—and they store up that knowledge so as to help them live wisely. They don't run around talking all the time, so when they speak, we trust that what they say is knowledgeable. In contrast, the fool is "babbling" all the time, talking without thinking. That "invites disaster," said the writer. We should seek to be people whose words can be counted on as having depth and wisdom.

A WORD FOR TODAY
Wisdom makes regular deposits in a knowledge account.

Lord, watch over every word I speak. Help me to consider my words and from where they come. Teach me how to treasure knowledge.

MAY 11

Make no mistake about it—both the Old and New Testaments describe a "day of judgment," a time when God will vanquish evil and make all things right. No matter how rich we are, our money will be worthless. We cannot purchase salvation—it was already purchased by the blood of Christ.

Of course, the writer did not know about Jesus Christ. All he knew was that a relationship with God was available and that God's people attempted to live by God's standards. "Right living" does not mean that good deeds can give salvation, for the New Testament clears that up for us. However, right living—a life lived through the power of the Holy Spirit because of one's belief in Christ—does indeed "save from death." It is not that we will never die. Instead, it pictures that death is not the end, but merely a step into the next life—an eternal one with God.

A WORD FOR TODAY
Real life inoculates against death.

Lord, may I learn to see my money (no matter how little or much I have) as your gift to me. Teach me how to use it wisely to meet my needs and then to do your work in the world.

Read
Proverbs 11

WHAT MONEY
CAN'T BUY
*Riches won't help
on the day of
judgment, but right
living can save you
from death.*
Proverbs 11:4

MAY 12

**Read
Proverbs 12**

LISTEN UP

*Fools think their
own way is right,
but the wise listen
to others.*
Proverbs 12:15

This verse has been taken many ways—with varying
results. At face value, this could mean that a teenager who listens to the advice of his friends to try
drugs is actually considered wise. Obviously, the
principle here goes far deeper, concerning both attitude and discernment. Foolish people think their
own way is right. They think they need no advice,
and so they refuse to listen to anyone who might
have experience, knowledge, or even just loving
concern for them. They foolishly limit their ability
to make good decisions.

"The wise listen to others" means that these people are able to discern to whom they should listen as
well as the wisdom of the advice offered. God often
does speak to us through other people, and so wise
people should seek counsel from others whom they
respect as spiritually sensitive. Wise people then can
consider the advice and experience of others as they
continue to seek God's guidance.

A WORD FOR TODAY
The wise pay attention.

*Lord, I ask you to show me how I should seek advice.
Reveal to me the people who can give wise advice. Teach
me how to discern and use the counsel I receive. Help me
to grow and learn so that I can give good counsel to
others who have need.*

MAY 13

This marks our fifth look at this Greatest Commandment. The first four have been general attempts to see the big picture of our relationship with God and our neighbor. Our remaining meditations on this passage will focus on individual aspects of the command.

For instance, when we quote or think about the first part of the verse, we tend to mentally shorten it to "Love the Lord with all your heart, soul, mind, and strength." We leave out the clearly repeated "all your"that introduces each human component. The summary may help us clarify the main point of the commandment, but it doesn't help us apply it very well.

The task of meditation forces us to consider some important questions: What is the difference between loving God with "all your heart" and loving God with "all your mind"? What does it mean to love God with "all your soul"? How does "all your strength" fit with the other three? Keep these questions in mind. Meditate toward answers on your own.

A WORD FOR TODAY
The greatest proverb—"Love God."

Lord Jesus, you said this was the most important commandment. Help me treat these words that way— seeking to understand and to put into practice your priorities.

Read
Proverbs 13

ALL OF WHAT?
Jesus replied, "The most important commandment is this: 'Listen, O Israel! The LORD our God is the one and only LORD. And you must love the LORD your God with all your heart, all your soul, all your mind, and all your strength.' The second is equally important: 'Love your neighbor as yourself.' No other commandment is greater than these."
Mark 12:29-31

MAY 14

Read
Proverbs 14

❦

CHECK
THE MAP
There is a path
before each person
that seems right, but
it ends in death.
Proverbs 14:12

Many people live in sin, never sensing that they are doing anything wrong. They are doing what pleases them, so it must be right, they reason.

In his letter to the Romans, Paul wrote, "When you were slaves to sin, you were free from the obligation to do what was right. And what was the result? You now are ashamed of the things you used to do, things that end in eternal doom" (Romans 6:20-21). Just because people "feel good" about what they are doing doesn't necessarily make it right. No matter how it "seems," it may be a pathway only to death.

So what *is* the right path—the one that *doesn't* end in death? It is the path we get on when we accept Jesus Christ as our Savior. We follow that path as we serve him in the world. On that path, we are truly set free to "do those things that lead to holiness and result in eternal life" (Romans 6:22).

A WORD FOR TODAY
You can walk in any direction, but only one leads to life.

Lord, walk with me. Help me to take steps in my life not because they "seem" right, but because I have sought your guidance and am walking closely with you.

MAY 15

It seems so obvious—why make it a proverb? When people's hearts are light and joyful, their faces reflect happiness; when people are sorrowful and brokenhearted, their spirits are crushed. While this may be true, does it *have* to be that way all the time?

The author may want us to consider how we react to the situations that come into our lives. It's easy to be happy when our hearts are glad; it's much more difficult to reflect deep joy when we are hurting. Yet all of us experience hurt, sorrow, and grief in our lives at one time or another. While we are not called to be happy about our difficulties, we can still reflect an attitude of strength and faith in God, refusing to let our circumstances crush our spirits. Such an attitude understands God's love and sovereignty and trusts him to be a "rock and fortress" through times of difficulty.

A WORD FOR TODAY
You externals will reveal your internals.

Lord, may my face reflect my love for and faith in you, regardless of my circumstances.

Read
Proverbs 15

HAPPY FACES
A glad heart makes a happy face; a broken heart crushes the spirit.
Proverbs 15:13

MAY 16

**Read
Proverbs 16**

DAY PLANNER
*We can make our
plans, but the LORD
determines our steps.*
Proverbs 16:9

This verse is not saying that we should make no plans. In fact, God says that wise people listen to others (12:15) and don't just follow whatever path seems right (14:12). Surely God does not want us to sit idly, waiting for him to make things happen in our lives. We must make plans, get advice, think carefully, pray, weigh the pros and cons, and use our God-given brains to take steps forward in life.

The writer is reminding us of God's complete sovereignty. As Paul made his plans to visit various countries in his ministry, at times God simply stood in the way and said "no" (Acts 16:6-10). The point is, we make our plans and hold them loosely, allowing God to intervene and make changes according to his will. What a wonderful promise! At no time do we ever need to fear that we will miss what God wants for us. As we move, he guides and directs.

A WORD FOR TODAY
God is in both the planning and the execution.

Lord, as I make my plans, help me to remember that you are sovereign. Wherever you want to take me is exactly where I should be.

MAY 17

How vivid is the picture of quarrelsome words opening a floodgate and letting loose a torrent of anger. However, this proverb is not telling non-confrontational people to keep their hurt and anger stopped up behind a dam. There is a place for talking through difficulties and differences of opinion—in fact, in healthy relationships, it *has* to be done.

The writer is advising us not to *begin* a quarrel. In other words, when we need to talk about some hurt or to deal with some anger, there is a way to start the conversation and there is a way *not* to start it. To begin with a volley of accusations or even a heated voice will start a quarrel and open the floodgates. How much better to drop the matter, at least for the time being. Then we can calmly find the right way to communicate how we feel and talk it through in a healthy manner.

A WORD FOR TODAY
Wisdom drains a resentment reservoir.

Lord, help me to deal in a right way with the hurts, disagreements, and concerns I have with people close to me. If I feel quarrelsome, help me to wait for a better time. Help me to speak calmly and to express myself clearly. Help me to listen to what the other person says to me.

**Read
Proverbs 17**

FLOOD LINE
*Starting a quarrel
is like opening a
floodgate, so stop
before a dispute
breaks out.*
Proverbs 17:14

MAY 18

**Read
Proverbs 18**

❧

READY
FOR BATTLE
*The name of the
LORD is a strong
fortress; the godly
run to him and
are safe.*
Proverbs 18:10

At times, we just need a place to hide. Life's circumstances begin to overwhelm us, problems mount, situations are out of our control. We know we have to deal with these things, but we just can't do it right now. Instead, we just want to get away and regroup.

God knows that life is like this. He knows that sometimes we feel like we can't handle anything more. So he provides himself as a fortress, a place of safety, a place to hide. With high walls, battlements, and soldiers on the lookout, our fortress is a place for us to run to and find safety. The gate swings open for us and locks securely behind us. There in the fortress we can talk to God, get his guidance, and receive his strength. We will indeed have to go out and face whatever is before us, but not before God has prepared us behind the walls of his fortress.

A WORD FOR TODAY
Escape to God.

Lord, I need you to calm my heart, give me rest, and then prepare me for what is ahead. Please be my strong fortress today.

MAY 19

The Bible makes no excuses for the realities of life. Some people will be wealthy; some will be poor. While we can blame all kinds of circumstances, the fact is clear that even some of the poorest people in one country are very rich by the standards of another country.

So what do we do about it? The Bible makes it very clear that God's people are to be concerned for those less fortunate. Obviously we ourselves cannot solve the entire problem of poverty; governments have tried to do that and often come up short. The most efficient and effective system involves individuals helping other individuals in whatever ways the Lord leads them. The promise is that in helping others we are helping the Lord, just the way Jesus described (Matthew 25:31-40). In addition, God promises to repay. But don't wait for a refund check in the mail. God's currency comes in many forms—not the least of which is great joy!

A WORD FOR TODAY
God settles every account.

Lord, let me be mindful of the needs of others. Show me how I can, with wisdom and sensitivity, help to meet those needs.

**Read
Proverbs 19**

A HELPING HAND
If you help the poor, you are lending to the LORD—and he will repay you!
Proverbs 19:17

MAY 20

Read
Proverbs 20

❧

TONGUE-
CONTROL

*If you claim to
be religious but
don't control
your tongue, you
are fooling yourself,
and your religion
is worthless.*

James 1:26

James makes the point that the tongue, while small, can cause lots of damage (James 3:5-6). We may know some people whose mouths always seem to get them into trouble, but we certainly don't expect that from people who "claim to be religious." Such people claim to have faith in the Lord, but if their mouths are out of control—either by use of profanity, gossip, or words that wound—then they are fooling only themselves about their faith. Their "religion is worthless" because it has made no change in their hearts.

Believers have received the Holy Spirit, and one of his fruits is "self-control" (Galatians 5:23). Self-control involves tongue-control. While we may not always be able to control the thoughts that fly into our heads at any given moment, we certainly ought to be able to control the words that seek to fly out of our mouths. The Holy Spirit promises to help us.

A WORD FOR TODAY
Words reveal both counterfeit and genuine faith.

Lord, help me to watch what I say. Give me self-control to think before I speak so that my words will reveal your Spirit in me.

MAY 21

God hates pride. Sure, God wants his people to realize how much he loves them; he wants his people to have strong self-esteem that comes from knowing their worth and value in his eyes. But God *hates pride*. Why? Because pride pushes us away from God. Pride says we don't need God watching over us. Pride says we don't want God in control. Pride says we are better than everyone else. Pride turned a glorious angel into Satan, so God knows the power of pride.

We would all agree with the second part of this verse—evil actions are sinful. But God also views "haughty eyes" and "a proud heart" as sinful. To look down on others and to separate oneself from God is to commit sin, just as surely as doing an evil act such as stealing. Pride is powerful and dangerous, so we must be ever on guard against it.

A WORD FOR TODAY
Living me-centered is living stuck in sin.

Lord, if I am haughty or prideful in any way toward anyone, please reveal it to me. Show me how to walk humbly with you and to treat others as I should.

Read Proverbs 21

WHEN PRIDE GETS IN THE WAY
Haughty eyes, a proud heart, and evil actions are all sin.
Proverbs 21:4

MAY 22

Read Proverbs 22

🍂

HUMBLE PIE

True humility and fear of the LORD lead to riches, honor, and long life.
Proverbs 22:4

God hates pride (21:4). He desires that we have "true humility." Humility does not mean weakness; true humility is a proper understanding of oneself in relation to God and to others. It understands sin but knows that God loved us enough to die for us. Humility understands that we have a place in God's plan, while we respect the place God has for others in his plan.

When we are humble and fear (respect) the Lord, God says this leads to "riches, honor, and long life." We must remember that a proverb is a "life observation," not necessarily a promise. Plenty of truly humble and reverent people have been poor, gone unnoticed, or died young. The proverb is saying that when people live this way, many times they receive these blessings simply because it is a smart way to live. We ought to strive to honor the Lord by how we live, regardless, for we will be pleasing him.

A WORD FOR TODAY
The fear of the Lord is the beginning of success.

Lord, help me to begin on the path toward true humility. Give me healthy self-esteem so that I can use my gifts for you, while always being aware that you gave me the gifts to use for your glory and to build up your kingdom.

MAY 23

It can be very difficult when we see "sinners" prospering—especially when they prosper well beyond us. We see blatantly dishonest people being rewarded for their dishonesty. People that we know are anti-Christian seem to be receiving God's blessings. Many who are living in ways that are socially acceptable but sinful are gaining fame, wealth, and power. It's difficult not to be envious as we try to please God and yet continue to struggle.

This proverb tells us not to envy them, but to continue to fear the Lord. The next verse tells us why: "You will be rewarded for this; your hope will not be disappointed" (Proverbs 23:18). No matter what happens in this life, we must continue to fear the Lord. He has promised to watch over and guide us in this life so that we accomplish exactly what he desires. And he has promised eternity in glory with him. It doesn't get any better than that!

A WORD FOR TODAY
Fear the Lord every day, one day at a time.

Lord, show me how to continue to trust in you, even when doing so seems to put me at a standstill while everyone else moves ahead. Help me not to be envious of them. Show me the riches of your glory and my blessings in you so that I have the right perspective.

Read
Proverbs 23

WHEN THEY
HAVE IT ALL
*Don't envy sinners,
but always continue
to fear the LORD.*
Proverbs 23:17

MAY 24

**Read
Proverbs 24**

TRANSPARENT
BEFORE GOD

*Don't excuse
yourself by saying,
"Look, we didn't
know." For God
understands all
hearts, and he sees
you. He who guards
your soul knows you
knew. He will repay
all people as their
actions deserve.*
Proverbs 24:12

Trying to play hide-and-seek with God is what we
might call a "no win" situation—for us. The context
of this verse is where someone is unjustly sentenced
to death and a person who could have helped
remained quiet (24:11), claiming he knew nothing.

The point is that God knows everything about us.
He knows our hearts, he sees us wherever we go, he
keeps watch over our souls. We may be able to hide
from people, fool them, and even make them think
one way about us when the opposite is true. But we
can never hide from God. He sees all, knows all,
understands all, and—eventually—judges all.

We should seek to live honestly, truthfully, and
respectably. While we don't have to wear our hearts
on our sleeves for *everyone* to see, we should at least
be transparent enough for people to know that we
are sincere in how we speak and what we do.

A WORD FOR TODAY
God knows everything.

*Lord, may I always remember your presence with me.
May I always remember that no matter what I say or do,
you know the truth. Teach me to live a life of sincerity
and truthfulness.*

MAY 25

"You can't have too much of a good thing," or so the saying goes. Yet even the sweet taste of honey can become sickening if one eats too much of it. And a stomach full of sweet honey feels sour!

In other words, we can enjoy what God gives us to enjoy, but we are wise to do so in moderation. It is our penchant toward overindulgence or misuse of God's gifts that leads to sin. A little wine may be fine—overindulgence leads to alcoholism. Food is for sustenance and often for enjoyment—overindulgence is gluttony. Our sexuality is a gift from God—misuse of it outside the bonds of marriage can lead to much heartache.

We can indeed have too much of—or find ourselves misusing—things that God intended for our good. How much wiser to know from where the gifts come and how to use them in order to please God.

A WORD FOR TODAY
Moderation even applies to good things.

Lord, thank you for all that you have given me to enjoy. Help me to use your gifts wisely.

**Read
Proverbs 25**

TOO MUCH
Do you like honey? Don't eat too much, or it will make you sick!
Proverbs 25:16

MAY 26

**Read
Proverbs 26**

🍂

NO LAUGHING MATTER

*Just as damaging
as a madman
shooting a deadly
weapon is someone
who lies to a friend
and then says, "I
was only joking."*
Proverbs 26:18-19

When an insane person starts shooting, lots of people end up hurt—or dead. Senseless shootings have made us question the sanity of those who wield lethal weapons to commit such horrible acts.

Yet consider the damage our words do when we tell lies to others. Now consider the damage done when telling a lie to a friend. Now consider telling a lie, getting caught, and then trying to say we were "only joking." A little saying goes, "What a tangled web we weave, when first we practice to deceive." Telling lies to our friends may cause situations that spin out of our control. Despite the movies that try to show humorous situations that arise from this—or unhappy situations that have a happy ending—the truth is that lying and then trying to cover up is like shooting a lethal weapon. No happy ending here. Be truthful. Lies are never a joking matter—not even among friends.

A WORD FOR TODAY
Lies hurt and kill indiscriminately.

Lord, teach me to see lies for what they are—as damaging as lethal weapons. Help me to value and practice truthfulness in everything I say and do.

MAY 27

Tucked in among the Beatitudes, we find Jesus'
statement of what we know as the Golden Rule.
Jesus gave it later in the Sermon on the Mount.
"Do to others whatever you would like them to
do to you" (Matthew 7:12).

To this profound relational principle, Jesus added
the teaching that God stands ready to bless this kind
of attitude, which sees others deserving nothing less
than what we hope to receive. This runs exactly
contrary to selfish human desires, which tend to
think of benefits only at the expense of or loss by
others. Rather than change the desire, Jesus simply
challenged us to enlarge it to include everyone. He
used this same principle in the second half of the
Great Commandment, "Love your neighbor as
yourself" (Mark 12:31).

The application of mercy, love, and simple kindness to others ultimately benefits us. God guarantees it.

A WORD FOR TODAY
Practice mercy.

*Lord, I know I pray "Forgive us our sins as we have for-
given those who sin against us" without really thinking
about what I'm asking. Teach me to extend mercy more
readily.*

**Read
Proverbs 27**

GUARANTEED EXCHANGE

*God blesses those
who are merciful,
for they will be
shown mercy.*
Matthew 5:7

MAY 28

FOLLOW
THE LEADER

*Those who lead
good people along
an evil path will fall
into their own trap,
but the honest
will inherit good
things.*
Proverbs 28:10

Jesus made a similar statement when he told his disciples, "If you cause one of these little ones who trusts in me to fall into sin, it would be better for you to be thrown into the sea with a large millstone hung around your neck" (Mark 9:42). Clearly, God does not take it lightly when anyone leads others into sin. He is especially harsh on spiritual leaders because they are trusted (James 3:1). A pastor, teacher, parent, or anyone else in spiritual leadership must be worthy of trust. A spiritual leader who leads others into sin will be punished severely. Leadership is a heavy responsibility.

Honest leaders, however, will reap the fruit of their honest leadership. The results, though they may take time, will be worthwhile. They will have students who will grow and mature and so be able to teach others (2 Timothy 2:2). And they will receive a commendation from the Lord.

A WORD FOR TODAY
Honesty plants seeds of abundance.

Lord, let me look at myself as those who follow me look at me. Reveal to me what kind of example I am to them. Show me where I need to improve.

MAY 29

What a very simple statement, yet how many parents fail to put it into practice. Afraid of being politically incorrect, or hurting their little child's psyche, or wanting to be best buddies with their child, too many parents are bypassing the command to discipline their children. Then they wonder why their kids give them nothing but unhappiness, fear, and worry.

Of course, the word *discipline* needs to be understood. Many parents either threaten but never follow through or are too harsh. Wise parents will discipline their children wisely. They will let the punishment "fit the crime." They will follow through consistently. They will also show love.

Does this *guarantee* happiness and peace of mind? The proverb tells us that this will be the general case. There will probably still be times of sadness and worry—for that is part of life. But parents who have wisely disciplined their children will find their efforts well rewarded.

A WORD FOR TODAY
Disciplining kids is worth the effort.

Lord, show me how to be wise when I have to discipline my children. Show me how to help them know my love for them even as I teach them how to act appropriately.

**Read
Proverbs 29**

LOVING
DISCIPLINE
*Discipline your
children, and they
will give you peace
of mind and will
make your heart
glad.*
Proverbs 29:17

MAY 30

Read
Proverbs 30

JUST TWO THINGS

O God, I beg two favors from you; let me have them before I die. First, help me never to tell a lie. Second, give me neither poverty nor riches! Give me just enough to satisfy my needs.
Proverbs 30:7-8

If God were to give you any two requests, would you choose these? Agur, the writer of this passage, requested only that he never tell a lie and that he not be too poor or too rich.

We can learn from this little prayer. This need not be the pattern for all that we request in life, but it reveals a heart that trusts completely in God and knows its own weaknesses. Agur wanted to never be dishonest—and we would do well to value honesty as highly. Agur also knew that riches might lead him away from his God, and intense poverty might do the same. So he asked God to take that into account and just meet his needs. We would do well to consider the natural outcome of some of our requests, understanding that what might seem good to us may *not* be good in the long run.

A WORD FOR TODAY
Learn contentment.

Lord, may I think through the requests I bring to you. Help me to remember that you have the big picture, that you know all things, and that you may at times even say no to my requests because you know my weaknesses better than I.

MAY 31

In this portrayal of what is known as the "virtuous wife," we find, among many other qualities, a woman of compassion. While no one woman is expected to exemplify perfectly every characteristic in this description, the general portrayal is a woman of wisdom, a fitting ending to a book about wisdom. This woman has wealth that she manages carefully, and yet she is willing to help the poor and open her arms to the needy.

Compassion is a vital need in our world today. Many of us are running around trying to gain more and more, never having enough, never content, never even considering offering help to those in need. We have plenty of excuses. But this woman of wisdom stood willing to help those who have less. Whether she gave money, time, or resources is unknown—and not really important. The point is, she gave. And so should we.

A WORD FOR TODAY
Busy people make time for others.

Lord, open my eyes to the needs of others. Show me how to be a person of compassion. Show me one person for whom I can do something compassionate today.

**Read
Proverbs 31**

OPEN ARMS
*[The virtuous wife]
extends a helping
hand to the poor
and opens her arms
to the needy.*
Proverbs 31:20

JUNE 1

GREED INDEED

*Such is the fate of
all who are greedy
for money; it robs
them of life.*
Proverbs 1:19

It starts simply enough. We need enough stuff to get by. We want the good things of life for ourselves and our loved ones. Soon, however, "enough" just doesn't seem like enough. Greed has gotten a hook into our heart. Solomon knew firsthand what greed could do: In the quest to get more in life, true life starts to ebb away. In this passage in this first proverb, he passes on the benefit of his experience.

What happens when greed takes over? As we long for more stuff, we gradually lose our relationship with the Giver. Without this connection to the Source of life, true life in its eternal richness gets lost. But if we seek to gain more and more of the rich relationship that God offers—through prayer, reading the Word, and worship with his people—God is pleased and will bless us. Let us, in a sense, become "greedy" for the riches of a life lived in close connection with God.

A WORD FOR TODAY
Greed never meets the need.

Lord, may I seek the riches that you offer and not those of the world. Make me greedy for a deep relationship with you.

JUNE 2

Good teachers and trainers know that their role in their students' lives is temporary. The student pilot will eventually fly solo. The intern will someday make independent diagnoses. The trainee truck driver will be alone one day behind the wheel of a big rig. All will have to make decisions and perform tasks alone, but only after they have learned and internalized all they have been taught.

God is the ultimate teacher and wants us to so learn and internalize his lessons that we "will find the right way to go." Just as a well-taught pilot does not panic when things go wrong but can instead call upon ingrained knowledge and skills, so we can be confident that, when the time comes, we can know what is right, just, and fair. How can we have this assurance? We can open our minds and hearts to God's wisdom, shown in his Word. With such knowledge comes a bonus: joy.

A WORD FOR TODAY
Training in wisdom is life preparation.

Today, Lord, teach me more of what is right, just, and fair in your sight. Thank you for the joy that comes with your wisdom and knowledge.

Read
Proverbs 2

FIND THE
RIGHT COURSE
You will understand what is right, just, and fair, and you will find the right way to go. For wisdom will enter your heart, and knowledge will fill you with joy.
Proverbs 2:9-10

JUNE 3

Read
Proverbs 3

❧

LET IT SHINE

*You are the light of
the world—like a
city on a hilltop
that cannot be
hidden. No one
lights a lamp
and then puts it
under a basket.
Instead, a lamp is
placed on a stand,
where it gives light
to everyone in the
house. In the same
way, let your good
deeds shine out for
all to see, so that
everyone will praise
your heavenly
Father.*

Matthew 5:14-16

At first glance, Jesus seems to be encouraging his followers to call attention to themselves. These are surprising words from the one who at other times condemned religious leaders who tooted their own horns. What could Jesus be thinking? Does he want his followers to have big heads?

The answer, of course, is no. The standing out and shining have a higher purpose: the praising of our heavenly Father. The light within us that deserves attention is the light of Christ, he who was and is the Light of the world (John 9:5; 12:46). People must know the source of the good and of the light—that it comes from the Light, not from a sunny disposition or a commitment to a good cause. These words of Jesus come from the Sermon on the Mount, not long after the Beatitudes, a list of the many ways God blesses us. We are called to a bold display of the bright goodness of God at work in us and through us.

A WORD FOR TODAY
Let your faith shine.

Today, Lord, give me the courage and the humility to let your light shine out through my life.

JUNE 4

Much of life is spent traveling, and a path is an apt image for the way we live. We choose a path. We cross paths. We follow a path. We stray from the path. But the author of this proverb had something much more literal in mind when he spoke of "the path of evildoers." Our feet can take us on paths that will lead us away from God.

If we have struggled with or even succumbed to a particular sin in the past, we are to steer clear of the places that will put us in a compromising position. A compulsive gambler would do well to pick Rapid City over Atlantic City for a vacation. One who has struggled with drinking should stay away from bars, especially when alone. As the proverb urges, pick a new destination, for life is a journey. In the Lord's Prayer, we ask God to "lead us not into temptation." Why would we then tell our feet otherwise?

A WORD FOR TODAY
Our companions and destination have a lot in common.

Lord, help me to stay on your path. Give me fellow pilgrims on the journey so that we can encourage each other not to stray.

**Read
Proverbs 4**

THE PATH
NOT TAKEN
Don't do as the wicked do, and don't follow the path of evildoers. Don't even think about it; don't go that way. Turn away and keep moving.
Proverbs 4:14-15

JUNE 5

THE VOW THAT
REFRESHES

*Drink water
from your own
well—share your
love only with
your wife.*
Proverbs 5:15

The idea of comparing drinking water with marital love is most certainly an image sent from God to the author of this proverb. After all, who better than God would know that, just as water refreshes us and even sustains our life, fidelity within marriage refreshes and sustains. In addition, just as there is no true substitute for water—despite all the colas, sports drinks, and simulated fruit juices—all other sexual relationships are impostors compared to that of husband and wife.

God loves the very concept of marriage and wants us to know that any other coupling is far from his best. He wants us to experience his best for each of us. We must never settle for imitation sex or even compromise another person's marriage. Let us concentrate on and be thankful for what and whom God has provided to each of us.

A WORD FOR TODAY
Grown-up love is faithful.

God, help me to hold on to your view of marriage. Give me strength to be faithful to you and, if it is your will that I marry, to the spouse you give to me.

JUNE 6

Honesty and good communication in relationships are elusive enough in and of themselves. God knows this well, just as he knows us well. God is therefore particularly upset by those who lie and promote disharmony within a family: *Hate* and *detest* are not words to be taken lightly.

The image of a person pouring out lies as one would pour out a watering can on a garden is vivid indeed. It shows an intention—not accidentally spilling, but *pouring*—that betrays a heart at cross purposes with God. In much the same way, sowing discord—as if planting a garden of disharmony in a family—indicates how far the guilty party has strayed from God's best in relationships. Such actions often grow out of small things—the "little white lie" that seems harmless but leads to a habit of falsehood, or the gossip and taking of sides that pits family members against one another. Let us guard our ways, striving to be people who tell the truth and promote harmony.

A WORD FOR TODAY
Troublemakers create a lot of trouble for themselves.

Today, Lord, give me your sense of truth and harmony, that I might be your force for good in my family, church, workplace, and neighborhood.

Read Proverbs 6

DISCORD VERSUS HARMONY
There are six things the Lord hates—no, seven things he detests: haughty eyes, a lying tongue, hands that kill the innocent, a heart that plots evil, feet that race to do wrong, a false witness who pours out lies, a person who sows discord in a family.
Proverbs 6:16-19

JUNE 7

Read
Proverbs 7

CAME OUT
AND
CAME ON TO
*You're the one I was
looking for! I came
out to find you, and
here you are!*
Proverbs 7:15

Some people stumble into temptation never realizing that "one thing can lead to another," and suddenly they find themselves inappropriately involved with someone. Then, there are other people who most certainly do not stumble into sexual sin; indeed, they march purposely toward it, seek it out, and finally say, "You're the one I was looking for!" In the movies or in novels, it can look romantic, even "destined to be," but God knows it for what it is . . . and so should we.

We must not be naive about the world. In order to safeguard our own and others' marriages, we must look out for those who would seek extramarital relationships, steering clear of them and any involvement with them. Those of us who are married must do whatever it takes to continually strengthen our marriages and our willpower.

A WORD FOR TODAY
We find what we're really looking for.

*Lord, you are such a good God for making marriage.
Give me your wisdom and strength to recognize any
challenge to my marriage or others' marriages.*

JUNE 8

Proverbs 8 gives one of the richest, most vivid personifications in the Bible: the traditionally abstract concept of Wisdom presented as a woman. She describes her creation so long ago, before anything else was created, and her appointment to a timeless role for the benefit of all humankind. Yet what she offers in this verse is so needed today. Indeed, we might mistake these words for the promises on the dust jacket of a self-help book: common sense, success, insight, strength.

Many people read the Bible—or, if they are honest, comment on the Bible without having read it—and say that God is inscrutable. They think that he enjoys confusing his people, that no one can even begin to know his ways. Yet here is Wisdom offering the insights of the ages, making herself visible and accessible. She foreshadows the clear teaching and godly advice of Jesus, the ultimate teacher. We would do well to read, listen, and humble ourselves before the wisdom of God.

A WORD FOR TODAY
Wisdom doesn't hoard her riches.

Lord, I thank you for your willingness to teach and guide me. Give me an open mind and a devoted heart.

Read
Proverbs 8

ADVICE AND
SUCCESS
Common sense and
success belong to me.
Insight and strength
are mine.
Proverbs 8:14

JUNE 9

**Read
Proverbs 9**

WISE,
WISER,
WISEST

*Instruct the wise,
and they will
be even wiser.
Teach the righteous,
and they will learn
even more.*

Proverbs 9:9

In the world of words, whether it be a newspaper column, a magazine article, a 945-page novel, or anything in between, one thing is certain: Everybody needs an editor. Even the best writers, out of sheer overfamiliarity with their material or good old human imperfection, need someone to point out the inconsistencies, the missing transitions, the faulty logic, the shaky plot lines. In fact, good writers have become good because of what they have learned from critique and instruction. The good get better. Those resistant to editing never improve and grow.

In similar fashion, the wise get wiser. They listen to the words of Wisdom. They "take it personally," but in the best sense of the phrase. Rather than allowing their feelings to be hurt, they listen and change, much as a writer reads all the red-pencil markings rather than wallow in self-pity and the claim that "no one understands my work." God has so much to teach us, so much that he has entrusted to Wisdom, who in turn entrusts it to us. We simply must be willing to be edited.

A WORD FOR TODAY
The good get better; the wise get wiser.

*Lord, I thank you for the persistent work of Wisdom.
Teach me to be wise. Teach me to be righteous.*

JUNE 10

How many times have you loved with all your heart? We often find it surprisingly easy. The idea of loving with our whole heart appeals to us. We understand and desire the intensity of such love.

Our problems arise from the objects of our affection: We love what we shouldn't love. In fact, it is easier to be wholehearted in our love for almost anything other than God. Jesus warned that our hearts tend to be wrapped around our treasures (Matthew 6:21), and few of us treasure God as we ought. Yet obedience begins by loving God with our whole heart. Jeremiah recorded this starting point, from which the Lord quoted above: "If you look for me wholeheartedly, you will find me" (Jeremiah 29:13).

What we don't seek and love with our heart, we will not love with our soul or strength. Since we will love God only to the degree that we have "found" him, we must intensify our search. We must persist in asking God to reveal himself to us, noting the way the character and mind of God were revealed in Jesus. Everything we need to know about love we find in Jesus.

A WORD FOR TODAY
The greatest proverb—"Love God."

Lord, show me one part of me that is not entirely committed to loving you. Give me your grace and strength to conform that part.

**Read
Proverbs 10**

WITH ALL
YOUR HEART
Jesus replied, "The most important commandment is this: 'Listen, O Israel! The LORD our God is the one and only LORD. And you must love the LORD your God with all your heart, all your soul, all your mind, and all your strength.' The second is equally important: 'Love your neighbor as yourself.' No other commandment is greater than these."
Mark 12:29-31

JUNE 11

Read
Proverbs 11

CAN YOU KEEP
A SECRET?
*A gossip goes
around telling
secrets, but
those who are
trustworthy can
keep a confidence.*
Proverbs 11:13

Many think of it only as a tongue twister, but its meaning rings true: Loose lips sink ships. Whether the ship represents a relationship, a reputation, a career, a person's faith, or the trust within a community, gossip and rumors can lead to disaster. What can seem harmless and fun eventually can cause disaster. Gossiping becomes a habit that needs to be stopped.

Even Christians can fall into the habit of gossip, often under the pretense of "sharing" or informing others "just so you can know how to pray for the poor dear." But today's proverb labels it for what it is: breaking a trust. If keeping a secret is hard for us, we can be assured that God is more than able to help us end this habit. It is that important to him. If we abide by the Golden Rule (would we want *our* secrets revealed?), pray for the person, and ask God for strength, he will see us through to be people of integrity who have better uses for communication than breaking a confidence.

A WORD FOR TODAY
Gossip is a form of treachery.

*Today, Lord, help me to be a person of integrity. Show
me how to avoid gossiping.*

JUNE 12

In many cultures, defending one's honor is not merely acceptable, it is mandatory. "What are you, a wimp?" our friends chide. "Are you going to let him talk to you that way?" Soon harsh words or even fists are flying. But the Bible prescribes a better way.

A wise person realizes that an insult says more about the insulter than the insulted. He or she takes a deep breath and takes the long view. Staying calm, in this case, becomes not a passive, wimpy reaction but an active response drawn from inner strength and assurance that what the other person thinks or says is not the final word. We take our cue from God himself; the prophets spoke often of his being "slow to anger." The apostle James, whose letter counsels us to be patient and calm in various situations, picks up the theme of today's verse from Proverbs when he writes, "Understand this, my dear brothers and sisters: You must all be quick to listen, slow to speak, and slow to get angry. Human anger does not produce the righteousness God desires" (James 1:19-20).

Read
Proverbs 12

STAY CALM
A fool is quick-tempered, but a wise person stays calm when insulted.
Proverbs 12:16

A WORD FOR TODAY
An insult has only as much power as we give to it.

Lord, help me to be "slow to get angry" and to stay calm in the face of insults, real or perceived.

JUNE 13

Read
Proverbs 13

FAST
FORTUNE?
Wealth from
get-rich-quick
schemes quickly
disappears; wealth
from hard work
grows over time.
Proverbs 13:11

If we want proof of the timelessness of the wisdom of the book of Proverbs, we need look no further than this verse. Whether solicited through pyramid scams, self-help books, infomercials on television, junk e-mail, or a dozen other means, get-rich-quick schemes are alive and well in our culture. Human nature has always been attracted to the fast track to fortune, but God has always known that the money rarely lasts, if it comes at all.

For the Christian, however, wealth should not even be a goal. Instead, obedience to God's call is our objective, with monetary rewards one of the possible—not promised—benefits. Hard work, no matter how large or small the task, is godly, and God will reward us in whatever way and in whatever amount he deems best for us and for his purposes. If we convince ourselves, and try to convince God, that we could do so much more for God's kingdom with a quick buck, we have taken our eyes off the real prize: the satisfaction of plain old hard work and obedience.

A WORD FOR TODAY
Easy wealth is a vapor.

Today, Lord, may I concentrate on you and on working hard at the tasks you have given me.

JUNE 14

The term "backsliders" is an interesting word. It implies that these people once had faith, that they used to be committed. Somehow these believers took a step back from God and slid away from him. We know that God is just, so if they are getting "what they deserve," that first step of retreat must have been conscious. They cannot claim to be innocent victims of circumstance or moan, in the words of a television character years ago, "The devil made me do it."

What do they get? More precisely, it is what they lose that matters: their relationship with God. This is the very thing that good, faithful people receive. We who remain "good" can stand proudly on the mountaintop in judgment of the backsliders, but the footing is shaky up there. We must remember that it may have been only one small, false step away from God that started the whole downward motion. God is the judge. It is for us to remain faithful and in prayer for our fellow hikers up the mountains of faith.

A WORD FOR TODAY
God will make final settlement.

Lord, I want a deep relationship with you. Help me keep my eyes on you and not in judgment of others.

Read
Proverbs 14

RECEIVING
REWARDS
Backsliders get what they deserve; good people receive their reward.
Proverbs 14:14

JUNE 15

Read
Proverbs 15

TRUTH OR
TRASH?

*A wise person is
hungry for
knowledge, while
the fool feeds
on trash.*
Proverbs 15:14

What a picture! Falsehood and dishonesty sit in the Dumpster, covered with spoiled leftovers and half-eaten sandwiches. In a quest for sustenance, some will actually choose these forms of "nourishment." But the real food lies somewhere else entirely, far from the Dumpster in the alley.

Truth is the true food that not only sustains us, but also helps us grow. Wise people recognize hunger for what it is and fill their mind and heart with truth. We can find this kind of nutrition in the Word, in solid teaching and counsel, and in humble prayer that asks God directly for it. Or we can settle for the quick and easily found snacks of lies and deception that the world offers. The axiom from computer programming will apply, however: garbage in, garbage out. The menu choice is ours.

A WORD FOR TODAY
Your mental diet determines your soul-health.

Today, Lord, I thank you for the feast of truth that you spread before me in your Word.

JUNE 16

Today's verse may conjure up images of celebrities or politicians who were riding high, did not see the precariousness of their proud position, and eventually fell from grace. We sometimes take secret pleasure in seeing such famous folk, their chests still puffed out, take a major tumble.

We need to note, however, that this verse is not addressed solely to those in the public eye. There is no preface that reads, "Hey, all you whose faces frequent the popular magazines, this message is for you!" No, God's word of warning is for all of us. Whenever the source of our pride is something other than God, whenever we have confidence in ourselves alone, we are in danger of losing altitude quickly. We must seek the proper perspective on ourselves in relation to our Creator. It is on the basis of Jesus' life and sacrifice, not our own accomplishments, that we have our worth restored. The proper source of our pride? The one who humbled himself and then was lifted up, Jesus Christ.

A WORD FOR TODAY
Pride will guide you over the cliff.

Today, Lord, may I stay proud of Jesus' work and not my own. Thank you that you will keep me from falling if I remain faithful to you.

**Read
Proverbs 16**

PRIDE AND
PRECIPICE
*Pride goes before
destruction, and
haughtiness before
a fall.*
Proverbs 16:18

JUNE 17

Read
Proverbs 17

GODLY
POSSIBILITIES
[Jesus] replied,
"What is impossible
for people is possible
with God."
Luke 18:27

He had seemed so earnest and eager for the truth. The rich, religious leader had genuinely wanted to know how to get eternal life. But when Jesus gave him the truth about salvation, he could not accept it. His earthly wealth meant more to him than heavenly treasure and Jesus' call to discipleship—and the Savior knew it. It was not the wealth itself that kept the man from salvation; it was his dependence on it.

The disciples, and we who read this story, heard from Jesus that because of this dependence it would be extremely difficult for the rich to enter the Kingdom of God. They wondered aloud if anybody could therefore be saved. Jesus replied with one of the most powerful statements in the Bible—with God, the impossible becomes possible. Anybody's dependence on wealth—measured in money, fame, friends or family, possessions, intelligence, giftedness, or any other currency—must be set aside in order to receive God's gift of salvation. The offer still stands today.

A WORD FOR TODAY
God loves to accomplish impossibilities.

Today, Lord, I thank you for the riches of salvation
that you offer. I accept the treasure in heaven that
you promise.

JUNE 18

Over the centuries, cultures and groups have devised all sorts of defensive buildings and barricades using the materials and technology of the time. Inside, the leaders and their people feel secure and protected. But time and again, history records that the city walls are scaled, the castle doors are rammed open, the wooden fort is burned to the ground, the steel beams melted. What was thought impregnable is soon found wanting.

So it is with people's dependence on wealth to defend them against all harm. Either the money does not last, or they find that no amount of it can protect them from the problems and losses of this life. Any one of us can be attacked by outside circumstances, disease, injury, broken relationships, or more. But the true defense is not found in anything but God who, if we trust him, will shield us from the crushing effects of life's problems. His promise, however, is his care in the midst of problems, not freedom from them. In the words of Martin Luther's powerful hymn, "A mighty fortress is our God, a bulwark never failing."

A WORD FOR TODAY
Wealth offers false security.

Today, Lord, may I rest secure in the fortress of your strength and love.

**Read
Proverbs 18**

OFFENSIVE
DEFENSE
The rich think of their wealth as a strong defense; they imagine it to be a high wall of safety.
Proverbs 18:11

JUNE 19

**Read
Proverbs 19**

WHILE THERE
IS HOPE
*Discipline your
children while there
is hope. Otherwise
you will ruin
their lives.*
Proverbs 19:18

When parents worry about ruining their children's lives, they often think of not giving them enough material things, not providing the shelter and food they need, or making them endure their parents' separation or divorce. All these circumstances certainly can affect girls and boys, but today's proverb has a bigger culprit in mind. Lack of discipline can actually ruin their lives, not merely produce annoying adults.

Why the strong language? Isn't the word "ruin" a bit extreme? No, because the lack of discipline establishes a pattern of behavior and attitude that will follow children until the day they die. They can lose out on the hope that the first part of the verse mentions—the hope of living a life that has been disciplined to love and serve God. Undisciplined people have an attitude of entitlement and an assumption that they are immune to punishment: If they got what they wanted as kids, then they will get what they want as adults. Parents can despair over this, or they can turn to God for the strength and consistency to discipline while there is still hope.

A WORD FOR TODAY
Good parenting recognizes limited time and opportunity.

Today, Lord, give all parents the strength and grace to discipline their children.

JUNE 20

According to an old saying, "It takes two to tango." In other words, responsibility for many forms of wrongdoing is shared. Today's verse expresses this truth in the context of spreading gossip, which is often a problem even among Christians. God detests gossip, as we can surmise from all the injunctions against it in the book of Proverbs alone. His directions for dealing with it, therefore, are certain and strong.

Part of the problem is that gossip is extremely contagious. What may seem like harmless, even positive, "sharing" is actually the telling of secrets, the revealing of parts of another person's life that are not ours to reveal. Because of the communicability of this disease of rumor, we must put the chronic gossiper into a sort of isolation ward. God does not mince words: "Don't hang around with chatterers," which we can infer is not just any kind of talk but specifically gossip. We will not "cure" a gossip; we will more likely be infected ourselves.

A WORD FOR TODAY
Loose lips sink a lot more than ships.

Lord, I want to be a person whose speech is positive and uplifting. Give me strength to avoid the gossipers in my life.

**Read
Proverbs 20**

TOO MUCH TALK

A gossip goes around telling secrets, so don't hang around with chatterers.
Proverbs 20:19

JUNE 21

Read
Proverbs 21

❦

MISTY MONEY

Wealth created by a
lying tongue is
a vanishing mist
and a deadly trap.

Proverbs 21:6

Financial matters may seem to be dry numbers, endless columns of stock quotes, boring business analysts on public television, and impersonal banks. In truth, however, money matters are highly emotional when you add to the picture siblings squabbling over inheritances, spouses arguing over debt, long-time business partners cheating each other, and a host of other scenarios. The stakes are high, God says, and he is not talking about casino odds.

The highest stakes, and therefore the suggestion of death in today's proverb about money, are found when wealth has been created by lying. English has a variety of terms for such wealth: *ill-gotten gain, dirty money, filthy lucre*. Lest we think God has only millionaires in mind, we should note that an amount of money is not specified here, only the manner in which it is gained. We must be honest in all our financial dealings and teach this to children from the time they are old enough to pick up a penny found on the sidewalk. If we are faithful in small things, we can learn to be faithful with more (Matthew 25:21).

A WORD FOR TODAY
Dishonest money comes with deadly strings attached.

Lord, I know that you are the source of true wealth. Give me your wisdom and commitment to honesty in all my handling of money.

JUNE 22

Many parents see part of their role as making good choices for their children. Certainly this is true for very young children. Adults decide what they will wear, what they will eat, where they will go any given day, and who will be their playmates. But the true job of parenting is teaching children to make their own choices as they grow, first in small things such as wardrobe, then branching out to include friends, college, career, life partner, and more.

Some parents find it hard not to make all the choices for their growing children, whether out of genuine concern or out of a selfish desire to fulfill their own dreams through their children. God gave his children free will and the guidance to use it; this is what earthly parents must do for their children. Life is full of so many choices. Paths converge and diverge before us constantly. We truly love our children when we show them how to consider options, weigh the evidence, pray, read Scripture for guidance, and seek godly advice before they choose. Just as a child's wardrobe choices gradually improve from the "interesting" ensembles of three-year-olds, children will gradually get better at the business of making choices.

A WORD FOR TODAY
The lessons of youth remain precious in adulthood.

Thank you, Lord, for the gift of choice. Help me to model and teach good decision making to the children in my life.

Read
Proverbs 22

PATHFINDERS
Direct your children onto the right path, and when they are older, they will not leave it.
Proverbs 22:6

JUNE 23

Read
Proverbs 23

❧

A FUTURE AHEAD

You will be rewarded for this; your hope will not be disappointed.
Proverbs 23:18

"You've got your whole life ahead of you!" we say, whether to the newly graduated or the newly disappointed in life or love. God wants us to maintain this long-term perspective as well. Today's verse must be seen in context; verse 17 says, "Don't envy sinners, but always continue to fear the LORD." It is easy to lose sight of our good future and reason for hope when those who do not follow God seem to be prospering.

Actually, God is not attaching a timetable to all this "future and hope" talk—he wants us to adopt a long, long-term perspective. His view of the future stretches way beyond our view, and he has hopes for us that we cannot yet imagine. We must look to our part: continue to fear God (in the sense of revering and being in awe of him) and hold on to our hope. We may have minidisappointments, but we have the God of the future with us.

A WORD FOR TODAY
If God holds our future, we can have hope.

Lord, I thank you that you have a future for me. I trust and hope in your goodness.

JUNE 24

When we picture a person whose heart is pure, we may easily picture a small child or an adult who has led a quiet, sheltered life. We smile fondly. Yet look at the reward that Jesus promises to such an individual: to see God! Does this mean that the Mighty One of the universe will make a personal appearance, rather like a celebrity making a visit to the pediatrics ward of a hospital? Or is the vision of God, rather, the ability to see him around us?

We cannot know exactly what Jesus had in mind that day up on the mountainside, when what came to be known as the Beatitudes began what came to be called the Sermon on the Mount. We can be certain only that the presence of God abounds nearby and within a person whose heart has been made pure by the blood of the Lamb, Jesus. God indeed blesses them . . . and this blessing can be ours.

A WORD FOR TODAY
We see God most clearly through pure hearts.

Today, Lord, I offer you my heart. I want it to be pure for you, for I want to see you.

Read
Proverbs 24

PURE IN HEART
God blesses those whose hearts are pure, for they will see God.
Matthew 5:8

JUNE 25

Read
Proverbs 25

ONCE TOO OFTEN

Don't visit your neighbors too often, or you will wear out your welcome.
Proverbs 25:17

Moderation is the watchword of many of the proverbs, and evidently this principle applies to relationships as well. The truth of this verse has proved itself through the centuries. For example, "wearing out one's welcome" is a well-known social faux pas and the premise for many a comedy.

The other side of the picture—going right along with not taking advantage of others' hospitality—is the need to extend one's own hospitality. We need to open our hearts and homes to others rather than to always be on the receiving end. Let ours be welcoming homes where people of all ages and situations feel welcome. Going along with this is separating the notion of hospitality from simply entertaining. When we attend more to our guests than to the angle of the cutlery, we will be most in the spirit of Christian hospitality.

A WORD FOR TODAY
Hospitality shouldn't be abused.

Lord, make my heart and my home the welcoming places they were meant to be.

JUNE 26

Solomon must have had considerable experience with gossip, if the number of proverbs dealing with the subject is any indication. Likening gossip to fuel is a powerful image and speaks to the destructive effects of idle talk.

A quarrel suggests that communication is impaired and trust is harmed, if not broken entirely. Such is also the nature of gossip, as the one talked about can no longer trust the gossiper with information. Some who gossip are unaware of the ill effects of their words. We may be aware of arguments, but we need to examine our part in "fueling the fire." If we guard our tongues and use our speech for good, we may be surprised as the animosity level goes down and the trust level between and among people goes up. Without the fuel of gossip, even the presence of small sparks of disagreement need not lead to a conflagration of argument.

A WORD FOR TODAY
Gossip is the oxygen that feeds the fire of arguments.

Today, Lord, help me speak positively of others . . . or not at all.

**Read
Proverbs 26**

QUENCHING
QUARRELS
Fire goes out without wood, and quarrels disappear when gossip stops.
Proverbs 26:20

JUNE 27

Read
Proverbs 27

WELCOME
WOUNDS
*Wounds from a
sincere friend are
better than many
kisses from an
enemy.*
Proverbs 27:6

Try as we might, it is easy to cringe when we hear the words, "Now, you know I wouldn't say this if I didn't care about you, but . . ." It is a rare person who does not mind being criticized. It may help to realize that there truly is such a thing as constructive criticism. True friends who offer constructive criticism are seeking to help us become better people; the wound is merely the means to that end. Motivation is the key; true friends have our best interests at heart.

Motivation is also the key when an enemy "kisses" us. He or she certainly does not have our best interests at heart; the motive is of the ulterior variety. Perhaps the goal is to trick us into thinking the person is a friend in order to gain an advantage over us. Or the hope may be merely to use us against another person. The question for us concerns the foundation of the relationship: Is it trust or distrust?

A WORD FOR TODAY
Genuine love risks pain.

Lord, help me to recognize my true friends and to accept the ways that you use them to make me a better person.

JUNE 28

"Cover your tracks." "Cover your bets." "Cover your rear." Solomon's own father, King David, attempted to cover his sin of adultery with Bathsheba with hypocrisy and more sin. He certainly suffered for it, and many of his relationships and dealings were hindered as a result. But he also experienced the truth of the rest of the verse: He confessed, he turned away from his sins, and he received God's mercy— that is, he did not receive what he deserved (see 2 Samuel 11:1–12:25).

Like people in Old Testament times, we are no strangers to the art of the cover-up. From high levels of government to the office building down the street to our own bedrooms, we "modern" human beings are tempted to sin and then further tempted to cover our sins. Eventually we are discovered or so wracked with remorse that the truth comes out. But the experience of David can be ours as well: We can confess, forsake our sins, and hold open our hands to receive God's mercy.

A WORD FOR TODAY
Confession plus repentance add up to mercy.

Lord, I praise you that you are a merciful God. Be merciful to me, a sinner.

**Read
Proverbs 28**

CONFESS AND
FORSAKE
*People who conceal
their sins will not
prosper, but if they
confess and turn
from them, they will
receive mercy.*
Proverbs 28:13

JUNE 29

WILD THING

When people do not accept divine guidance, they run wild. But whoever obeys the law is joyful.
Proverbs 29:18

Running wild or happily obedient? Are those the only choices for humans? Solomon says yes, and his life is testimony to the truth. He stopped listening to and following God's will, drifting further and further away from God. People need not be dashing through the streets to be effectively running wild. If our lives are out of control, it is not always apparent to passersby. Rejection of God's guidance can take many forms and can run at many speeds.

Making the journey God's way are the people who are obedient . . . and happy. Listening to and following God's rules, we acknowledge that the one who made us did not lose interest and move on to another project. If he guides us by communicating his laws, it is with the motivation of loving us and knowing what's best for us. In short, he knows better than we do what makes us deep-down happy.

A WORD FOR TODAY
Happiness is a by-product of living God's way.

Lord, I thank you for loving me and knowing me so well that even your laws have my best interests at heart.

JUNE 30

Slander is a serious charge; it represents an attack on a person's character. When this attack threatens a person's livelihood, the damage increases. The accused may turn on the accuser, and the latter's judging attitude may backfire. The accuser also then is accused, and the cycle of character assassination continues.

We each must be responsible for our own behavior. Judging and accusing others is not our responsibility. Following God's will and ways is a full-time occupation; no time should be left for "tattling." If reporting infractions is a requirement of our job description, that is another matter, and procedures must be followed. But slander has a different motivation, for it desires to damage another's character. The Christian has no call to this mean-spirited behavior. We are called to faithfulness to our own responsibility and empathy for other people.

A WORD FOR TODAY
A false recommendation will backfire.

Lord, help me to keep my eyes on my own behavior. Help me view my coworkers as fellow sojourners.

**Read
Proverbs 30**

THE COST
OF SLANDER
*Never slander
a worker to the
employer, or the
person will curse
you, and you will
pay for it.*
Proverbs 30:10

JULY 1

**Read
Proverbs 1**

EXPECTING
TROUBLE

*I have told you all
this so that you may
have peace in me.
Here on earth you
will have many
trials and sorrows.
But take heart,
because I have
overcome the world.*
John 16:33

Everyone experiences trials and sorrows in this life.
However, Jesus reminds us that these are limited to
this earth only. We can "take heart" because Jesus
has overcome this world, and as a result of his death
and resurrection, we too know that "overwhelming
victory is ours through Christ, who loved us"
(Romans 8:37).

Because we have been made right with God, we
can approach him in confidence. Not only did Jesus
overcome the world, but we also "may have peace"
in him. This is not a random promise but a theme in
Scripture, as found in two powerful confirmations.
The first is in John 14:27: "I am leaving you with a
gift—peace of mind and heart. And the peace I give
is a gift the world cannot give. So don't be troubled
or afraid." The second is found in Philippians 4:6-7:
"Don't worry about anything; instead, pray about
everything. Tell God what you need, and thank him
for all he has done. Then you will experience God's
peace, which exceeds anything we can understand.
His peace will guard your hearts and minds as you
live in Christ Jesus."

A WORD FOR TODAY
The world offers trouble; Jesus offers peace.

*Lord, grant me peace as I endure the trials and sorrows I
face, and help me to look forward in hope to the eternal
glory I will share with you in heaven.*

JULY 2

Read any book on success and the number one ingredient is having a plan. Major corporations do not achieve success through procrastination, households cannot run smoothly without organization, and students cannot fully apply themselves unless they make wise use of their time. To achieve our goals, we need to have a plan.

God's will for us is to reach our full potential in life, whatever that may be. Having a map is essential if we want to reach that goal. However, the second part of this verse reminds us that having a plan is not the end of the matter. God is in control of everything. Only a firm understanding of who we serve will enable us to avoid the pitfalls of success, whether in business or in ministry. All our planning is for nothing if the goal is not part of God's plan.

A WORD FOR TODAY
Wisdom protects.

Today, Lord, as I make my plans, help me to remember that you are in control and that my ultimate goal in life is to glorify you. Guide my paths today and speak to me about the direction I should go.

**Read
Proverbs 2**

A LIVING
STRATEGY
Wise choices will watch over you. Understanding will keep you safe.
Proverbs 2:11

JULY 3

**Read
Proverbs 3**

WISDOM'S
APPRAISAL
*Wisdom is more
precious than
rubies; nothing
you desire can
compare with her.
She offers you long
life in her right
hand, and riches
and honor in her
left. She will guide
you down delightful
paths; all her ways
are satisfying.*
Proverbs 3:15-17

"Wisdom" has come to mean many things in today's society, but here it refers specifically to God's wisdom. When we seek wisdom and understanding from God, we are consciously making a decision to reject the ways of the world and to desire what the world cannot appreciate.

God's ways are higher than our ways. God created this world and everything in it. He alone knows what is best for us. Seeking wisdom is seeking communion with God. It means laying aside what we think is the best way of doing things and finding through the Bible how the Lord would have us live instead.

The promises in the proverb describe a satisfying life, a life without regrets. Wise living may not always be easy living, but the paths are delightful along the way. The truly wise seek to know God, who desires to be known. Nothing compares with the joy of knowing him (Philippians 3:7-8).

A WORD FOR TODAY
Wisdom: one of God's most precious gifts.

Today, Lord, please teach me about your wisdom and help me to gain a deeper appreciation for all that I can learn from you.

JULY 4

Righteousness is the state of being "right" with God. In the Old Testament, the path to righteousness was through obedience to the law. But people, in their sinfulness, were not even able to be obedient. We cannot obtain righteousness by ourselves—it is a gift from God. There is nothing we can do to earn it. We are so buried in sin that only Jesus, being free from sin, has the power to pull us out and make us right with God. When we choose Jesus, when we reach for that hand he holds out to us, we are reaching out to the light.

Salvation is like the dawn of a new day—a fresh start and the more we seek God, the brighter it gets. Whereas righteousness is a life with God, wickedness is a life apart from God. It can only be darkness because without God's light in our lives we have no meaning, no purpose, no way to understand this world. How wonderful that God, in his grace, shines the light of Jesus into our darkness. No wonder one of Christ's titles is "bright morning star" (see Revelation 22:16).

Read Proverbs 4

NEW DAY
The way of the righteous is like the first gleam of dawn, which shines ever brighter until the full light of day. But the way of the wicked is like total darkness. They have no idea what they are stumbling over.
Proverbs 4:18-19

A WORD FOR TODAY
Right living is also "light" living.

Today, Lord, help me to remember that in you I am a new creation; I have left the darkness and chosen to walk in the light. Speak to me today about the ways I can walk more closely with you and shine brightly for your kingdom.

JULY 5

**Read
Proverbs 5**

SACRED
RESERVOIR

*Why spill the water
of your springs in
the streets, having
sex with just
anyone? You should
reserve it for
yourselves. Never
share it with
strangers.*
Proverbs 5:16-17

Sexual purity is not a very popular topic of conversation today. In movies, television, and books, sex is portrayed as something that is "no big deal," something we have a "right" to, whether or not we are married. Society seems blind to the rampant spread of sexually transmitted diseases and the epidemic of divorces. Immorality gets flaunted while virtue is held up for ridicule.

But God calls us to a higher standard. He created sex as something special that would happen within a marriage relationship only. God did not create it as something to be treated lightly, abused, or shared with strangers. When we have sex outside of marriage, for whatever reason, we are disobeying God, plain and simple.

In the powerful imagery of this proverb, those who derive life from the springs must guard them. Otherwise, they will become polluted and of no good to anyone.

A WORD FOR TODAY
Marriage means dedicated springs.

Today, Lord, help me to have the strength to resist the temptations of this world and to remain pure in your sight.

JULY 6

Parents have a crucial role to play in contemporary society. There are more and more pressures on families today as they attempt to function within a world that rejects truth, traditional notions of marriage and family, and basic moral guidelines for living. One of the basic building blocks of society is under attack, and there is little recognition of the chaos that will follow if the family structure should collapse.

Teaching cannot be left to schools or churches; the primary people in a child's life are his or her parents. The responsibility is unavoidable. But this proverb is not just for parents; it also calls on children to listen to their parents. This proverb conveys the words of a loving heavenly Father saying to children, "More than anyone else in this world, your parents love and care for you and desire to see you fulfill your potential. As your parents are listening to what I teach them, you should also be listening to what they are teaching you."

A WORD FOR TODAY
Parents are a valuable resource.

Lord, help me to be a great parent to my children and a great son or daughter to my own parents. Impress your commands on my heart and fill me with love for my family members.

**Read
Proverbs 6**

TWO-WAY
STREET
*My son, obey your
father's commands,
and don't neglect
your mother's
instruction.*
Proverbs 6:20

JULY 7

Read
Proverbs 7

FALSE
ADVERTISING
Come, let's drink
our fill of love
until morning.
Let's enjoy each
other's caresses,
for my husband
is not home.
He's away on
a long trip.
Proverbs 7:18-19

When no one is around and, seemingly, no one will find out, it is very hard to resist the temptations of this world. A little lie here, a furtive glance there, a curse uttered in anger. These transgressions seem small and insignificant at the time, but they are sin nonetheless.

In these cases Satan scores a double victory. Not only are we doing something that goes against God's will, but we are doing so because we don't think anyone is around. At that moment, we have accepted the bold-faced lie that we can get away with something because "no one is watching." And that, perhaps, is the greater problem, for it means we have forgotten that God is with us always. No one else may see you, but God does, and your sin breaks his heart. It is a lie from Satan that we can enjoy sin while no one is around, while the coast is clear. It ignores God's high standards for us and, worst of all, it ignores God's presence in our lives.

A WORD FOR TODAY
Secrecy is a false excuse.

Today, Lord, remind me of your wonderful presence in my life. Help me to remember that you are with me always and that I can turn to you for strength when I feel weak.

JULY 8

Of these four ways to love God, loving him with "all your soul" may be the least familiar. The soul doesn't get much attention these days, but it should. Jesus pointed out the danger of being extremely successful at the cost of our soul (Matthew 16:26). He taught that our soul is the one thing about ourselves that we dare not lose. Loving God with all our soul means loving him in any and every way that goes beyond our heart, mind, or strength. In other words, we are to love God even when we don't feel like it.

Here are three training exercises in loving God with your soul: (1) Read, meditate, and imitate those psalms that mention the soul in action (such as Psalms 23, 31, 42, 62, 63, 103); (2) learn several of the popular worship choruses that express love for God; and (3) practice using them to train your soul in loving God. The next time you become aware that you're not actively loving God, use one of these resources to love him anyway.

A WORD FOR TODAY
The greatest proverb—"Love God."

Today, Lord, keep me thinking about my soul. Help me to appreciate how precious a gift from you it is. Help me never to exchange it for something cheap.

Read Proverbs 8

SOUL-LOVE
Jesus replied, "The most important commandment is this: 'Listen, O Israel! The LORD our God is the one and only LORD. And you must love the LORD your God with all your heart, all your soul, all your mind, and all your strength.' The second is equally important: 'Love your neighbor as yourself.' No other commandment is greater than these."
Mark 12:29-31

JULY 9

Read
Proverbs 9

HEALTHY FEAR

Fear of the LORD is the foundation of wisdom. Knowledge of the Holy One results in good judgment.
Proverbs 9:10

Most of us are familiar with John 3:16, "For God loved the world so much . . ." He loved us so much that he provided a way out of our sin through the death of Jesus Christ. So what does it mean to "fear" him? This does not mean that he is "out to get us."

However, stopping to contemplate the personhood of God should put us in complete awe. God created everything. He made this world. He put the planets in motion. He designed the universe. Shouldn't we fear someone with that much power? It's beyond the scope of our imagination to even begin to think about who God is. He is beyond definition. Even a label of *omnipotent* seems somehow limiting for the one who invented power. *Omniscient* is a joke for the one who made thought, language, and words. Our God is a mighty God. He isn't an old man with a long beard; he isn't the best of several other gods. He is the only God.

God is not only the foundation of wisdom, he is the foundation of everything. God is worthy of our utmost awe and worship.

A WORD FOR TODAY
Knowing God includes the right kind of fear.

Today, Lord, give me a glimpse of who you are and what you can do in my life. Help me to fear you more, so that I might come into a deeper relationship with you.

JULY 10

It seems pretty obvious to most Christians that we should not "squander" our money on sinful activities. But at the same time, we sometimes try to "get around" this proverb by altering God's definition of sin to fit our current situation. For example, we may feel good about not spending money at a certain store or subscribing to a particular magazine. However, we might then go and pour more money than is perhaps wise into our house or car.

When we stop to realize that it is all God's money, there is a shift in perspective. Turning to God for advice and guidance on what we spend and where can only enhance our lives. We are enriched not through the things we purchase but in the direction we are led to use our funds for the glory of God's kingdom. When we choose to spend our earnings without consultation or guidance from God, we often squander the financial opportunities that God has presented to us.

A WORD FOR TODAY
Stewardship satisfies.

Today, Lord, help me use your blessings to enhance my life and others in accordance with your will. Help me to avoid the pitfalls of my sinful heart and to focus on serving you in everything that I do.

Read
Proverbs 10

STEWARDSHIP
The earnings of the godly enhance their lives, but evil people squander their money on sin.
Proverbs 10:16

JULY 11

**Read
Proverbs 11**

LEADERSHIP BACKUP

Without wise leadership, a nation falls; there is safety in having many advisers.
Proverbs 11:14

Without God's direction in our lives, we would be hopelessly lost in sin. Indeed, whenever we try to strike out on our own path and go in a direction different from God's, we invariably fail. The same is true at all levels—in the family, in a church, at a business, and in government. It is impossible to have wise leadership without the presence of God, for true wisdom comes from God alone.

Furthermore, every leader needs good advisers. From the president of the country down to the family unit, we all rely on a close-knit circle of friends and counselors for advice and guidance. Sometimes, when we are far from God, it is only the wise counsel of a spouse or close friend that can bring us back. Thank God for the good advisers in your life.

A WORD FOR TODAY
Wise leadership isn't optional.

Today, Lord, remind me that true leadership is based on you and you alone, that your wisdom is the source of life. Please use the people in my life to guide and mold me and keep me on the path that you have set for me.

JULY 12

Just about every courtroom drama revolves around someone not telling the truth. The judge and jury have to figure out who is being honest and who is not. As Christians living in the world, no one should ever have to call our truthfulness into question. With the Holy Spirit dwelling within us, there is no reason why we cannot tell the truth. Yet we continually slip up, and little untruths quickly become big lies.

Part of the problem lies in our perspective. In any given situation in our day-to-day routine, it can be very easy to come up with a good reason for not telling the whole truth. But this proverb calls our attention to a larger purpose, a bigger calling. We are all witnesses for Christ and his love. We are living, breathing examples of the work he did for us on the Cross. Our witness to the world should be honest and true, for if our truthfulness is called into question on small things, how can we expect people to believe us about the massively important truths of salvation and forgiveness?

A WORD FOR TODAY
Stand on truth.

Today, Lord, give me the courage to stand firm for you. Help me to be an honest witness, proclaiming your truth to the world in all that I do.

**Read
Proverbs 12**

WITNESS STAND
An honest witness tells the truth; a false witness tells lies.
Proverbs 12:17

JULY 13

Read
Proverbs 13

❧

LONG-TERM
HOPE
Hope deferred
makes the heart
sick, but a dream
fulfilled is a tree
of life.
Proverbs 13:12

Read the front page of any newspaper and it's hard not to get depressed at the state of the world. Wars, unrest, fighting, terrorism, natural disasters, diseases, failing economies—the list goes on and on. How can we have any hope in such a fallen world? Some Eastern religions gloss over these troubles and suggest that through meditation we can remove ourselves from caring about the suffering around us. Others try to accept it all as just being the way the world works. For them, there is no meaning or purpose, just a hard life followed by death. But neither of these worldviews are true, and neither of them is God's will for us.

This proverb says that when hope is deferred, it makes the heart sick. But God wants us to have enduring hope—hope for a future, hope for the return of Jesus Christ, hope for a time when all suffering and persecution will end. Some might call this hope nothing more than the foolish wishes of a child who doesn't yet understand the harsh realities of life. But the proof is in Jesus Christ. His life, death, and resurrection are the reasons for our hope. We may not get what we hope for in this world, but the one in whom we hope will never fail us.

A WORD FOR TODAY
Hope in God will not be deferred.

Today, Lord, grant me a deeper sense of hope for the future. Fill me with an abundance of your love, and help me to look forward with a longing heart for your return.

JULY 14

As Christians, we have nothing to fear anymore.
Satan has lost the war once and for all, and we
can move forward in full confidence. However,
there is a difference between confidence in Christ
and overconfidence, or pride in ourselves. There
is no trial, tribulation, or struggle that is too great
for Christ to deal with, but there are many things
that we cannot. We should be confident because
of Christ and through Christ, but not outside of
Christ. The foolish blunder forward with too
much *self*-confidence.

Furthermore, it is foolish to rush forward and,
out of pride, think that everything will be okay.
Christians are not immune to stupidity. God will
often allow gracious lessons in humility and endurance to occur because we have confused confidence
in ourselves with confidence in him. Instead, we
want to live with a wise caution that makes decisions neither out of fear and anxiety nor out of
prideful overconfidence.

A WORD FOR TODAY
Fools rush in; the wise take their time.

*Today, Lord, I want to be your servant. You have shared
your wisdom with me through your Word and through
your church, but I pray for extra guidance as I go out
today. I pray that you would help me to be cautious and
prudent, not rushing into anything prematurely.*

**Read
Proverbs 14**

INFORMED
RISK
*The wise are
cautious and avoid
danger; fools plunge
ahead with reckless
confidence.*
Proverbs 14:16

JULY 15

*[Jesus] said, "How
hard it is for the
rich to enter the
Kingdom of God!
In fact, it is easier
for a camel to
go through the
eye of a needle
than for a rich
person to enter the
Kingdom of God!"*
Luke 18:24-25

There are two things here that we know Jesus was
not trying to say. First of all, it is not impossible for
rich people to be born again. God has blessed each
one of us differently, and while one person may have
been born in poverty, another may have been born
into wealth. God can use people in all walks of life,
no matter how much money they have. Surrendering our will to him, first, is imperative because
unless we are born again, there is nothing we can
do for God. Second, we do not need to be poor in
order to be good Christians. The Bible does not say
that we must sell everything we own in order to be
holy.

That said, it is often much harder for wealthy
people to be exposed to God's Word and for it to
sink in and take root. The problem lies most often
with the distractions of the world. Cars, houses,
schools, jobs, 401k plans—the amount of time
spent each day worrying or thinking about money
tends to outweigh devotional time. This is why having money makes it so hard to worship God—and
why Jesus offered stern warnings to those with
wealth.

A WORD FOR TODAY
Sometimes hard things are worth doing.

*Today, Lord, help me to clear away the distractions and
the lies of this world and focus on you and your eternal
wisdom.*

JULY 16

Do you remember the first time that you read the words of Jesus? Do you remember the thrill of reading something that you knew deep down in your heart was absolutely, eternally true? Throughout the Bible, it is experiences with this absolute Truth, the Creator of the world, that drive the changes in people's lives, make leaders out of the most unlikely people, and shape the fate of nations.

True wisdom can come only from God—through praying, having quiet times, reading his Word, and earnestly seeking his will. But most of all, wisdom will come from an attitude of service and obedience. No amount of Bible study or church activity can cover up our hearts before God. He can bless us only when we are genuinely seeking to follow him.

God also uses some of his followers as teachers and leaders, who must pass on their understanding to others. They have a responsibility to seek God's wisdom first and foremost because they are teaching not what they know, but what they have been taught by God. Presentation is important too. When the words are pleasant, instruction is appreciated and taken to heart. And when the source is truth, instruction is not just appreciated, but actively sought.

A WORD FOR TODAY
Both how you speak and what you say are important.

Today, Lord, help me to find wisdom in your Word and share it openly and confidently with others.

Read
Proverbs 16

WISDOM
SENSITIVITY
The wise are known for their understanding, and pleasant words are persuasive.
Proverbs 16:21

JULY 17

Read
Proverbs 17

THE HIGHEST COURT

Acquitting the guilty and condemning the innocent—both are detestable to the LORD.
Proverbs 17:15

We've all heard stories about prisoners being set free after spending years in prison for a crime they did not commit. Whatever the reason, the results are always devastating. It fills our hearts with joy to hear of an innocent man being set free after a false imprisonment.

Regardless of what we see on the news or read in the papers, God keeps tabs on everything. This proverb tells us about God's response when he sees lies take precedence and the innocent condemned. The story of Jesus is the ultimate wrongfully accused story—a man who came to save us, who had done nothing wrong at all, was imprisoned, tried, and convicted without a fair trial.

This is the depth of God's love for us. Although he despised the situation, he used it to defeat Satan and his lies once and for all and to grant us all eternal life. Although as sinners we were part of the crowd that called for Jesus to be crucified, now that we are born again we have right standing with God and the ability to live a life that is pleasing to him.

A WORD FOR TODAY
The gray area between guilt and innocence is a steel curtain.

Today, Lord, I choose you. I choose honesty and truth, and I pray that you would help me to live out these ideals today as I face so many different challenges from Satan. Protect me and give me the strength that I need to stand firm for you.

JULY 18

At some point in our lives we've all rushed to give advice without listening to the complete story. On the other end of the spectrum, almost everyone has had the misfortune of receiving advice before being allowed to finish explaining first. This proverb encourages us to rein in our tongues and listen more carefully than we usually do. It is then easier to give accurate and helpful advice and avoid the pitfalls of pride.

Why is this true? Often when we speak too quickly, the advice we give turns out to be the first thing the person has already tried. Listening can help us realize how little help we have to offer and remind us to ask for wisdom and help from God on behalf of our friend. Waiting to hear the whole story is itself the action our friend needs the most from us. Our attention conveys care and concern in ways we can't measure.

A WORD FOR TODAY
Listening avoids a lot of pointless repetition.

Today, Lord, I want to hear all the facts before passing judgment. Help me to rein in my tongue and focus on listening to other people.

Read
Proverbs 18

TONGUE BITING
Spouting off before listening to the facts is both shameful and foolish.
Proverbs 18:13

JULY 19

Read
Proverbs 19

REPEAT
OFFENDERS

Hot-tempered people
must pay the
penalty. If you rescue
them once, you will
have to do it again.
Proverbs 19:19

Tough love gets rave reviews from those who have learned its lessons. Those in the middle of undergoing the tough-love experience, however, rarely like it! Hot-temperedness is simply one of numerous character traits that cannot be corrected or eliminated by cooperation. If a hot temper proves effective to move or cower people, that behavior will continue.

Trying to help a hot-tempered person requires calm and the use of effective negative consequences. One such consequence, described as a "penalty" by this proverb, is the cost created by hot temper: fines, repair charges, restrictions, or restitution. If a hot-tempered person is shown in any way that others are willing to "cover the costs" of his or her behavior, the behavior is simply reinforced.

Tough love is hard on the one being loved and on the one loving. We want to help. But we aren't helping when we deflect the consequences that can teach a valuable lesson.

A WORD FOR TODAY
Tough love allows pain to teach.

Today, Lord, I pray for the hot-tempered people in
my life. If I'm one of them, I include myself in my
request for your help. Teach me to pay attention
to the penalties.

JULY 20

Almost all of us have, at some point, insulted a parent in some way (just think about when we were teenagers), and yet we are still here, alive. So obviously, this proverb is not saying that a word uttered in anger, frustration, or ignorance against a parent will result in a bolt of lightning from on high.

However, that said, insults result from anger. Anger expressed outwardly comes from anger in the heart, which is the same emotion that can lead to many other dreadful and hurtful acts. Jesus said that although the law condemns murderers, those who are merely angry with another will be judged also (Matthew 5:21-22). Anger is not part of God's plan for us or for the world. It is a sinful emotion that tends to lead to more sin and more hurt. We need to repent and seek forgiveness for any time that our anger takes control in our lives, and turn to God for the patience and strength that only he can provide.

A WORD FOR TODAY
Parental respect includes what we say.

Today, Lord, as yesterday, I need you to help me with anger. Help me to put your Holy Spirit in command instead, so that you are in complete control of my life.

**Read
Proverbs 20**

VERBAL
HONOR
*If you insult your
father or mother,
your light will be
snuffed out in total
darkness.*
Proverbs 20:20

JULY 21

**Read
Proverbs 21**

HEARING AID

*Those who shut
their ears to the
cries of the poor
will be ignored
in their own
time of need.*
Proverbs 21:13

Anyone who lives in a big city hears cries from the poor every day. Even in the suburbs, homeless people are out on the streets. This is aside from the working poor, who may not be living on the street, but barely make it from day to day. The situation in developing countries is even worse—the quality of life is often terrible, running water may not be available, children are homeless, and wars destroy entire towns. Sometimes we are tempted to deal with all this suffering and heartache by steeling our hearts against it, blocking it out. There is, after all, only so much we can do.

But nowhere in the Bible does God call on one individual to fix all the problems of the world. That is his job, not ours. Jesus told us, "Those who are last now will be first then" (Matthew 20:16). In the meantime, we are called to respond to the leading of the Holy Spirit in our lives. What can a dollar do for a homeless person? Maybe not much at all, but that's not for us to decide ahead of time. If you feel a tug on your heart, don't let Satan rationalize it away, but respond freely and openly. Let God worry about what happens to it.

A WORD FOR TODAY
Those who don't listen won't be heard.

Today, Lord, give me a heart for the poor. It is hard to see so much suffering and not shut it out. It's a greater burden than I can bear. But you can bear it, Lord. And so, while I know I can't help everyone, I pray that you would give me an opportunity today to help one person.

JULY 22

"I want to work for world peace." It's a cliché we hear all the time—on TV, in newspapers, from world leaders and local leaders, politicians and beauty queens. Rarely is any real action taken, however. On the one hand, this is understandable; world peace is a mammoth task that no one person could ever hope to achieve.

However, while we may not be able to stop all fighting and wars across the globe, we can do much to heal wounds and bring peace to our local communities and personal relationships. We can stop yelling at our children and our spouses. We can stop fighting with extended family members whom we don't like or can't get along with. We can stop honking furiously at the person in front who stopped us from cruising through a yellow light. These simple acts are completely within our ability and absolutely under our control. At every difficult and stressful moment we have a choice—to escalate the problem or to defuse it. With the Holy Spirit in our lives, we should always be working for peace and glorifying God in the process.

A WORD FOR TODAY
Peacemaking begins at home.

Today, Lord, help me work for peace in my community. Help me make the right choice when a stressful situation arises. Fill me with your love and patience and the ability to defuse such situations rather than escalating them.

Read
Proverbs 22

PEACEMAKERS
God blesses those who work for peace, for they will be called the children of God.
Matthew 5:9

JULY 23

STAYING ON THE WAGON

Do not carouse with drunkards or feast with gluttons, for they are on their way to poverty, and too much sleep clothes them in rags.
Proverbs 23:20-21

Lust, greed, power, money, laziness, self-righteousness, anger, and avarice—these are all things on which we can gorge ourselves. They may not be as obvious to others as the overconsumption of alcohol or food, but they are equally bad because they take control away from the Holy Spirit. And when we grab the steering wheel away from the Holy Spirit, it's going to result in a car wreck—guaranteed.

Yes, drinking too much liquor will eventually lead to bankruptcy, but too much greed, anger, lust, or laziness will also bankrupt us spiritually, taking us out of the presence of God. Although it's easy to point our fingers at those we know who are struggling deeply with such sins, we are fooling ourselves if we ignore the times we indulge ourselves as well. But though there may be pleasure in sin for a time, it always ends. Furthermore, when we get away from the presence of God, we can't be moving forward at the same time. We come to a dead halt spiritually. No more building up treasures in heaven, no more being used by God here on earth, no more anything. And unless we turn back, we will face spiritual poverty.

A WORD FOR TODAY
Gluttony, drunkenness, and laziness add up to poverty.

Today, Lord, help me to identify the places in my life where I am most in danger of overindulging my sinful heart. Keep me from temptation, and help me to keep the Holy Spirit firmly in control of my life.

JULY 24

We may hate to admit it, but sometimes we are glad when things start to go wrong for someone we don't like. Maybe it's an adversary at work who suddenly gets fired, or a neighbor we don't like who has to move away. Finally, we think to ourselves, they are getting what they deserve.

God calls us to a higher standard, however. Sure, we can rejoice when our enemies start to experience persecution in the way they persecuted us, but that misses the most fundamental truth of Christianity—forgiveness. It should pain us when anyone experiences trouble and difficulty. It should be a sad moment when others stumble and fall. Such occurrences should cause us to pray and show love and kindness. When our "enemies" are outside the church, it is a powerful testimony to the true life-changing power of Jesus Christ when we shed a tear for their troubles instead of laughing in glee.

Within the body of believers, it is even more imperative to step forward and help those who stumble, however much we dislike or disagree with them. We are brothers and sisters in Christ.

A WORD FOR TODAY
Loving means weeping at an enemy's disaster.

Today, Lord, fill me with love for my enemies. It is hard sometimes to love them or treat them kindly when they have abused me so much. Lord, I know that you have the power to help me. Soften my heart, and help me to love more freely.

Read
Proverbs 24

WASTED
CHEERS
Don't rejoice when your enemies fall; don't be happy when they stumble.
Proverbs 24:17

JULY 25

Read
Proverbs 25

❦

HARD WORDS

Telling lies about
others is as harmful
as hitting them with
an ax, wounding
them with a sword,
or shooting them
with a sharp arrow.
Proverbs 25:18

When you were a child, you may have heard the phrase, "Sticks and stones may break my bones, but words will never hurt me." It's a popular saying, but the Bible tells us otherwise. Whereas a stone might cause a bruise on the surface, it heals quickly and there are rarely any long-term negative consequences. Words, on the other hand, pierce to the soul and can cause long-lasting damage.

Of all the words that sting, lies are the worst. They slander our name; they spread dissension; and they destroy relationships, families, businesses, and churches. They lead to more lies and more lies again to cover up the first lies. Satan deceived Eve with a lie in the Garden of Eden. The bottom line is that lies cause far more damage than any other weapon invented by man. Thankfully, the solution is simple—don't tell lies. The command is not just for kids who stole a cookie or didn't do their homework—it's for everyone, of every age, of every station in life.

A WORD FOR TODAY
Words hurt more deeply than sticks and stones.

Today, Lord, help me to stand up for truth. I know it
in my head and I can say it with my lips, but help me
to feel it in my heart and live it with my life.

JULY 26

Touch a lit match to a piece of paper soaked in gas and you'll have a fire on your hands before you know it. Likewise, if you make friends with a quarrelsome person, don't be surprised when quarrels start to break out! But there is more to this proverb than this simple correlation.

The application of proverbs always starts best "at home." This proverb provokes a good question: "Am I a quarrelsome person?" Or perhaps, "When am I a quarrelsome person?" Almost every heated discussion or confrontation has one or more important forks in the road. If any of the participants is in a quarrelsome mood, the fork taken will likely lead to a fight.

Think of the last fight you had with a spouse or a friend. Can you remember the fork? Did the argument become a fight because you took the quarrelsome fork in the road? Would it have been better to call a time-out?

A WORD FOR TODAY
People with chips on their shoulder are magnets for conflict.

Today, Lord, help me admit my weaknesses. Help me not to avoid truthful discussions but to avoid ruining them with a quarrelsome attitude.

Read
Proverbs 26

SPARKS!
A quarrelsome person starts fights as easily as hot embers light charcoal or fire lights wood.
Proverbs 26:21

JULY 27

Read
Proverbs 27

🐦

GENERATIONS
Never abandon
a friend—either
yours or your
father's. When
disaster strikes, you
won't have to ask
your brother
for assistance.
It's better to go to
a neighbor than
to a brother who
lives far away.
Proverbs 27:10

A good friend is hard to come by. We make many acquaintances throughout life, but a friend who sticks with us through thick and thin is a special gift from God. As such, we should treasure the friends that we have.

As counselors in times of need, prayer partners, advisors, and friends can be used by God to teach and guide us. But although our friends may have played a special role in our lives, we sometimes let these relationships slip through the cracks, and those friends become mere acquaintances again.

The Bible urges us to put the extra effort into these relationships to keep them going. We need a body of believers around us, a close group of friends who are also believers to support and pray for us. A tight-knit community is much harder for the enemy to break into.

Although the proverb seems to imply that we should favor friends over family, it really just emphasizes the special nature of a close friend. Family will always be there. But close friends are the first level of defense and support in our lives, and should be treasured as such.

A WORD FOR TODAY
Friendships should bridge generations.

Today, Lord, I thank you for the friends that you have blessed me with; they are truly assets that I treasure very much. I pray for their protection, and I hope that you will continue to bless these relationships over the course of this year and the years to come.

JULY 28

A stubborn heart has stood in the way of many people from becoming Christians. Such a heart refuses to change or listen to reason. And the sad result is that they will never know the redeeming love of Jesus Christ. But don't give up on the stubborn! They need as much prayer, and sometimes more, than those who seem more receptive to hearing about the Cross.

People who fear to do wrong, on the other hand, are a joy to meet. They are more receptive and responsive to the gospel. They often have a high awareness of their sins and find the news of forgiveness in Jesus Christ truly good news! Those who are stubborn may take longer and be a harder audience, but "serious trouble" often has a way of softening people. That's more than enough reason to persist in praying and caring for the stubborn people in our lives.

A WORD FOR TODAY
Thank God for hearts that fear to do wrong.

Today, Lord, make me aware of someone who fears to do wrong. Give me the wisdom and words to encourage and speak to that person about you.

Read
Proverbs 28

THE STUBBORN
HEART
Blessed are those who fear to do wrong, but the stubborn are headed for serious trouble.
Proverbs 28:14

JULY 29

HORN-FREE ZONE

When you give to someone in need, don't do as the hypocrites do—blowing trumpets in the synagogues and streets to call attention to their acts of charity! I tell you the truth, they have received all the reward they will ever get.
Matthew 6:2

This proverb seems so easy. We can give a gift or otherwise help someone in need, but we don't go out of our way to tell everyone how great we are for doing it. What's so difficult about that? But then we see a homeless person outside a grocery store and everyone is ignoring him, so we offer to buy him some groceries. The desire to tell everyone about our "good deed" is a strong one!

Jesus makes a serious point. The hypocrite gives to charity or helps a poor person but thinks in his heart: "It's *my* gift that is helping that person," or "If it weren't for *me*, this charity would be lost." Such an attitude takes God out of the picture and marks hypocrites—those who confess God with their lips but in their hearts feel that they are the ones making things better on this earth.

All good things come from God, and he uses us all in different ways. But our gifts and deeds are worthless apart from him. He is the one doing the work; he is the one changing lives and hearts, not us. It is a blessing and a privilege to be a part of any work for God, and we should always consider it as such.

A WORD FOR TODAY
Genuine giving is not attention getting.

Today, Lord, help me to give freely of my time and money for the glory of your kingdom. Help me to remember throughout all I do that you are the one in control, not me.

JULY 30

Respect. Honor. Talk to any teacher or parent today and you'll hear how much they struggle with kids who don't have any respect for their elders. Note how children dishonor their parents. It's a growing problem, and one that we can't ignore.

Lack of respect is at the heart of mockery; you don't mock someone whom you respect. People who have become Christians should have a deep understanding of respect. Before we met Christ, we mocked God with our rebellious hearts and lives. We disrespected and dishonored God. We were convinced that our way was better than his, but the end result of such a life is death, with no hope for eternal life. Repentance and salvation changed that.

Our relationship with our parents should reflect our relationship with God. We are bound by respect for God to honor them.

A WORD FOR TODAY
Parental disrespect yields unexpected troubles.

Today, Lord, I thank you for my parents and all that they have taught me. I pray that you would bless them and keep them safe.

**Read
Proverbs 30**

R-E-S-P-E-C-T
The eye that mocks a father and despises a mother's instructions will be plucked out by ravens of the valley and eaten by vultures.
Proverbs 30:17

JULY 31

Read
Proverbs 31

CONFIDENT
LAUGHTER
[The virtuous wife]
is clothed with
strength and
dignity, and she
laughs without fear
of the future.
Proverbs 31:25

Many women today find it hard to understand their roles and identity. On the one hand, they are expected to be 100 percent female and fulfill all the typical female "norms" and responsibilities. On the other hand, they are also expected to be just like men, competing, working, and living like men. The result is doubt and fear and confusion. It's hard enough to live up to one set of expectations, but to live up to two sometimes opposing expectations is impossible.

A woman whose life is planted firmly in the Lord's hands is able to live free from these societal constraints, and instead live according to the way God made her. A life built on Christ's redeeming power and the wisdom of the Lord opens the heart to a source of strength that comes only from a relationship with God. True dignity comes from a firm belief in God's love for each one of us. And such a woman can indeed laugh at the future—not in mockery, but with confidence, for there is nothing to fear when she is walking with the Lord.

A WORD FOR TODAY
A wise woman is comfortable with herself in the present.

Today, Lord, I give you all my fears and doubts. You created me. You love me. You alone know what is best for me. I put my life in your hands and seek your will.

AUGUST 1

A memorable distinction we learn from watching children is the difference between hearing and listening. Sure, children hear what adults say. "Stop that." "Come here." But do they listen? The answer to that question is, "selectively," at best. Many parents are mystified by a child's uncanny ability to hear the tinkling of the neighborhood ice-cream truck still blocks away, while feigning acute deafness when being summoned for dinner from the next room.

In the same way, we may "hear" what God says through a pastor or our own personal Bible study. But are we really listening to God? Listening implies open hearts as well as open ears. As with children, obedience is the sign that listening has taken place. When we listen to God in this way, he promises to pour out his wisdom on the soil of our hearts. We grow wise as a result.

A WORD FOR TODAY
Listen to wisdom!

Today, Lord, make my ears quick to listen to your voice. Make my heart ready to respond with obedience.

**Read
Proverbs 1**

HEARING TEST
Come and listen to my counsel. I'll share my heart with you and make you wise.
Proverbs 1:23

AUGUST 2

Read
Proverbs 2

TURN IT OFF

Wisdom will save
you from evil
people, from those
whose words are
twisted.
Proverbs 2:12

The story is told of an unfortunate woman whose accelerator became stuck as she was leaving the parking lot of a local bank. The "self-propelled" station wagon bolted across four lanes of traffic, sideswiped two telephone poles, and steamrolled a postal box before finally boomeranging into the evacuated lobby of the bank. Her teary testimony about her foiled attempts to wrangle the "wild beast" into reverse, neutral, or even park was silenced when the officer at the scene asked, "Did it occur to you to turn off the ignition?"

Sometimes common sense eludes us when we need it the most. What disastrous chain reactions common sense can avoid! Often the precursor to wisdom, common sense is an insider's tip. It's the voice inside that alerts us to others' mischievous motives and questionable quandaries. Common sense makes us take note that something's not quite right. Wisdom follows in the form of a choice—a decision not to partner with impiety. Fools, too, hear the same voice—they merely decide to ignore it.

A WORD FOR TODAY
Wisdom decides whom to listen to.

Today, Lord, may I use common sense in dealing with others in order to choose wisely. Save me from foolish mistakes.

AUGUST 3

Sometimes in our rush to "do" the next thing on the horizon, we don't take time to think things through. As a result, we stumble into the future, fueled only by a dream. When we slow down and focus on the future goal, we can steady our gaze with a firm grasp on a good plan.

Before treading on new ground, it is a good idea to take a look over our shoulder. Enthusiasm is a poor substitute for common sense and discernment. Pinpointing prior mistakes in previous ventures decreases our chances of repeating them. Also, incorporating the insights of those who have already achieved similar life goals (buying a home, adopting a child, etc.) ensures that our own choices will be laced with an honorable legacy. Most important, we must diligently seek God's counsel along the way. Goals change, and so do our plans for reaching them. Fortunately, we can rely on God's relevant advice whenever a change of course might be wise.

A WORD FOR TODAY
A lot of worry can be avoided with common sense and discernment.

Today, Lord, help me to pattern my plan for the future after your godly ways.

Read
Proverbs 3

WORTHY
COMPANIONS
My child, don't lose sight of common sense and discernment. Hang on to them, for they will refresh your soul. They are like jewels on a necklace.
Proverbs 3:21-22

AUGUST 4

HEART
WOUNDS

Guard your heart
above all else, for it
determines the
course of your life.
Proverbs 4:23

Ever wonder why a single, well-placed paper cut can create such relentless agony? Even the smallest task like folding letters or jotting a note becomes an impossible feat—comparable to water torture. How can such a small thing command such focus from the entire body?

The Bible refers to the human heart as facing a similar experience. The condition of our heart affects each undertaking, without exception. Sure, our lips may let a lie slip past them, but our heart feels the pain. Our fingers may deal a dirty hand to a neighbor or business partner, but our heart is soiled. Guarding our hearts from leading the rest of our members to sin is a full-time job.

Thankfully, God is willing to take control. He alone can safely monitor an irregular heartbeat—one that can be arrested by sin at any moment. Through Christ's death on the cross, we can surrender our heart to his keeping.

A WORD FOR TODAY
Check your heart security.

Today, Lord, I surrender the leanings of my heart to your keeping.

AUGUST 5

At times life seems like a mystery: We park in the driveway and drive on the parkway. We say feet "smell," and our noses "run." Likewise, Jesus' method for finding true life may sound like a riddle. Yet, it is no mystery because his truth has been tried and proven. A significant few have discovered that the secrets to a life of happiness go something like this: "Go last to be first." "Lose to win." "Die to live." Jesus' words are an ill fit with our natural instincts, yet they are a salve to our spiritual nature. Surrendering selfish pursuits allows us to experience the joy of fulfilling others' needs. Giving up personal gain is the gateway to outrageous satisfaction from God's hand.

We must, however, understand that it is impossible to grasp Jesus' intent unless we take him at his word. Experience is the best way to unravel the riddle.

A WORD FOR TODAY
"Lose to win; die to live"—Jesus' words.

Today, Lord, I will give up finding my own route to satisfaction so I can find favor with you instead.

Read
Proverbs 5

SOLID SAVINGS
If you try to hang on to your life, you will lose it. But if you give up your life for my sake, you will save it.
Matthew 16:25

AUGUST 6

Read
Proverbs 6

WISDOM
STORAGE

*Keep their words
always in your
heart. Tie them
around your neck.
When you walk,
their counsel will
lead you. When you
sleep, they will
protect you. When
you wake up, they
will advise you.*
Proverbs 6:21-22

A popular female humorist, Erma Bombeck, titled
one of her books, *Family: The Ties that Bind . . . and
Gag.* How often the words our parents spoke to us
in our childhood find their way into our lives, applying just enough pressure to remind us of their timelessness. Regardless of our family experience, the
wisdom of the more experienced has girded us
throughout our lives. Whether it was a trusted
teacher growing up, a godly grandparent in our
young adulthood, or a colleague in our first job,
most of us have gleaned guidance from others.

Proverbs is just such a collection. It serves as a
permanent document of godly wisdom. Were these
words written in today's culture, the author might
suggest entering words of wisdom in our PDAs or
planners—whatever paints a picture of a constant
companion. God is able to remind us of the wisdom
garnered from others in our moments of need. The
words we have stored in our minds and memories
can serve to lead, protect, and advise us day by day.

A WORD FOR TODAY
Wisdom is worth thinking about . . . any time.

*Today, Lord, I am grateful for those who have influenced
my life. Remind me of their wisdom and ways when I
need it.*

AUGUST 7

A scientific experiment once proved that a frog would, strangely, allow itself to boil to death if placed in lukewarm water that was then gradually heated to a boil. If placed in boiling water first, it naturally leaped to safety. However, the gradual increase in temperature lulled the frog into a false sense of security, for it hardly noticed its weakening muscles until too late to jump to safety.

Sound familiar? Perhaps we can't remember the last time we viewed life from the inside of a kettle. But how about being flattered to death within the walls of our own workplace? It starts out slow—a subtle need for people's approval. The extra attention we may receive for a job well done feels nice, soothing. However, we can find our resolves gradually weakened by the warm feelings we get from having our ego stroked. Our craving for affirmation from others can lead to a number of questionable ethics on the job. We may join the office gossip loop to feel included. We may fudge figures to appear successful to our boss. When it boils down to pride, there's a lot to be learned from the frog in the kettle.

A WORD FOR TODAY
What sounds good may not be good.

Today, Lord, I praise you for the ways you have protected me from myself. Help me be alert and prepared for temptation of all forms.

Read
Proverbs 7

JUMP!
She seduced him with her pretty speech and enticed him with her flattery.
Proverbs 7:21

AUGUST 8

**Read
Proverbs 8**

SURE
OUTCOME
*[Wisdom says,]
"I love all who
love me. Those
who search will
surely find me."*
Proverbs 8:17

Fifty-one weeks, three days. That's the average amount of time an individual spends in a lifetime looking for lost keys. Wouldn't it be nice to know that once we began searching for a needed item, its location would be instantly revealed? No more wracking our brains to remember the last time we saw it, used it, or heard it. What time we would save from looking between sofa cushions or underneath beds. Instant gratification, guaranteed.

The Bible says that what the natural world cannot offer, the spiritual realm does. Those who seek for wisdom will surely find it. If we treasure wisdom, wisdom will prove invaluable in return. God will not withhold his counsel from us when we earnestly desire to have it—he promises to richly reward our efforts. Satisfaction, guaranteed. With a guarantee like that, what are we waiting for? Let the search begin!

A WORD FOR TODAY
Wisdom rewards those who love her.

Today, Lord, I pray you will lead me down new paths in my hunt for wisdom. May I search out your ways with all my heart.

AUGUST 9

It's not a pill, a diet, or a complicated daily regimen; however, it is the top technique for increasing our longevity. It has nothing to do with guava juice, gravity weights, or wrinkle analysis, yet it does wonders for our health and vitality. Don't look for it on the Home Shopping Network anytime soon. It can't be sold, bartered for, or bought, yet its value is priceless. Men and women have turned to it with guaranteed results throughout the centuries. It boasts the longest running ad history of any product—its formula has been unchanged since its inception.

Known as wisdom, it is both prescribed and described within the pages of the Bible. Whoever takes wisdom to heart will experience the quality of life we were meant to share. It relieves stress under pressure. It cures our heartaches and changes our attitudes. It offers perspective on persecution. Wisdom can lance our emotional ailments and thereby increase our physical health as well. Indeed, is it any wonder that it is the greatest health secret of the ages?

A WORD FOR TODAY
Take wisdom like daily vitamins.

Today, Lord, I need help applying wisdom to my life's ailments. Deliver me from my insistence on fixing my own pain. Instead, may I lean on your counsel.

**Read
Proverbs 9**

LONGEVITY
*Wisdom will
multiply your days
and add years to
your life.*
Proverbs 9:11

AUGUST 10

OVERLOOKING THE OBVIOUS

People who accept discipline are on the pathway to life, but those who ignore correction will go astray.
Proverbs 10:17

Correction is a blessing; constructive criticism is a gift. However, no one looks forward to receiving either one! The Bible concedes that discipline is not enjoyable, but it is necessary for our growth.

We can consider it this way: Suppose a fellow driver points out that we have a flat tire. How ridiculous it would be for us to get mad at the person who pointed out the flat. If we continued driving with our flat tire, we would then become a hazard for others on the road, as well as causing damage to our car.

Those who refuse to be corrected allow pride and insecurity to take the wheel. They are a road hazard on the pathway to peace. It's best that we stay out of their way. In contrast, the person who responds to discipline is able to enter the roadway again—better equipped for the future.

A WORD FOR TODAY
Correction is a needed traffic sign.

Today, Lord, open the parts of me that I have closed off to correction. May your discipline bring me up to speed on the pathway of life.

AUGUST 11

Hearses do not have trailer hitches—a reminder that when our time comes to take a ride in a hearse, whatever we have amassed on earth is staying right here. Believers and unbelievers alike have the same return on material investments—they will all lie in the dust at the end of our earthly life. While a corporate culprit may take in hoards of ill-gotten gain (holed away in Swiss accounts), a righteous person's portfolio is more diversified. As any financial advisor will reveal, it is the length of the term, not the amount of the investment, that matters.

Earthly gain for the moment cannot compare to an eternal reward. A virtuous person maintains a heavenly account of spiritual rewards that has thousands upon thousands of years to accrue unlimited interest. Understandably, Wall Street has nothing on heaven. One measures wealth in a teacup over time; the other doles it out in perpetual waves across eternity. The godly can amass untold heavenly wealth from a lifetime of Christlike living.

A WORD FOR TODAY
Godly rewards are long term.

Lord, help me keep my sights set on the long-term benefits of loving and serving you.

Read
Proverbs 11

LEFT BEHIND
Evil people get rich for the moment, but the reward of the godly will last.
Proverbs 11:18

AUGUST 12

**Read
Proverbs 12**

MINDFUL LOVE

*Jesus replied, "The
most important
commandment is
this: 'Listen,
O Israel! The LORD
our God is the one
and only LORD. And
you must love the
LORD your God with
all your heart, all
your soul, all your
mind, and all your
strength.' The second
is equally important:
'Love your neighbor
as yourself.' No other
commandment is
greater than these."*
Mark 12:29-31

When Jesus quoted Deuteronomy 6:5, he purposely included the *mind* as one of the personal channels of our love for God. By doing so, he clarified the scope of our relationship with God. We are expected to love the Lord completely, so our love must be conscious and thoughtful.

In a world where faith is often described as a characteristic of people who don't think, Jesus' words point to the importance of engaging our minds as a central aspect of what we believe. Jesus spoke of himself as the Truth (John 14:6). The Bible repeatedly claims to be true and reliable (Psalm 19:7-11; Psalm 119:151; 2 Timothy 3:16).

Truth keeps the mind healthy. Every day, our minds have to digest large quantities of mental junk food. If we do not include truth in our thought diet, we will have malnourished minds. The daily discipline of thinking about God's Word will result in spiritual health.

A WORD FOR TODAY
The greatest proverb—"Love God."

Lord Jesus, teach me to apply my mind to think about you and your Word as part of loving you.

AUGUST 13

Just like the full-body rush we feel when we dive into a swimming pool on an August afternoon, getting the right instruction in the time of need can't be beat. But not just any kind of instruction will bring us relief.

Unfortunately, soliciting instruction from the wrong source is like diving into the deep end of failure. This proverb encourages us to seek the counsel of the wise. Think of it as creating an advisory board for our lives. Imagine eight empty chairs around a large conference table, with Christ seated at the head. These chairs represent where our most trusted advisors reside in our minds. One chair represents someone we would turn to in financial areas, another chair is for our spiritual advisor, another seats the one called upon for family concerns, and so on. In times of need, the benefit of their resources and experience may be only a phone call away.

A WORD FOR TODAY
Wise instruction is a cool drink to the thirsty.

Today, Lord, I am thankful for the times I have received godly advice from good people. Bless them today for their faithful work.

Read
Proverbs 13

LIVING WATER
The instruction of the wise is like a life-giving fountain; those who accept it avoid the snares of death.
Proverbs 13:14

AUGUST 14

Read
Proverbs 14

GOOD NEIGHBORS

It is a sin to belittle one's neighbor; blessed are those who help the poor.
Proverbs 14:21

If this proverb referenced only our literal neighbors, some of us would be hard pressed to find a financially challenged one in the bunch. We can broaden the principle revealed in the proverb by considering anyone in a poor, pitiful situation to be "one's neighbor." Ironically, the poorest "neighbors" of all can include those who may be substantially wealthy, yet without a friend in the world. They find themselves at the top, yet in the unenviable position of loneliness. Our "neighbors" are those who have gone through a messy divorce, bankruptcy, or other public humiliation and suddenly find their social circle has shrunk significantly. Those whom the world finds easiest to belittle—perhaps in fear of becoming like them and sharing their fate—are our neighbors.

The Bible reminds us that it is wrong to ride with the tide of public opinion when it belittles those in need. Instead, we are called to help our neighbor by offering friendship and the reassurance of support. We are commanded to welcome those "survivors" whom society has "voted off the island." In fact, we are to consider them as close as . . . neighbors.

A WORD FOR TODAY
We can always find need among our neighbors.

Today, Lord, keep my eyes fixed on those from whom I'd rather turn away. Move me to help them however I can.

AUGUST 15

Imagine being offered a luxurious townhome filled with all the comforts and conveniences money can buy. It is the ultimate townhome in terms of finery and decor. There is only one stipulation: The quarters must be shared with one, modest-sized elephant. That's all—the zenith of luxury living offered in exchange for enduring a gigantic problem.

The reality of this ridiculous illustration is no exaggeration for some folks. Some people have the freedom to buy anything their hearts desire, yet they are confined by mammoth-sized grief, divorced families, spoiled children who haven't spoken to them in years, so-called friends who use them for position, or impatient lawyers bringing bad news. For them, that fleeting but terrifying feeling just before retiring at night is that the weight of their growing grief may one day trample them. Meanwhile, the God-fearing family with comparably little material wealth sleeps soundly in their beds. The Bible teaches that God's awesome presence is a believer's true treasure.

A WORD FOR TODAY
It's *who* you have that counts.

Today, Lord, I praise you for being my true treasure. Help me value my relationship with you above all else.

Read
Proverbs 15

REAL TREASURE
Better to have little, with fear for the LORD, than to have great treasure and inner turmoil.
Proverbs 15:16

AUGUST 16

Read
Proverbs 16

GOSSIP CROP
A troublemaker
plants seeds of strife;
gossip separates the
best of friends.
Proverbs 16:28

Gossip is to a friendship what weeds are to a garden. As weeds choke a garden, so gossip saps the strength and chokes the growth of relationships. The Bible highlights dozens of friendships and relationships built on qualities like trust, affection, mutual purpose, and mission. Such words characterize the intense bond between biblical characters like David and Jonathan and Paul and Silas.

When we gossip with close friends, a subtle change affects our friendship. Our dearest friends may become haunted by the persistent thought that maybe they would find their own name as our hot topic in another social circle. Who's to say we wouldn't slice and dice them, too, if the opportunity arose? We may never betray a best friend by gossip, but human nature allows the suspicion to remain. By publicly dismantling another person's dignity, even within the intimacy of a close circle of friends, we have demonstrated the destruction we are capable of.

A WORD FOR TODAY
Gossip and friendship don't mix.

Today, Lord, help me deal with gossip in a godly way.
Help me spread only good news instead.

AUGUST 17

We can choose our friends, but not our families.
A less touted observation is the Bible's reminder
against cafeteria-style loyalties with friends or family members. We don't have the option to pick and
choose *which* friends or family members we will be
loyal to at which times. When families run into hard
times, Proverbs boasts that the idea of the family
unit was birthed for just such a purpose. Similarly,
true friends are not only loyal; they are *always* loyal
in their intent. Going the second mile is second
nature to the believer. If a friend or family member
is in need, a believer does whatever is possible to
meet that need.

Why such an emphasis on loyalty? Christian
relationships—friendships or marriages or families—
are to model Christ's own relationship with believers
as a witness to the world. In fact, the Bible emphasizes that the world will take note of our loyalty or
lack thereof. How well we demonstrate our willingness to honor a commitment to family or friends is
a strong testimony for or against the legitimacy of the
Christian faith.

A WORD FOR TODAY
Be a loyal sister or brother.

*Today, Lord, I am aware of friends and family members
with whom I have struggled. Motivate me to work on
my commitments as a testimony to your grace.*

**Read
Proverbs 17**

LESSON ON
LOYALTY
*A friend is always
loyal, and a brother
is born to help in
time of need.*
Proverbs 17:17

AUGUST 18

❦

RUN DOWN
The human spirit
can endure a sick
body, but who can
bear a crushed
spirit?
Proverbs 18:14

Although believers are privy to supernatural experience, we are not superhuman. While we dwell on this earth, we will get mud on our shoes and rain on our heads. We may become well acquainted with illness, disease, calamity, and catastrophe. Through all this, God can infuse the human spirit with courage to bear up through whatever earthly trials come our way. Though we may reach the depths of depression, we can endure because of the hope of Christ.

However, the Bible teaches that the ultimate sadness is the devastation of a crushed spirit apart from Christ. God infuses the spirit with life; sin bears down on the spirit with ever-increasing pressure, crushing it with hopelessness. These broken lives pass us in the aisles of grocery stores and stand in line beside us at the theater. They are a reminder that we are unable to save ourselves from the hopelessness of life without Christ. Whatever believers may experience, we can endure because of Christ. However, no one can bear up alone under a life with no hope.

A WORD FOR TODAY
Christ can crush-proof your spirit.

Today, Lord, I know I can endure my trials because
I am relying on you. Encourage my spirit and make
me strong.

AUGUST 19

How many people gain a promotion only to lose their principles along the way? How many business tycoons focus their mental energies on gaining material fortune only to lose their families due to neglect? As pitiful as these stories are, Jesus points to a more frightening proposition. It is possible to gain everything this life has to offer and yet lose our souls. We risk losing the only thing we take with us from this life into the next: our soul. Jesus proves the point of his proverb in the form of a question—not a mandate. No one can answer for us—we each must answer his inquiry for ourselves.

What will we benefit from our earthly gains? When we are caught up in a materialistic moment, we can lose sight of what really matters in light of eternity. Jesus reminds us that preparedness is essential when it pertains to eternal life.

A WORD FOR TODAY
Why would you trade a priceless gift for anything less?

Today, Lord, many things will attempt to draw my focus away from what really matters. Steady my gaze and tighten my grip.

Read
Proverbs 19

PRICELESS
SOUL
What do you benefit if you gain the whole world but lose your own soul? Is anything worth more than your soul?
Matthew 16:26

AUGUST 20

**Read
Proverbs 20**

DIVINE BACKUP

*Don't say, "I will get
even for this wrong."
Wait for the LORD to
handle the matter.*

Proverbs 20:22

There are a few select phrases that delight the ears of almost anyone: "Let me do the dishes" or "Who wants this last piece of cake?" for example. Moreover, there are particular words that just feel good on the tongue: "I have the day off" and "I think I'll take a nap" are near the top of the list. However, there is a unique phrase (with many variations) that we may love to say but dread hearing from anyone else: "I will get even."

Vengeance—it's the variation on a theme repeated throughout literature, prose, history, film, and fantasy. Whenever we are harmed, we rush to our idea of justice. Taking matters into our shaky hands, we often handle the situation poorly. Instead, the Bible offers a panacea to personal injury: wait. Wait on God to handle the matter. Like a mother arranging for the father to "deal the goods" to an undisciplined child, so we can bequeath our right to repay. We can summon our heavenly Father to right the wrong according to his ways.

A WORD FOR TODAY
Give God room to work.

*Today, Lord, grant me the wisdom to wait. When
I am hurt, angry, or frustrated, help me to set vengeful
thoughts aside.*

AUGUST 21

Justice is a two-sided proposition. One side represents the joy we experience when we see a wrong righted. An abuser is arrested. A criminal is caught. If we are on the proper side of justice, fear is unnecessary. We can relax and rejoice when justice is administered in a situation. In contrast, those who receive its penalty experience another side of justice altogether. Guilty participants ponder life in the penitentiary as punishment for their crime. The penalty that accompanies justice angers an unrepentant delinquent. Such indignant offenders don't want justice to be rendered in their case.

Ultimately, justice is a joyous experience for believers because of the certainty of heaven's reward. Likewise, evildoers find nothing to celebrate. Final justice will rest upon them. The Bible warns us to be on the proper side of justice—both in an earthly and eternal sense. We can then live without fear and with great joy, celebrating God's justice on earth and in heaven.

A WORD FOR TODAY
Justice sounds good until our evil is exposed.

Today, Lord, may I stand for what is right in all situations and rejoice.

**Read
Proverbs 21**

JUSTICE
ASSURED
*Justice is a joy
to the godly, but
it terrifies evildoers.*
Proverbs 21:15

AUGUST 22

**Read
Proverbs 22**

DEBT SERVICE
*Just as the rich rule
the poor, so the
borrower is servant
to the lender.*
Proverbs 22:7

Analogy is a favorite tool of Proverbs. Comparing two items demonstrates the relationship between them. In this case, the rich rule the poor because of the balance of power. Their relationship is dependent upon the concept of supply and demand. The rich have what the poor need. In the same way, this proverb exposes the balance of power between a lender and a borrower. A servant is dependent upon another in the same way borrowers become dependent upon a bank or other lender. Whether or not we should borrow money is not at issue.

This truth simply emphasizes the seriousness of such a move. The comparison is a vivid picture of our commitment to repaying our debt. Though we may enjoy the benefit of a loan, the balance of power remains in the lender's hands. We ought to fully understand the dependent relationship that is created whenever we borrow money. Understanding is the first step to applying what the Bible teaches about integrity and money.

A WORD FOR TODAY
Debt enslaves.

*Today, Lord, help me realize that I am indebted to you
for all of my resources. May I be a good manager of what
you give to me.*

AUGUST 23

When spiritual hunger strikes, we have options. We can starve, we can bargain-hunt in earthly resources, or we can turn to God for what we need. Too often, we are tempted to go to the convenience store of earthly resources instead of God's Word. We pick up a bargain brand of humanism in place of God's truth. Instead of scriptural self-discipline, we take home the latest self-help CD. We would rather skim a horoscope than whisper a prayer for wisdom.

In contrast, Proverbs is a shopper's paradise—a wealth of resources at our fingertips. We can pick up exactly what we need: a handy answer to that nagging problem, a bit of advice concerning a family member. This particular proverb contains a shopping list of the essentials for Christlike living. They are a saint's staples—a farmer's market of fundamentals—as if they were called out by a hungry soul to a hastening shopper: "While you're out, get Truth. Also get Wisdom if you see it. Discipline. And one more thing: Good judgment." We can make a meal out of these goods that will truly satisfy our soul.

A WORD FOR TODAY
We sell the truth when we ignore it.

Today, Lord, thank you for the resources you have given me in Scripture. Help me to turn to your Word for my daily needs.

**Read
Proverbs 23**

WISDOM
SHOPPING
Get the truth and never sell it; also get wisdom, discipline, and good judgment.
Proverbs 23:23

AUGUST 24

WISE JOURNEY

*Don't fret because
of evildoers; don't
envy the wicked.
For evil people
have no future;
the light of the
wicked will be
snuffed out.*
Proverbs 24:19-20

When the ruthless beat out the righteous for the next promotion at work, we may begin to envy them. When the malicious go unpunished, the disparity between what seems fair and what is reality causes great frustration. We become convinced that if we are "nice," we are destined to "finish last." However, that's just it: We're not finished yet. Like a hiker cresting the top of a mountain peak only to see the horizon littered with higher and higher peaks, we must remember that our journey has just begun.

Life on earth—for the godly and the ungodly—is but one peak from God's perspective. Many people may cheat to climb higher, stepping on the heads of the righteous for a foothold. However, while they may enjoy the pinnacle experience of life on earth, sadly it will be their only summit. The Bible teaches that there is no future for evildoers. While the righteous will continue to ascend for eternity, evildoers are "snuffed out" and doomed to descend into darkness.

A WORD FOR TODAY
Be with God when the lights go out.

Today, Lord, may I not waver between worry and envy when it comes to the wicked. Help me to trust that righteousness will win out in the end.

AUGUST 25

Early radar systems functioned with such dulled sensitivity that they often picked up a flock of birds as a formation of planes. Imagine the resulting mishaps, wrong landings, and missed calculations! In the same way, our sluggish sensitivity to others' needs causes us to misfire when it matters most. We are often too preoccupied with ourselves to pick up on others' feelings or emotions. Instead, we carry on with our own cheery selves—indifferent to those with heavy hearts.

This proverb vividly illustrates coming upon someone in need, only to leave that person in worse condition! Proverbs sharpen our radar images, teaching us to notice. Instead of overlooking and further saddening a person who already feels ignored, we can stop and take note. Practicing the proverbs makes us helpful in that moment. Instead of unrealistic platitudes or other efforts likened to vinegar in a wound, we can learn heartfelt ways that offer salve to someone who is hurting.

A WORD FOR TODAY
Practice wise encouragement.

Today, Lord, I want to be tuned in to the needs of others. Show me how to be helpful with my words and actions.

Read
Proverbs 25

SENSITIVE
REPERTOIRE
Singing cheerful songs to a person with a heavy heart is like taking someone's coat in cold weather or pouring vinegar in a wound.
Proverbs 25:20

AUGUST 26

Read
Proverbs 26

POSTHUMOUS AWARDS

God blesses those who are persecuted for doing right, for the Kingdom of Heaven is theirs.
Matthew 5:10

Like wearing rival colors at our alma mater's home football game, the Bible teaches that godliness is countercultural, often resulting in persecution. We can be thankful that the typical Western experience of persecution is not life threatening, but it remains uncomfortable; aggravating; and, at times, lonely. We may be ostracized from social events because of our faith. We may undergo criticism for upholding standards for our children—sometimes even within our own ranks. Persecution in the workplace may mean being passed over for promotions. Amid all our persecution, God's promise is his presence and power.

Like a medal of honor, the Kingdom of Heaven is a reward for such endurance. However, just as veterans alone know the true value of a medal of honor, we will realize the truth of this verse only if we experience it. The goal is not a higher rating on the persecution meter. Rather, we should be concerned only with how overtly we live out our faith.

A WORD FOR TODAY
Endurance is a test of Kingdom citizenship.

Today, Lord, there are those who don't understand what I am about. Encourage me with a spirit of rejoicing whenever I am misunderstood.

AUGUST 27

Like a linguist, Proverbs explores the power of the tongue in a number of different ways. It weaves together the words we say and the motives behind them to create revelations about human nature. At first glance, the emphasis in this proverb appears no deeper than a chuckle—clearly, this neighbor is not a morning person. However, consider the motive of the zealous greeter. Why was the greeter up at such an hour? Why go out of the way to call for the neighbor's attention? Perhaps the pleasant greeting was a form of flattery with a person of influence—one with high standing in the community. Maybe that person had something the eager greeter desperately wanted. Whenever we trip over ourselves to get another person's attention, we present a questionable motive. Are we trying too hard to impress? Are we attempting to elevate ourselves in society or the workplace instead of waiting on God's direction?

Proverbs reminds us that such a venture often meets with disappointment. We can actually lose ground with such a "greeting." Better to wait on God's timing than force our own.

A WORD FOR TODAY
Consider another's need.

Dear Lord, I know that I have tried too hard sometimes to impress someone. Help me to maintain pure motives in all my interaction with others.

Read
Proverbs 27

SUNRISE
EXUBERANCE
A loud and cheerful greeting early in the morning will be taken as a curse!
Proverbs 27:14

AUGUST 28

DANGEROUS SPEED

The trustworthy person will get a rich reward, but a person who wants quick riches will get into trouble.
Proverbs 28:20

Late-night TV's sleep-inducing, snowy rendition of "The Star-Spangled Banner" (signaling that the television is going to bed before we are) has new competition in town: the dawn of the infomercial. Now, we can enjoy back-to-back testimonials from fellow insomniacs who ordered the latest moneymaking-ploy package and retired in an Italian villa six months later.

The Bible warns us of the get-rich-quick scheme, but not because making money is inherently evil. Money is not the issue. The pursuit of money is more the point. Those who want money above all else are destined for troubling temptations: Tax evasion. Fraud. Debt. Chapter 13.

When we want to be faithful more than we want to be rich, a funny thing happens: Money finally finds its proper place in our lives. We begin to see the fruit of faithfulness, such as ripened relationships nourished by integrity, as a more valuable commodity. Though our bank statements may never be summoned as a television testimonial, the quality of our lives will testify to our rich reward.

A WORD FOR TODAY
Better to be counted on than count your riches.

Today, Lord, help me want to be faithful above any other earthly desire. Lead me to taste and enjoy the fruit of being trustworthy.

AUGUST 29

Miss Manners, Peggy Post, and Martha Stewart make a robust living off the premise that some things are just not done. The published pontiffs of politeness agree: Opening our mouths with our foot nearby is one of them. This proverb reminds us that someone who speaks without thinking is worse off than the fool who doesn't know any better. There is hope for fools to recover gracefully—no one expects anything from them. However, when it comes to being able to inflict pain with our words, friends, not fools, have the edge.

Proverbs reminds us that our tongues contain the power to ravage a friendship when our speech is not in sync with our minds. Until we have prayed through a piece of advice for a friend, we have no right to share it. Unless we have thought through our own responsibility in a matter, we can't adequately bring up a grievance against another person. Thinking it through before speaking our minds can save many people a lot of wasted and hurtful words.

A WORD FOR TODAY
Think before engaging the tongue.

Today, Lord, may my words be few. Give me wisdom to speak only what is important and encouraging today.

Read
Proverbs 29

GRACEFUL LIVING
There is more hope for a fool than for someone who speaks without thinking.
Proverbs 29:20

AUGUST 30

DENIAL IS
NO RIVER
An adulterous
woman consumes
a man, then
wipes her mouth
and says,
"What's wrong
with that?"
Proverbs 30:20

The bully of the big screen is a familiar stereotype.
The bully walks into the school cafeteria and
snatches a meatball sandwich out of a scrawny kid's
fumbling fingers. After gorging on the poor kid's
meal in plain view, the remorseless bully eyeballs
the cowering crowd and says incredulously, "What
are you lookin' at?" End of scene.

The star of this proverb acts out a similar screen-
play—only with much higher stakes. It is a frightening picture of how we can be so driven by our sinful
appetites that it becomes impossible for us to be
remorseful. The imagery is of a woman wiping her
mouth to get rid of her indulgence. It warns us of
times when, instead of repenting of our actions, we
justify them. Not only are we steeped in sin; we
cease to see our sin as sinful. Many people call such
action a choice, a mere lifestyle like any other. But
Scripture is clear: Sin has consequences.

A WORD FOR TODAY
When we get our way, we lose our way.

Today, Lord, may I remember what it is like to be truly
sorry for my sins. Teach me how to repent.

AUGUST 31

Which is easier: giving instructions or following them? While it is often easier to make up the rules than to follow someone else's, life requires us to be adept at both. In the same way, leadership is both leading and following.

This proverb gives us insight into a person's reputation for leading. How often do we run across an authority figure whose words are wise each time he or she speaks? How many in positions of power follow the rule of kindness in exercising their role? If others can express similar affirmations about our style of leadership, then we are in sync with scriptural command. However, too often, leaders are memorable for less than godly reasons.

Leadership may be a heady experience, though it should never be a "head trip." When we use kindness as our governing rule, we will honor, not abuse, those who are under our authority—from coworkers to family members. Our reputation for leading others should emerge from a commitment to wisdom and kindness.

A WORD FOR TODAY
Genuine leadership includes kindness.

Today, Lord, I want to strive for a reputation that honors you. May my words be wise and my actions result in kindness.

Read
Proverbs 31

WISDOM
APPLIED
*When she speaks,
her words are wise,
and she gives
instructions with
kindness.*
Proverbs 31:26

SEPTEMBER 1

Read
Proverbs 1

AN AWESOME
GOD
When they cry for
help, I will not
answer. Though they
anxiously search for
me, they will not
find me. For they
hated knowledge
and chose not to fear
the LORD.
Proverbs 1:28-29

In 1988 Rich Mullins wrote a worship song titled, "Awesome God." Its familiar lyrics highlight biblical events that display the awe-inspiring character of God. The chorus begins and ends giving honor to God's greatness. Indeed, our God is awesome—in the fullest sense of the word. Although we often hear of God's great love for us and his mercy toward us, we must never forget his incomprehensible grandeur. Hebrews 10:31 says that it is "a terrible thing to fall into the hands of the living God." And Galatians 6:7 warns us, "Don't be misled—you cannot mock the justice of God. You will always harvest what you plant."

Our wise, powerful, and loving God earnestly desires to fellowship with us. But if we "hated knowledge and chose not to fear" him, we will find the heavens as hard as iron, and our God as elusive as vapor. Let us always approach our God with a healthy respect for his majesty and holiness.

A WORD FOR TODAY
Don't lose your awe of God.

Today, Lord, take my hardened heart and make it fear
you. Show me the glory of your righteousness and the
beauty of your ways.

SEPTEMBER 2

When God created us in his image and for his glory, he gave us gifts. He made us unique by giving each of us certain abilities, talents, and character traits in a combination no one else possesses. Later, when we became believers, certain spiritual gifts were added to the original package (see 1 Corinthians 12).

Each of us has different gifts and in differing measures, but God would have us all use them for his purposes. Sometimes we doubt that we're gifted, or we're not sure how to use our gifts in the situations in which God has placed us. As we remember that the very air we breathe is a gift from our Creator, we can trust that he has total creative rights over all his creation and that he will guide us in the use of our giftedness.

Accordingly, as we remember his goodness and kindness toward us, we can come before him and say, "Father, all that I have is yours, and I lay it at your feet." Then, we can go out into the world, determined to use the gifts that he has given us to glorify his awesome name.

A WORD FOR TODAY
What you rightly use you can't lose.

Today, Lord, help me recognize my gifts and use them in ways that glorify you.

Read Proverbs 2

A USEFUL GIFT
To those who use well what they are given, even more will be given, and they will have an abundance. But from those who do nothing, even what little they have will be taken away.
Matthew 25:29

SEPTEMBER 3

**Read
Proverbs 3**

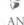

AN
INCLINATION
TO SERVE

*Do not withhold
good from those
who deserve it
when it's in your
power to help them.
If you can help
your neighbor
now, don't say,
"Come back
tomorrow, and then
I'll help you."*
Proverbs 3:27-28

Have you ever met someone whose good intentions were just on the other side of a winning lottery ticket? You know, the kind of person who says, "If I just win this money or that sweepstakes, I'll do all these wonderful things."

We may all fantasize about what we would do with a million dollars, but God wants to use us to do wonderful things right now. We must remember that our Father's heart overflows with love and compassion for the poor and hurting. As we walk more fully in his will, we should reach out to help those in need with whatever resources we already possess.

This proverb points out how easy it is to withhold help from others under the excuse that we need what we have in order to have even more to give in the future. Such an attitude actually betrays a tendency to never give at all. Remember, Jesus promised a reward to those who did good to others, for he likened it to doing good to him (Matthew 25:40).

A WORD FOR TODAY
Good intentions don't count without action.

Today, Lord, show me someone who needs to be shown your love in a practical way, and use me to meet that person's need.

SEPTEMBER 4

We all know that our tongues are powerful. Through them, we have the power to build up a hurting friend or to mercilessly tear down those who have offended us. But do we realize that the words we speak reveal the true character of the innermost depths of our hearts? There is a direct connection between what we say and who we actually are.

Jesus said, "For whatever is in your heart determines what you say" (Matthew 12:34). So, when we engage in "perverse talk" and "corrupt speech," we show the very sinfulness of our own hearts. In order to "avoid," we may have to consider the company we keep. Our prayers should echo the psalmist's: "May the words of my mouth and the meditation of my heart be pleasing to you, O Lord, my rock and my redeemer" (Psalm 19:14).

A WORD FOR TODAY
Be absent from certain conversations.

Today, Lord, change my heart so that the overflow of my lips is pleasing to you.

Read
Proverbs 4

THE POTENT TONGUE

Avoid all perverse talk; stay away from corrupt speech.
Proverbs 4:24

SEPTEMBER 5

**Read
Proverbs 5**

❦

MARITAL BLISS

*Let your wife be
a fountain of
blessing for you.
Rejoice in the wife
of your youth.*
Proverbs 5:18

When God created people in the Garden of Eden, he created us male and female. In his wisdom, our Father created two distinct sexes that would each represent his glory throughout his creation. But he didn't stop there. God ordained that the two would become one flesh, and so present a picture of Jesus and his church (Ephesians 5:22-32), united by love. We need look only briefly at the world around us to see how that image has been attacked and distorted.

The proverb, meant for a son, highlights the effects and blessings of a healthy marriage. The "let" indicates how important it is for marriage partners to allow or expect each other to be a benefit in their lives. When we "rejoice" in our spouse, we allow him or her to know the significant and wonderful difference he or she is making in our lives.

May we recommit ourselves to loving and serving each other and to showing forth the love of God through our families.

A WORD FOR TODAY
Marriage is for life.

Today, Lord, teach me to better love and serve my family and to rejoice in the blessings that you have given me.

SEPTEMBER 6

We don't like to be told that we are wrong. It is an affront to our pride. And so, in our self-assuredness, we often push ahead with our own plans, presuming that we know better than God. It's the same lie that Adam and Eve bought into in the Garden. Satan said, "You won't die!" (Genesis 3:4), and they believed him instead of God, turning their backs on the Father.

The proverbs tell us over and over again that it is the fool who spurns correction. An honest look at our own lives and hearts will show us that God is infinitely better equipped to be Lord of our lives. Therefore, let us humble ourselves and seek his direction. Then, when we fail and need correction, we will have another opportunity to demonstrate that we do trust him to straighten us out.

A WORD FOR TODAY
God's Word lights the way.

Today, Lord, teach me the way of life. Soften my heart to yield to your truth and to rejoice in the beauty of your commands.

**Read
Proverbs 6**

REPROOF
FOR LIFE
*Their [parents']
command is a
lamp and their
instruction a light;
their corrective
discipline is the
way to life.*
Proverbs 6:23

SEPTEMBER 7

**Read
Proverbs 7**

SIN'S
ATTRACTION

*He followed her at
once, like an ox
going to the
slaughter. He was
like a stag caught
in a trap, awaiting
the arrow that
would pierce its
heart. He was like a
bird flying into a
snare, little knowing
it would cost him his
life.*

Proverbs 7:22-23

Oh, the compelling attractiveness of sin! Even though we know that what we're pursuing will destroy us, our hearts lust after that which can give us only passing pleasure at best. This proverb pictures that all-too-familiar moment when we consciously decide to go our own way. The sinful temptation may not be as obvious, but our sudden fall shares similarities with the young man's choice.

The apostle Paul wrote candidly about his struggle: "I don't really understand myself, for I want to do what is right, but I don't do it. Instead, I do what I hate" (Romans 7:15). We love our sins so much that we follow them blindly to our destruction. May God revitalize our hearts and open our eyes to the reality that "everything else is worthless when compared with the infinite value of knowing Christ Jesus" (Philippians 3:8).

A WORD FOR TODAY
Giving in is giving up.

Today, Lord, show me the folly of my sinful ways. Help me to desire your righteousness more than anything that this world has to offer.

SEPTEMBER 8

Why would it matter that the first thing formed in all Creation was wisdom? Before God began to create the physical items—earth, stars, moon, animals, fish, plants, and planets—God decided on a *way,* an approach, he would use in Creation. That way was wisdom. Creation didn't result from a random, miscellaneous approach to building an intricate system. God may have created instantly, but he didn't create haphazardly!

We've discovered that even what appears to be in chaos in the universe exhibits order at some level. Wisdom shouts from the organization, intricacy, balance, and wonder of Creation. God decided, by using wisdom, that every molecule of Creation would give evidence of its Creator. This is why the psalmist was stating a profound truth when he wrote, "The heavens proclaim the glory of God. The skies display his craftsmanship" (Psalm 19:1).

A WORD FOR TODAY
God created with wisdom.

Today, Lord, teach me to see myself and those around me as incredibly precious, made for your glory, and created through wisdom.

Read
Proverbs 8

PRIORITY IN
CREATION
*[Wisdom says,] "The
LORD formed me
from the beginning,
before he created
anything else."*
Proverbs 8:22

SEPTEMBER 9

Read Proverbs 9

🍃

STRONG LOVE

Jesus replied, "The most important commandment is this: 'Listen, O Israel! The LORD our God is the one and only LORD. And you must love the LORD your God with all your heart, all your soul, all your mind, and all your strength.' The second is equally important: 'Love your neighbor as yourself.' No other commandment is greater than these."

Mark 12:29-31

The phrase "all your strength" must not lead us to the conclusion that a robust and energetic love for God would be something impressive. We sometimes read this verse as if Jesus said, "Love the LORD your God with . . . all your great strength." Instead, we ought to quietly consider that what he meant was, "Love the LORD your God with all of what little strength you actually possess."

Jesus measured qualities like strength and faith by comparing them to mustard seeds (Matthew 17:20). In the context of the great commandment, if heart-love is characterized by spontaneity, then strength-love involves a conscious effort. For instance, attentive worship takes energy. If we stay out late Saturday night, we may fall asleep during our worship on Sunday morning. What are we communicating to the Lord when we say "I love you" while yawning? The "little strength" we have should come as a result of effort expended for the Lord, not because we are too tired to give even our leftover strength to God.

A WORD FOR TODAY
The greatest proverb—"Love God."

Today, Lord, help me to love you with everything I am, in everything I do.

SEPTEMBER 10

Sometimes, we just like the sound of our own voices. We may be tired, excited, or angry; but we need to tell *someone* what's on our mind. Yet how often in the midst of those talkative times do we say something that we later regret? Whether it's a juicy bit of gossip or a rash comeback, our intemperate tongues can bring upon us a multitude of troubles.

That's why God counsels us to guard our words. "Too much talk," says this proverb, *"leads to sin."* The wise observation has to do with percentages; the more we talk the greater the chance we will say something we regret. Silence allows us to not only avoid error but provides added time to consider what we are going to say before we actually say it!

A WORD FOR TODAY
Wise silence is golden.

Today, Lord, help me to speak in ways that honor you. Help me to be silent when that honors you as well.

**Read
Proverbs 10**

A VERBAL
FLOOD
*Too much talk leads
to sin. Be sensible
and keep your
mouth shut.*
Proverbs 10:19

SEPTEMBER 11

Read
Proverbs 11

GOD'S VALUE SYSTEM

The LORD detests people with crooked hearts, but he delights in those with integrity.
Proverbs 11:20

Our value system and God's value system are often at odds. Whereas we may admire someone for his or her intelligence, beauty, athletic ability, or charisma, God may remain unimpressed. The Old Testament tells the story of Samuel going to anoint a new king of Israel after Saul had disobeyed God. Samuel came to the sons of Jesse, and he saw David's oldest brother, Eliab, a tall, handsome man. But God spoke to Samuel, saying in part, "I have rejected him. The LORD doesn't see things the way you see them. People judge by outward appearance, but the LORD looks at the heart" (1 Samuel 16:7).

God is not interested in anything else as much as he is interested in our hearts. It's the place where his presence is rooted or absent in our lives. When God looks in our hearts, he wants to find integrity. May we summon the courage to give him our everything, no matter what the cost, and to be people of integrity.

A WORD FOR TODAY
God sees our "covers" and our "contents."

Today, Lord, guard my heart from the twisted path and show me how to walk in the integrity of your ways.

SEPTEMBER 12

When a carpenter begins to build a house, his primary concern is a proper foundation. He knows that no matter how beautiful or well built the rest of the structure is, if the foundation isn't solid, the whole building will go awry. It may take time, but gravity will eventually prove whether or not a foundation is plumb and true.

So it is in our lives. If we build our values and priorities on the foundational truth of the one who claimed to be truth—Jesus (John 14:6)—then time will bear witness to the rightness of our choice. However, if our foundations aren't true, then all our flimsy facades will be exposed for the shams that they are. We must pursue God's truth as if our lives depended on it. They do!

A WORD FOR TODAY
Truth keeps a life-house standing.

Today, Lord, lead me into your eternal truth. Show me where I have built on wrong foundations, and help me to build on the truth.

**Read
Proverbs 12**

A WORTHY
FOUNDATION
Truthful words stand the test of time, but lies are soon exposed.
Proverbs 12:19

SEPTEMBER 13

Read
Proverbs 13

A HEALTHY
INDECISION
Wise people think
before they act; fools
don't—and even
brag about their
foolishness.
Proverbs 13:16

Oh, those pitiful fools! First, they don't fear God, saying that he doesn't even exist. Then, they make rash decisions and brag about their foolishness. How we pity them—that is, until we realize that sometimes those characteristics strike a little too close to home.

We all have moments of foolishness. We can be thankful that God hasn't given up on us. He may discipline or reprove us, yet as the apostle Paul said, "I am certain that God, who began the good work within you, will continue his work until it is finally finished on the day when Christ Jesus returns" (Philippians 1:6). Let us be prudent in our decision making, choosing to rely on God and his wisdom rather than bragging about our foolishness.

A WORD FOR TODAY
Think, act, and then think some more.

Today, Lord, help me to lean on you. Keep me from rash decisions. Teach my heart to be patient.

SEPTEMBER 14

There are a great many causes of concern in our lives, covering a broad range of importance. Will our income cover our expenses? Will there be a nuclear war? Are my children safe? Will I get cancer? Is there anything I'm missing that I should be worried about?

In the midst of these concerns, there exists a God who has always been and always will be. He created us; he loves us; and he knows our past, present, and future. How great our confidence can be when we bask in the glow of his sovereignty and goodness. We can turn to God—not only in the midst of our hardship but also in the midst of our prosperity. We can find our identity and value in him. He will always be a refuge—to us and to our children.

A WORD FOR TODAY
Trusting God offers children an inheritance.

Today, Lord, teach me to place my whole trust in you.
I want you to be my eternal, unshakable refuge.

Read
Proverbs 14

A LASTING
PEACE
Those who fear the
LORD are secure; he
will be a refuge for
their children.
Proverbs 14:26

SEPTEMBER 15

Read
Proverbs 15

THE ULTIMATE
FEAST
A bowl of vegetables
with someone you
love is better than
steak with someone
you hate.
Proverbs 15:17

We all long for intimate fellowship with people who care about us enough to speak the truth and love us enough to endure our weaknesses. The book of Proverbs is filled with definitions of true friends. A favorite of many is Proverbs 17:17: "A friend is always loyal, and a brother is born to help in time of need."

When we are with true friends, we don't worry about every little thing we say, we don't try to make awkward conversation during times of silence, and we don't bother composing an appealing facade. We are free to be who we are. It is in that atmosphere of love and acceptance that true fellowship is found. What's on the menu isn't nearly as important as who is sharing the meal with us. We should always strive to be a "bowl of vegetables" friend to those around us.

A WORD FOR TODAY
Companionship transforms cooking.

Today, Lord, help me to be a friend to those around me. Teach me to value them above earthly pleasures.

SEPTEMBER 16

Whether we are working our way through Proverbs or turning to the New Testament, the Bible doesn't compromise its position regarding our tongues. We are repeatedly warned to guard our mouths, to think first, and to be slow to speak. While we may reason that our speech isn't so bad, we would do well to consider that God probably knows more about it than we do. Our tongues have an incredible potential to destroy people. Careless words can cripple friendships, jeopardize relationships, and bring great amounts of hurt into people's lives.

James offers us a proverb with a particularly devastating judgment. "No one can tame the tongue." We may be helpless, but we're not hopeless. What is impossible for people is not all that difficult for God. We need God to sanctify our tongues and to make our speech edifying and holy.

A WORD FOR TODAY
God can control our tongues.

Today, Lord, help me to tame my tongue. Keep me from speaking evil.

**Read
Proverbs 16**

TAMING
THE BEAST

People can tame all kinds of animals, birds, reptiles, and fish, but no one can tame the tongue. It is restless and evil, full of deadly poison.
James 3:7-8

SEPTEMBER 17

Read
Proverbs 17

WITH
OPEN EYES

It's poor judgment to guarantee another person's debt or put up security for a friend.
Proverbs 17:18

When we fell into sin in the Garden of Eden, we fell hard. Our very natures became corrupted, and one of the main areas where that sin is manifest is in our financial decisions. We love money. We love the power and fun that buying and owning things brings. One of the danger signs that we may be spending beyond our stewardship responsibility occurs when we have to ask someone to cosign with us for a loan. What kind of friends are we if we ask others to take responsibility for our debts?

Jesus cautioned us about loving money, saying, "You cannot serve both God and money" (Matthew 6:24). Paul warned that "the love of money is the root of all kinds of evil" (1 Timothy 6:10). In this atmosphere of corruption, the above proverb provides us with a welcome caution.

A WORD FOR TODAY
Be cautious before guaranteeing someone else's debts.

Today, Lord, help me to understand how you would have me handle my finances. Help me to have my financial decisions reflect your priorities.

SEPTEMBER 18

There's a classic story of a powerful king who was building a mighty new capital for his empire. At the culmination of the construction, he summoned all the wise men of his kingdom and asked them to inscribe a sign that would hang over his castle as an eternal testament to his accomplishment. So, the wise men collaborated and debated for days. When all their work was done, they unveiled their bit of eternal wisdom. Its message: "This Too Shall Pass."

Change is a constant in our lives. Every day brings new challenges and new blessings, and we are fools if we try to live in the past. Churches stagnate under lifeless traditions. People stagnate under empty rules. God created us to be creative, just as he is. The truth of God's Word often comes to us as a new idea; until a certain moment, we were not ready to hear it. If we remain open to the Scriptures, we will discover that they always have a new lesson to teach us.

A WORD FOR TODAY
Practice wise curiosity.

Today, Lord, help me to be open to new things. Challenge the parts of my life that have lain dormant for too long, and bring new life to me.

**Read
Proverbs 18**

SEEKING
WISDOM
Intelligent people are always ready to learn. Their ears are open for knowledge.
Proverbs 18:15

SEPTEMBER 19

Read
Proverbs 19

❧

LIFELONG LEARNING

Get all the advice and instruction you can, so you will be wise the rest of your life.

Proverbs 19:20

The Bible teaches that we are wise to honor our elders. This verse tells us that those who are wise have probably reached that level after years of hard work and experience. Some of the greatest storehouses of godly wisdom are found in the elder members of our families and churches. Are you an older saint? Share your hard-earned wisdom with those who follow you. Are you younger? Pursue those who have so much to share.

So how do *we* become wise? By seeking advice and instruction, acknowledging that we don't know it all and that we have much to learn. One of the great motives for gratitude in our lives comes when we realize how many people have given us gifts of wisdom along the way. We can benefit greatly from the counsel of others, for they can help us to avoid their mistakes along the way.

A WORD FOR TODAY
Let wisdom keep pace with age.

Today, Lord, keep me humble and teachable. Grant me wisdom to walk in your truth.

SEPTEMBER 20

When we go to a foreign country for the first time, the changes can be overwhelming. Besides the differences in language and currency, cultural differences may catch us unawares. At those times, knowledgeable and reliable guides are worth their weight in gold.

This principle can be seen in all of life. If we are honest, we can all admit to experiencing moments when we are simply overwhelmed. The weights and concerns of this life can crush us beneath their mercilessly relentless load. But Jesus told us that he would always be with us (Matthew 28:20); that he would send the Spirit to guide us into all truth (John 16:13); and that we have no need to fear, for our Father cares for us (Luke 12:6-7). We should always turn to him as our guide, for then we can walk in confidence that he is directing our steps.

A WORD FOR TODAY
Trust God and take steps.

Today, Lord, help me to look to you as my guide. Incite in me a passion to pursue your path as the way of ultimate satisfaction and joy.

Read
Proverbs 20

A RELIABLE
GUIDE
The LORD directs our steps, so why try to understand everything along the way?
Proverbs 20:24

SEPTEMBER 21

Read
Proverbs 21

❧

HONORABLE PURSUITS

*Whoever pursues
righteousness and
unfailing love will
find life,
righteousness, and
honor.*

Proverbs 21:21

The world is full of pursuits that seem worthy. However, we can easily spend too much time seeking out those pursuits that are the most elusive, such as financial security, fame, or power. At times, we even "catch" what we are pursuing, only to find that it cannot satisfy our desires. To adapt one of Jesus' warnings, we may catch the whole world, but if we've left our soul behind in the process, we've actually lost everything (see Matthew 16:24-26).

According to this proverb, there are some goals worth pursuing in life—righteousness and unfailing love. The first points to the quality of our relationship with God. To pursue *righteousness* is to desire to reflect God's character, to pursue God himself. The second points to the quality of our human relationships. To pursue *unfailing love* is to strive to love our neighbor as ourselves.

God promises us that if we pursue these goals, we will find the true worth of life and gain what we can never lose.

A WORD FOR TODAY
Worthwhile pursuits include valuable by-products.

Today, Lord, teach me to follow hard after you. Excite my heart to desire your righteousness and unfailing love.

SEPTEMBER 22

When God called Abraham to leave his home and family and to set off as a wanderer, he made a great promise to Abraham: "I will make you into a great nation. . . . All the families on earth will be blessed through you" (Genesis 12:1-3). Abraham was blessed to be a blessing to all the families of the earth. In the same way, God continues to bless his people so that they can be blessings to others. God shows us his goodness and blessing—not for our own selfish fulfillment, but so that we can be channels of blessing to those in need.

The wonder is that God chooses to use us, imperfect and sinful as we are, to bless those around us. "Remember this—a farmer who plants only a few seeds will get a small crop. But the one who plants generously will get a generous crop" (2 Corinthians 9:6). The measure of our generosity is the degree to which we give to those who cannot give in return.

A WORD FOR TODAY
Look for ways to give to others.

Today, Lord, thank you for your great blessings in my life. Teach me to be generous, to be a blessing to others. Give me an opportunity to give to those who are in need. Grant me compassion to reflect your love as I do so.

Read
Proverbs 22

SOWING TO
RIGHTEOUSNESS
Blessed are those who are generous, because they feed the poor.
Proverbs 22:9

SEPTEMBER 23

Read
Proverbs 23

🐟

SUFFERING
BLESSINGS

*God blesses you
when people mock
you and persecute
you and lie about
you and say all sorts
of evil things
against you because
you are my followers.
Be happy about it!
Be very glad! For a
great reward awaits
you in heaven. And
remember, the
ancient prophets
were persecuted in
the same way.*
Matthew 5:11-12

Jesus warned us that we would be persecuted. "Since they persecuted me, naturally they will persecute you" (John 15:20). So did the apostle Paul. "Yes, and everyone who wants to live a godly life in Christ Jesus will suffer persecution" (2 Timothy 3:12). So what are we to expect? Trouble.

God's value system and the world's value system are in direct opposition. In the above verses, however, Jesus gives us a wonderful promise: A great reward awaits us in heaven. Not only that, but we can also expect that our suffering will produce a more intimate, authentic relationship with our Lord, as was the case with Job. After suffering the loss of his family, his livestock, and his health, Job said to God, "I had only heard about you before, but now I have seen you with my own eyes" (Job 42:5). In his sufferings, Job met God. The principle remains true for us as well (1 Peter 4:14).

A WORD FOR TODAY
Hard times highlight hope.

Today, Lord, grant me the courage to stand for your righteousness. Help me to treasure you above the approval and flattery of people.

SEPTEMBER 24

In the famous statue that adorns the entrances of many courts, the woman called Justice wears a blindfold. The implication is clear: She is blind to the criteria that we normally use to distinguish among ourselves, whether physical appearance, riches, or rank. So, too, this proverb points to justice on earth and the justice to come in the last day.

We know that "God has no favorites" (Galatians 2:6). As Jesus told the apostle John, "Let the one who is doing harm continue to do harm; let the one who is vile continue to be vile; let the one who is righteous continue to live righteously; let the one who is holy continue to be holy. Look, I am coming soon, bringing my reward with me to repay all people according to their deeds" (Revelation 22:11-12).

An awareness of God's promise of eventual and absolute justice ought to lie behind every judgment we make. Otherwise, we place ourselves in the position of being liable for God's judgment.

A WORD FOR TODAY
Playing favorites is playing with fire.

Today, Lord, help me to walk in righteousness. Help me to not attempt to excuse my offenses against you.

Read
Proverbs 24

UPHOLDING
RIGHTEOUS-
NESS
Here are some further sayings of the wise: It is wrong to show favoritism when passing judgment.
Proverbs 24:23

SEPTEMBER 25

Read
Proverbs 25

GODLY OPPOSITION

If your enemies are hungry, give them food to eat. If they are thirsty, give them water to drink. You will heap burning coals of shame on their heads, and the LORD will reward you.
Proverbs 25:21-22

What is our natural reaction toward our enemies? Don't we generally seek their ruin, rather than their well-being? But Jesus reversed the order: "You have heard the law that says, 'Love your neighbor' and hate your enemy. But I say, love your enemies! Pray for those who persecute you!" (Matthew 5:43-44). The apostle Paul reminded us to leave room for God's vengeance, rather than seeking our own, and ended by saying, "Don't let evil conquer you, but conquer evil by doing good" (Romans 12:21). Perhaps our kindness in the face of adversity will help to change our enemies' hearts and draw them to the Savior.

There is probably no greater training ground for the soul than the endurance course of treating enemies with kindness. If our vision of the Lord's pleasure and reward are not clear or large enough, we may not even try. Perhaps the image of Jesus, forgiving his enemies while hanging on the cross, will help us endure—that, and the help he will give if we ask.

A WORD FOR TODAY
Enemies present opportunities to bless someone.

Today, Lord, help me to love my enemies. Show me your heart toward those around me, that I may walk in the love that comes only from you.

SEPTEMBER 26

Proverbs can be illustrated by life experiences—some childhood lessons make a lasting impression.

A young man told the story of his father, a carpenter. When the young man was just a boy, his father and he were building a deck for a model home. The plans called for a hot tub in an enclosure on the deck, but the builder didn't want to pay for a hot tub to just sit in a display home. So, they built an enclosure in the shape of a hot tub and fashioned a wooden lid to cover the opening. It looked like a hot tub, but there wasn't actually one there. The redwood they used was beautiful, but ultimately it was of little worth. It was just a shell covering an empty space.

In the same way, we can pursue beautiful veneers in our lives that cover the coarseness of our cores. True godliness must penetrate every fiber of our being. It searches the recesses of our hearts and lays us bare before the Almighty.

A WORD FOR TODAY
Your externals need to accurately reflect your internals.

Today, Lord, show me my sin. Grant me a repentance that leads to refreshing (Acts 3:19-20). Take your truth to the core of my being.

Read Proverbs 26

DECEPTIVE FACADES
Smooth words may hide a wicked heart, just as a pretty glaze covers a clay pot.
Proverbs 26:23

SEPTEMBER 27

Read
Proverbs 27

❧

A PROPER TOOL

As iron sharpens iron, so a friend sharpens a friend.
Proverbs 27:17

Imagine a carpenter who has a dull saw blade and takes it to his workshop for sharpening. What does he use to restore its usefulness? He knows that a piece of wood, a bar of soap, or some other "soft" item is not going to do the job. If he wants to sharpen his saw, he needs a sharpener that is made of steel—strong and tough.

Like that craftsman, we can improve our usefulness to God by having friends who sharpen us. "Don't be fooled . . . for 'bad company corrupts good character' " (1 Corinthians 15:33). We may choose to hang around those who flatter us, those who deceive us, or those who manipulate us, but in the end, they cannot "sharpen" us. They are soft, and so will we be. However, if our friends are pursuing godliness and desiring God's highest, then they will sharpen us, as surely as iron sharpens iron. Let's pursue relationships that bring us closer to God and challenge us to live for him alone.

A WORD FOR TODAY
Real friendships keep us sharp.

Today, Lord, help me to learn godliness from those around me. Teach me how to be a friend that would sharpen others.

SEPTEMBER 28

In Genesis 25:21-34, we are told the story of Jacob and Esau. Jacob, though younger, was the child of promise. God had decided to use him to continue the lineage begun by Abraham and Isaac. But Jacob wasn't content to wait for God's plans. He schemed to take what by law belonged to his brother. So when Esau came to Jacob starving with hunger, Jacob sold him a bowl of lentil stew and a piece of bread. The price? Esau's birthright, which came with being the firstborn. Esau exchanged his birthright for table scraps.

We can look at this story from the distance of several thousand years and see Esau's folly. But what trifles do we settle for in our lives? Our Father offers us incredible blessings if we would love him, but how often do we despise his offerings and seek out our own provision (Jeremiah 2:12-13)? The wrong, the cheap, and the momentary are never worth enough to exchange for what God can give us.

A WORD FOR TODAY
Compromise can sell out your soul.

Today, Lord, teach me to value most what is infinitely valuable, namely you.

**Read
Proverbs 28**

A GREATER
COST
*Showing partiality
is never good, yet
some will do wrong
for a mere piece of
bread.*
Proverbs 28:21

SEPTEMBER 29

Read
Proverbs 29

ETHICAL
WORK

A servant pampered
from childhood will
become a rebel.
Proverbs 29:21

You discover during a downpour that your home has a leaky roof. You call the roofers and ask them to come and replace the shingles. But when they show up, you tell them to sit down, have some lemonade, eat some cookies, and chat awhile. You ask about their families, their business, and what you can do to help them. If the roofers were your sons, you would be acting like any normal parent. But if they were only your hired help, you would be considered a fool to pay them for sitting around. In fact, you would discover that the longer they sit around "on the clock," the less motivated they will be to fix your roof!

God has called us to work in a way that reflects his character. Our work is important because it is the fulfillment of God's mandate to Adam and Eve to "fill the earth and govern it. Reign over the fish in the sea, the birds in the sky, and all the animals that scurry along the ground" (Genesis 1:28). Remember, "Whether you eat or drink, or whatever you do, do it all for the glory of God" (1 Corinthians 10:31). Our relationship with God is often evaluated by others on the basis of the way we work.

A WORD FOR TODAY
Character must be trained.

Today, Lord, help me to work for your glory. Show
me how to honor you through my occupation.

SEPTEMBER 30

The book of James gives us a very thorough picture of faith. James writes about its true nature, "So you see, faith by itself isn't enough. Unless it produces good deeds, it is dead and useless" (James 2:17). And again, three verses later, "How foolish! Can't you see that faith without good deeds is useless?" God would have us live out our Christianity in a manner that impacts every area of our being: our values, our financial decisions, how we spend our time, how we talk.

Sometimes, we may ponder, "What does God want me to do with my life?" Yet if we read the Bible, we find that God gives us many plain, unchanging commands. Love justice, seek truth, love God and our neighbor, minister to the orphan and widow in their distress, bring healing to the sick and freedom to the prisoner, give our cloak to the one who has need of it, honor God, fear God, delight in God, and many, many more. We need to pursue God in faith, and do what he commands.

A WORD FOR TODAY
Beware the sin of omission.

Today, Lord, teach me to hear your voice and to be obedient to your call. I yield myself to you. I ask that your will would be done in my life.

Read
Proverbs 30

AN EFFECTIVE FAITH
Remember, it is sin to know what you ought to do and then not do it.
James 4:17

OCTOBER 1

Read Proverbs 1

GOD'S FEAST

They rejected my advice and paid no attention when I corrected them. Therefore, they must eat the bitter fruit of living their own way, choking on their own schemes.
Proverbs 1:30-31

God does not leave us to fend for ourselves. He gives us corrective advice that will sustain us through life. Ironically, while we desire to eat the choicest fare, we often choose our own fruit—and have to experience its bitter taste in our mouths.

It seems ridiculous that a mere human would disregard God's all-knowing, loving guidance. Our arrogance leaves us confused and lost. The dangerous outcome is separation from God as we "eat the bitter fruit of living [our] own way."

God, however, offers his help even when we choke on sin. His words point out our shortcomings, so we know not to live that way anymore. He promises us the nourishment of his food if we follow his ways. While we don't deserve his feast, he nonetheless offers it to us if we choose to accept it.

A WORD FOR TODAY
God's Word is the sustenance of life.

Today, Lord, help me to listen to your advice. When I struggle to heed your Word, help me to trust in you so that I will not choke.

OCTOBER 2

There's no time for side trips when we're on the road of obedience to God. On this road, each step aligns with God's commands and respects his wishes. Proverbs 2:16 and 19 warn us about straying off the road, even if we try to justify it as a brief "detour." Many tangents turn out to be dead ends, especially if they lead to the kinds of women mentioned in these verses. Straying from obedience to meet with either one is unfortunate. The promiscuous woman represents the temptation to sin. The immoral woman symbolizes sexual corruption and the lies that lead up to her door. Both kinds of women are dangerous because their deceit lures us from our commitment to follow God's commands.

Maybe a mere visit doesn't seem like a big deal. Once we are in their company, however, returning to the right track is a struggle. The last two sentences (verse 19) do not leave room for second chances. Once you shut the doors behind you, the path you've followed is lost. But there is grace to keep us on the right track. Meditating on Scripture will save us from any traps along the way. This is the wisdom the book of Proverbs encourages.

DOOMED DETOURS

Wisdom will save you from the immoral woman, from the seductive words of the promiscuous woman. . . . The man who visits her is doomed. He will never reach the paths of life.
Proverbs 2:16, 19

A WORD FOR TODAY
Sometimes wisdom resorts to blinders and earplugs.

Please remind me throughout this day, Lord, to seek your wisdom instead of sin.

OCTOBER 3

Read
Proverbs 3
🍃

COPYCAT

Don't envy violent
people or copy
their ways.
Proverbs 3:31

At first glance, this proverb appears to be of little help. It's unethical to be violent. Society condemns it. If we pause for a deeper look at Proverbs 3:31, however, we will see that it is actually a significant warning to Christians to not get sucked into sin.

The wisdom lying beneath the surface of this proverb warns us not to be jealous of power, fame, and possessions. Unfortunately, violent people can be rich, not only with money but with influence and reputation. While being violent is not a socially acceptable quality, having power, taking control, and demanding attention are very attractive ones. We may disapprove of the violence, but admire the perks that come with it.

Violence is a conspicuous sin, but envy brews quietly inside. Jealousy eventually wells up and spills out as action. The power you may desire convinces you to copy a "bad guy's" tactics. This is how sin starts. God understands that, so he warns us clearly with this proverb. Sometimes we don't know what we need to hear. Thankfully, God tells us anyway.

A WORD FOR TODAY
Envy can lead to a dangerous form of imitation.

Today, Lord, help me to recognize the times when I am
envious of people. Teach me how to model myself after
you.

OCTOBER 4

Obedience is not an accident—it is a choice. Just like little children, Christians decide whether or not they will follow their Father's commands. Keeping in line is not easy, however. As our divine Parent, God encourages us by offering a plan for success and then adds a promise of safety to spur us onward.

God does not assume our passivity. Each phrase of Proverbs 4:25-26 contains action that propels a believer along a path of obedience. These spiritual principles closely parallel the rules for keeping a compass heading in the wilderness. We take a sighting on a distant, immovable object in the direction we must go, and then walk directly to it. When we reach that object, we take another sighting and repeat the process until we arrive at our destination.

God knows that in order for us to make it in the wilderness of this life, we have to continually keep our sights on his commands. Sharpening our focus to remove any distractions, we map out our route and then discipline ourselves to follow it. God's Word provides an immovable object that can keep us traveling in the right direction.

A WORD FOR TODAY
Don't detour from the straight and narrow.

Today, Lord, guide me as a little child in the way of obedience, and continue to bless me with your promises.

**Read
Proverbs 4**

AN ACTIVE
TRACK
*Look straight ahead,
and fix your eyes on
what lies before you.
Mark out a straight
path for your feet;
stay on the safe
path*
Proverbs 4:25-26

OCTOBER 5

Read
Proverbs 5

FRONT
PAGE NEWS
The LORD sees
clearly what a man
does, examining
every path he takes.
Proverbs 5:21

If every sin we commit were printed on the front page of *The New York Times,* we might live life in a slightly different fashion. While we think most of our sins are hidden from the public eye, they are always exposed to God. He sees what we do and where we go, and he knows our thoughts and motives.

Our attitude determines how we will live in the presence of God's omniscience. We will either be joyful or resentful. A joyous perspective rests secure under God's watch. (We are never out of God's protective reach.) A resentful perspective considers God's presence to be threatening and controlling. (One can never get a moment of privacy.)

God's watch over us convinces us of something else, however: He loves us. He knows us better than anyone else does. Only a caring father would keep such a steady eye on us.

A WORD FOR TODAY
God never blinks.

Today, Lord, I thank you for your ever-present watch on
my life, that you care about me enough to take an active
interest in my life.

OCTOBER 6

Exchanging an old, rusty car for a new, shiny one is hardly a risk—it's a fantastic swap. But almost nobody would trade a classic Porsche for a teenager's clunker. It is easy to risk something that you do not value. As Solomon warns his son in Proverbs 6:26, it is not worth risking a valuable possession to indulge a sin. The possession at risk in this proverb is sexual purity.

The truth is, exchanging purity for sin is not a fair trade. There are far more consequences than we can predict. The consequences may or may not be immediate. A sin such as adultery may not automatically lead to the loss of house and family—sometimes, terrible sins remain a secret. But they create a wall between ourselves and God. Eventually, we will be poorer than if we were in poverty. Without repentance and forgiveness, such sins may, as this proverb clearly warns, cost us our very lives.

A WORD FOR TODAY
Adultery is also self-treachery.

Today, Lord, give me the strength to make the right choices.

**Read
Proverbs 6**

AN UNFAIR
TRADE
*A prostitute will
bring you to poverty,
but sleeping with
another man's wife
will cost you your
life.*
Proverbs 6:26

OCTOBER 7

Read
Proverbs 7

FROM
HEAVEN'S EYE

*Don't store up
treasures here on
earth, where moths
eat them and rust
destroys them, and
where thieves break
in and steal. Store
your treasures in
heaven, where moths
and rust cannot
destroy, and thieves
do not break in and
steal. Wherever your
treasure is, there the
desires of your heart
will also be.*
Matthew 6:19-21

From your perch in heaven someday, the life you spent on earth will look very different. All the materialistic details of your life will remain here. The world will forget you in a moment or two, but the Lord will continue to love you for eternity.

In this passage, Jesus is instructing Christians where they should set their priorities. Jesus is not saying, "Live with the bare minimum. Sell your clothes, cars, home, and quit your job." Instead, he is saying, "Don't love your things; love your God." Where you set your eyes and direct your feet, there your heart will follow.

The moment you stand before God, you won't care how many cars you owned or that your house was the biggest on the block. Standing before Jesus, you won't be grieving over that stock market slump or that deal you lost. If you have treasured Jesus Christ during your life, then your heart will be fulfilled in that moment.

A WORD FOR TODAY
Treasure what matters.

Today, Lord, help me to keep in mind the eternal ramifications of what I accomplish.

OCTOBER 8

Imagine the top CEO of the nation leaving his job to become a janitor. Who would intentionally throw away status, power, and money to pick up a job at the bottom of the ranks? Proverbs 8:27 is a reminder that Jesus did precisely that.

It is easy to forget that Jesus demoted himself to become a mere man. How do we reconcile the image of the all-powerful God with the face of the man, Jesus? All existence was at his design as he directed and molded each detail of the earth. Why did Jesus fit so well in the world? He created it his size.

Even before the world's creation, the fullness of God dwelled in Jesus. God answers our question for us, however, pointing out that his ways and thoughts are beyond our understanding. How can we not be amazed, honored, and humbled by his choice to sacrifice his life for ours?

A WORD FOR TODAY
Wisdom is timeless.

Today, Lord, I call you mighty and powerful, and I thank you that you loved me enough to leave your throne in heaven to save my soul.

**Read
Proverbs 8**

WHAT JESUS
LEFT BEHIND
*I was there when
he established the
heavens, when he
drew the horizon
on the oceans.*
Proverbs 8:27

OCTOBER 9

Read
Proverbs 9

A WISE CHOICE

If you become wise,
you will be the one
to benefit. If you
scorn wisdom, you
will be the one to
suffer.
Proverbs 9:12

The essence of Proverbs is a choice: Will we pursue wisdom or not? No one can make this decision for us. The kind of person we decide to be touches every aspect of our lives. Proverbs 9:12 is a reminder that there are consequences to the choice we make.

Ideally, we would all scoop up wisdom as our prize and live happily ever after—but we don't. In fact, we often choose to grumble over God's commands. We don't want to hear advice from anyone. Even though God is clear that wisdom leads to a fulfilling life, we sometimes choose the opposite.

A tendency to make good decisions or bad decisions soon becomes a habit. Despite our poor decisions, however, God is persistent to warn us of the consequences. He lets us be responsible for our decisions. He is always hoping that, in the end, Christians will choose what's right.

A WORD FOR TODAY
Wisdom is a choice and a life.

Today, Lord, I want to do what is wise in your eyes.
Thank you for your guidance.

OCTOBER 10

Sometimes doing the "right" thing seems boring—even irritating. For example, stopping for a red light is a nuisance, while speeding through the intersection on a yellow is tempting. What keeps drivers braking for a red light?

From a practical point of view, most drivers realize that red lights are sensible tools. For the foolish driver, however, running a light may seem like fun, only the thrill doesn't last. That type of irresponsible behavior doesn't lead to genuine happiness. It leads only to a wrecked car—and perhaps wrecked lives.

While we may not enjoy putting on the brakes, we appreciate traffic rules for protecting us from danger on the road. This proverb reminds us that wise conduct is the first step toward happiness. If we make a habit of acting wisely, we grow accustomed to its benefits. Soon, wise conduct becomes a pleasure.

A WORD FOR TODAY
Your fun reveals who you are.

Today, Lord, pinpoint what I may be doing foolishly, so that with your help I can correct the situation.

Read
Proverbs 10

DRIVING
TOWARD
HAPPINESS
Doing wrong is fun for a fool, but living wisely brings pleasure to the sensible.
Proverbs 10:23

OCTOBER 11

Read
Proverbs 11

CHARACTER
OVER BEAUTY
*A beautiful woman
who lacks discretion
is like a gold ring
in a pig's snout.*
Proverbs 11:22

A pig wearing luxurious jewelry? That's absurd. Two applications of this proverb would be that (1) men should not desire the beautiful but indiscreet woman, and (2) women should not aspire to be like her. The pig prompts images of laziness and ignorance. Pigs eat trash and live in filth. A pig's stench follows it wherever it goes, leaving traces everywhere. A pig would have no idea of the value of a gold ring in its snout.

Beauty is wasted if a person reeks of immorality. Loveliness is marred by thoughtless behavior. If we emphasize appearance over character, we soon find ourselves laughingstocks as our beauty fades. God prefers a genuine faith and wisdom—they comprise true beauty.

A WORD FOR TODAY
Character sticks out.

Today, Lord, bless my efforts to condition my character rather than my appearance. Thank you for a gift that will not fade.

OCTOBER 12

You may not notice a genius standing in a crowded room, but it won't take long to zero in on a fool. According to this proverb, a fool announces his poor judgment simply by the nature of his words. This proverb implies the arrogance of a fool who throws words in people's faces. The wise are not being smug by holding their tongues; they are refusing to parade their knowledge before others. Wise people choose their words carefully. Unlike the wise, however, the foolish run out of words to say, but continue to babble.

The difference between a wise person and a fool is the ability to have quiet confidence. For example, Jesus did not need to advertise his knowledge. He simply spoke and acted wisely, and people noticed.

The tongue controls the entire body, and therefore can be a dangerous weapon or a helpful tool. We direct our speech not so much by deciding when to speak, but when to be quiet. Only then will people notice our wisdom—and it won't take a word from us to tell them.

**Read
Proverbs 12**

SPOTLIGHTING
FOOLS
The wise don't make a show of their knowledge, but fools broadcast their foolishness.
Proverbs 12:23

A WORD FOR TODAY
Wisdom practices humility.

Today, Lord, I will refrain from broadcasting my knowledge. Show me when to speak and when to keep my mouth shut.

OCTOBER 13

Read
Proverbs 13

FRIENDS
IN FAITH
Walk with the
wise and become
wise; associate
with fools and get
in trouble.
Proverbs 13:20

The quality of our friends reflects our quality. Jesus understood the importance of choosing who would surround him during his ministry. The twelve disciples didn't just happen to become his inner circle; he deliberately picked each man. In the same way, we should choose our friends thoughtfully and carefully.

Friends influence which movies we see, which games we play, and which books we read. They have an impact on our lifestyle. This proverb uses the verb "walk," hinting at the mutual journey between friends. Just as Jesus went into the mountains to pray over his decisions, we too should seek God for guidance in initiating relationships. We can expect to be affected by our friends. Socializing with people who do not honor God in their words or actions soon nudges us to do the same. At first, it may not be intentional to dishonor God, because it happens subtly. But gradual compromise leads to full rebellion, which in time causes pain and suffering apart from God. A good friend will lead you closer to, not further from, God.

A WORD FOR TODAY
Your companions will influence your destination.

Today, Lord, I will consider how my relationships glorify
you. Please show me how I can improve the quality of
my company.

OCTOBER 14

In answer to an honest question, Jesus provided a pair of central priorities for life. These two (love for God and love for neighbor) form an unbreakable bond. John recorded the following crucial test: "If someone says, 'I love God,' but hates a Christian brother or sister, that person is a liar; for if we don't love people we can see, how can we love God, whom we cannot see?" (1 John 4:20).

Jesus taught in these "love-orders" that God expects a public as much as a private relationship with us. People think too often that they can love God without anyone else finding out. But secret love for God seldom lasts. Real love for God leads to love for those whom God loves. The order is important. The Son of God himself gave us permission to express love for him by loving others (see John 13:34-35). Think of your neighbor as the last person you failed to treat with love. That's a good starting point to put this command into practice.

A WORD FOR TODAY
The greatest proverb—"Love God."

Lord, please let me actually "see" my neighbors today. Help me move toward loving by the simple act of ceasing to ignore them. I want to learn to love you through them.

Read
Proverbs 14

GOD AND NEIGHBOR
Jesus replied, "The most important commandment is this: 'Listen, O Israel! The LORD our God is the one and only LORD. And you must love the LORD your God with all your heart, all your soul, all your mind, and all your strength.' The second is equally important: 'Love your neighbor as yourself.' No other commandment is greater than these."
Mark 12:29-31

OCTOBER 15

Read
Proverbs 15

A WORD
OF ADVICE

*Plans go wrong
for lack of advice;
many advisers
bring success.*
Proverbs 15:22

Columnist Ann Landers fed advice to an estimated 90 million readers. Other advice-giving radio hosts have large audiences, as well. Their success has been based on this fact: We all have plans and problems that we can't handle on our own. Sometimes an outside perspective is just what we need to see our situation clearly.

While such general advice may be helpful, we can access wise counseling through an alternate venue: the Christian community. This advice comes with accountability and perspective. A radio host doesn't know his or her callers except from what they say. Those in the Christian community know us.

Proverbs 15:22 directs us to seek advice from a number of wise friends. This proverb, however, doesn't tell us to follow every piece of advice we receive—we accept advice in light of the Bible. Advice should never contradict what God says in the Scriptures. Pursuing advice while at the same time studying the Bible helps us to avoid disasters we would otherwise suffer on our own.

A WORD FOR TODAY
Several wise heads are better than one.

*Today, Lord, I ask you to point me toward wise friends.
Use these people to send me your wisdom.*

OCTOBER 16

Imagine how well you could get to know God in a lifetime. Throughout life, the moments of crisis, joy, faith, and perseverance all provide opportunities to deepen our relationship with God. Gray hair, hopefully, is evidence of wisdom gained over the years. A long life is the reward for rejecting sinful instincts for godly wisdom.

A godly life involves making wise choices, which are usually the smarter, safer ones. This kind of life leads a person to naturally live longer than someone who isn't making wise choices. The godly person may suffer the same temporal consequences for sin that the ungodly suffer, but a godly person has the hope of forgiveness and eternal life. The ungodly live with the weight of unforgiveness and the dread of eternal hopelessness.

Gray hair (a crown of glory) can be worn joyfully by those who are reflecting on a life's walk with the Lord. Not only have these people spent their lives with God, they also anticipate uninterrupted fellowship with him in heaven.

A WORD FOR TODAY
Godliness brings quality to old age.

Today, Lord, I thank you for my life. Let me use it to serve you and get to know you better.

Read
Proverbs 16

JOY FOR THE
GOLDEN YEARS
Gray hair is a crown of glory; it is gained by living a godly life.
Proverbs 16:31

OCTOBER 17

Read
Proverbs 17

❧

A SPOONFUL OF JOY

A cheerful heart is good medicine, but a broken spirit saps a person's strength.
Proverbs 17:22

Though sorrow is burdensome, it is still possible to choose joy. Proverbs 17:22 implies that there is a choice between remaining mired in misery or taking the antidote—a joyful attitude.

Poor circumstances are plentiful, but joyful attitudes are a little harder to come by. It's tough for a Little League player sitting in the dugout with a broken arm to smile. It's a struggle for a young widow to get accustomed to an empty home. Harsh circumstances drain our bodies and minds of strength, leaving us weak and overwhelmed with pain. A cheerful heart may seem out of reach. But if we decide that trusting in God will get us back to a cheerful outlook, we will have taken the first step of joy.

This proverb is a gentle warning that when sorrow strikes, we must not get bogged down for too long. We need the clouds to part and a sunny attitude to come through. Jesus is standing ready to help you rise above the pain.

A WORD FOR TODAY
Joy is a valuable choice.

Today, Lord, I will choose to have a cheerful heart. Let my joy be contagious to the people around me.

OCTOBER 18

Judges can't get by with swift, impulsive decisions in court. They don't make a final ruling until they have heard both sides of their cases. Making a well-informed judgment requires questioning, listening, and patience. Analyzing numerous stories leads a judge to a knowledgeable decision.

We should listen to the stories people feed us with exactly the same caution. This proverb is a useful tip for wise listening: Judge a speaker's words by putting them beside someone else's. We should be objective and fair, not putting too much weight in our initial assumptions. We must not be gullible or hasty. Instead, we should be swift to test what people claim. To "cross-examine" is to be discerning and to pursue the truth.

A WORD FOR TODAY
Don't lose the truth among the sides of a story.

Today, Lord, help me to consider carefully the stories I hear. I want to learn how to listen, to question, and to trust people.

Read
Proverbs 18

THE WHOLE
STORY
The first to speak in court sounds right—until the cross-examination begins.
Proverbs 18:17

OCTOBER 19

Read
Proverbs 19

ON TRACK
You can make
many plans, but
the LORD's purpose
will prevail.
Proverbs 19:21

People tend to like what they can plan, maneuver, and control—hence the popularity of PDAs, reservations, and retirement packages. This proverb can be viewed as God pulling the rug out from under us. We can plan as much into the future as we would like, but nonetheless, God is going to have his own way. All our planning seems to be pointless.

It takes the right attitude to understand that this verse is consoling, not annoying. To be annoyed at God's ultimate authority over the future is to assume that he is not looking out for our best interest. Rather, God hopes to bless his people to a higher measure than we can imagine. A better attitude regarding Proverbs 19:21 is one of relief, that no matter how we chart our own courses, God is poised to keep us on the right track. If as Christians we are sincere in our desire to see God glorified, then we will not argue when God's purpose overrules our own.

A WORD FOR TODAY
Don't plan to leave God out.

Today, Lord, I admit that your purpose overrides my
own. I am flexible; don't let my desires get in the way
of yours.

OCTOBER 20

God loves a cheerful giver—not a nervous, anxious giver. He delights in a promise or gift presented wholeheartedly to him. And who can blame him? God doesn't *need* anything. It's the love and commitment behind the gesture that God enjoys.

The ominous tone of this proverb is the warning to not disappoint God. "Rash" is a dramatic word choice, but it is appropriate. The proverb makes its point: Don't rush into a vow that you haven't thoroughly considered. Going back on your word isn't wise. Instead, contemplate your promises before offering them to God. He takes you seriously. He doesn't misplace your promise among the countless prayers he receives at any given moment.

If we pause to assess the motives and reasoning behind our gifts and promises to God, we will not have to fear the consequences. Then God will be at leisure to enjoy the love behind each one.

A WORD FOR TODAY
God doesn't take our vows lightly.

Today, Lord, I will hold my tongue and contemplate what I have promised you. I don't want you to ever doubt my integrity or my dedication to you.

Read
Proverbs 20

DO YOU PROMISE?
Don't trap yourself by making a rash promise to God and only later counting the cost.
Proverbs 20:25

OCTOBER 21

**Read
Proverbs 21**

WITHIN ARM'S
LENGTH

*Come close to God,
and God will come
close to you.*

James 4:8

God isn't pushy. He waits for us to make the next move. He is always accessible to us, eager and willing to talk. He has already moved as close as his will and plan will allow him to come. Now, it's our turn. This proverb is an open invitation to get together with God. You need not RSVP. Simply show up and God will be right there.

How close is "close"? Is it within an arm's length? Ten feet? Twelve inches? There is an implied intimacy that we can share with God in the word "close." The closeness is not a literal distance, but a special presence of the Lord. It's in his presence that we put aside our self-focus and train our thoughts to be on him.

If we are drawing near to God, we are naturally leaving something else behind—our pride. Along with our pride, we leave behind our worldly thoughts. God replaces all this with himself. It is in this intimacy that there is freedom to grow in our relationship with him. This is where we get to know the Almighty God.

A WORD FOR TODAY
God responds positively.

Today, Lord, I want to draw near to you so that I can get to know you better. Please draw close to me.

OCTOBER 22

After reading this verse, it's obvious which side God favors. He is not afraid to be partial; he "preserves" those who act wisely and frustrates those who are "treacherous."

What spills over from this proverb is a reminder that God is omniscient, able to read the mind of every person. He knows what people will do before they do it. He can intervene where necessary and allow what he chooses. Knowing this, Christians would be smart to stick to a clean course. If we act in a deceitful, dishonest manner, we should expect God to thwart our plans. It is as if the proverb is warning us, "Don't bother with your evil ways. He is sure to catch you."

But while the proverb warns what will happen if we err, it also promises what will happen if we obey. What a wonderful promise! If we strive for wisdom, God will shield us. This promise, coming from the almighty God, should make our choice obvious as well.

A WORD FOR TODAY
God is involved.

Today, Lord, I praise you that you are omniscient. You know all my thoughts and longings. Thank you for caring enough to listen.

Read
Proverbs 22

ON YOUR SIDE
The LORD preserves those with knowledge, but he ruins the plans of the treacherous.
Proverbs 22:12

OCTOBER 23

**Read
Proverbs 23**

❧

A JOYFUL
SMILE

*Give your father
and mother joy!
May she who gave
you birth be happy.*
Proverbs 23:25

A drawing on the refrigerator door, a picture inside a wallet, a graduation announcement—these are symbols of precious memories. Children bring joy to their parents throughout childhood. This proverb reinforces that natural affection parents feel for their children. It also encourages children, regardless of their ages, to act in ways that make their parents happy.

They bring a smile to God's face, too. God is pleased when Christians nurture positive family relationships. That means putting other people before ourselves. It means holding on to God's Word during tough times.

So, how do we please our parents? By finding out what God's Word says and following it. Out of respect to our parents and reverence to God, we accept the commandments and open ourselves up to receive the rewards. Obeying God is not only in our own best interest. It benefits our parents, too.

A WORD FOR TODAY
Consider blessing your parents.

Today, Lord, I will make the extra effort to live the way you want me to. I want to please you, my heavenly Father.

OCTOBER 24

Sometimes it seems to not be in our best interest to tell a friend the truth. He might get mad at us. Yell at us. Even end our friendship. But friends who tell the truth, despite possible repercussions, are rare.

Regardless of whether we want to share the truth or whether the other person wants to hear the truth, honesty ought to reign over all. The truth, though it may conjure up hurt and bitterness, always stands on its own in the end.

Jesus didn't do people favors by candy coating the consequences of sin. He taught people about the agony of it and the need for repentance. Jesus could have danced around the issue. But because he loves people, he would rather tell the hard truth than let them relax and be content with their sin.

As Proverbs 24:26 states, it is an honor to be told the truth. Telling the hard truth is an act of courage, risking hurt feelings so that a friend can hear what's important. A friend who is willing to take that risk is a true friend indeed.

A WORD FOR TODAY
A hurtful truth may be a precious gift.

Today, Lord, I will tell the truth in love. Help me to hear and to accept the truth from my friends.

**Read
Proverbs 24**

TRUE WORD,
TRUE FRIEND
*An honest answer
is like a kiss of
friendship.*
Proverbs 24:26

OCTOBER 25

Read
Proverbs 25

A TASTE FOR AMBITION

It's not good to
eat too much
honey, and it's
not good to seek
honors for yourself.
Proverbs 25:27

Eating too much honey is not sweet. This simile in Proverbs 25:27 compares honey with pride. This comparison is notable because it highlights the tendency for people to overindulge themselves on pleasurable things. In this case, it is specifically self-glorification. The proverb teaches the usage of appropriate boundaries, marking anything past that as "too much."

Dwelling on things that glorify ourselves is like craving delicious food. We crave it, so we indulge. The craving is satisfied, but we continue to hoard the food, consuming more than we can contain. Soon the tastiness of the indulgence diminishes. It is no longer as good as the first bite, becoming exactly the opposite: disgusting.

The purpose of this proverb is to spare us the disgust. Most people who get sick from overeating come to detest the food and avoid it altogether. Understandably, it is desirable to take credit for our work. Too much of a good thing, however, swiftly becomes idolatry.

A WORD FOR TODAY
Beware of too much of a good thing.

Today, Lord, help me to crave your Word.

OCTOBER 26

People with hateful hearts will do you no good. Though they may try to persuade you of their good intentions, Proverbs 26:24-25 says to remain wary of them. Sooner or later, their true motives and intentions will come out.

So how do Christians recognize people who are evil? Just as people can't contain the joy in their hearts, so it is impossible to keep evil from overflowing. The last line of this proverb stresses that these people's hearts are full of evil. That leaves no room for anything else.

Christians can determine the evil in a person's heart by watching his or her actions. Words may disguise them for a time, but evil people will eventually act on the content of their hearts. This is a crucial proverb for our times, when a lot of interaction takes place between faceless persons talking over the Internet. People who can manipulate words have a distinct advantage. This kind of communication must be carried out with extreme caution, lest we find ourselves tricked by someone's words whose actions reveal "many evils."

Read
Proverbs 26

A FALSE FRONT
People may cover their hatred with pleasant words, but they're deceiving you. They pretend to be kind, but don't believe them. Their hearts are full of many evils.
Proverbs 26:24-25

A WORD FOR TODAY
Real motivation is eventually revealed.

Today, Lord, I will keep an eye open for evil that wants to harm me. Help me to be discerning.

OCTOBER 27

Read
Proverbs 27

🍐

SHARING A PIECE OF HIS FRUIT

As workers who tend a fig tree are allowed to eat the fruit, so workers who protect their employer's interests will be rewarded.
Proverbs 27:18

God has chosen us to take care of the world and to tell people about Christ. God's promise in Proverbs 27:18 applies to us when we are faithful with the jobs we are given. God is the employer; we are the workers.

In a broad sense, Christians are called to be stewards of the world. We are allowed to eat its fruit, to enjoy many good things. We must never forget, however, that the world is not our eternal home, nor does it ultimately belong to us. Part of our duty is to "protect" our "employer's interests." God also grants to us individual jobs that are unique to our capabilities and talents.

There is a sense of justice in this proverb. God knows how well we are performing and how much we will be rewarded. The proverb is an invitation to work with him and share in his goodness. It is extraordinary that God offers to reward us. As servants of the Master of Creation, humans should be ready to serve him for nothing. But he chooses to let us enjoy his benefits, to eat his fruit though we could never work enough to truly deserve it.

A WORD FOR TODAY
God blesses those who work for him.

Today, Lord, I will be aware of my responsibilities. I will serve you and realign my focus to your purposes.

OCTOBER 28

Most people need to feel uncomfortable before they see a need to change their perspectives or behaviors. But people don't like discomfort, and they don't like change. Matthew 11:6 emphasizes the need for discernment regarding these feelings. Why do we feel a burden when we hear Jesus speak? Why do his words turn some people away while convicting others to hear him out?

It takes humility to see that Jesus' words are meant to correct us, not to antagonize us. They are spoken to guide us, not alienate us. His motive is to love us, not to turn us away. Recognizing God's intentions allows us to enjoy the gifts he has for those who aren't offended. Jesus risked rejection in order to save us.

A WORD FOR TODAY
Stay boldly true to Christ.

Today, Lord, I will remember that you had my best interest in mind when you inspired the Bible. I will remember that when I study your Word.

**Read
Proverbs 28**

YOUR
REACTION
TO JESUS
*God blesses those
who do not turn
away because of me.*
Matthew 11:6

OCTOBER 29

KEEPING COOL

An angry person starts fights; a hot-tempered person commits all kinds of sin.
Proverbs 29:22

"Hot-tempered" describes a person who reacts quickly and badly. A hot temper leaves no time for questions, reconsideration, different perspectives, or changes of heart. This kind of character assumes the worst before the best. How many ways can an angry person mess up? Today's proverb tells us that such people get into "all kinds of sin."

Compare the ill-tempered person with Jesus. What were the occasions for his anger? His anger did not add to the evil in a circumstance. He used his angry emotions as a red flag signaling that something was not right.

If we hesitate before acting on our angry feelings, we can avoid fights and quarrels. By modeling ourselves after Jesus, we can handle anger in a way that does not cause us to sin.

A WORD FOR TODAY
Uncontrolled emotions lead to disaster.

Today, Lord, I will hesitate before losing my cool. I don't want to fight or sin against you.

OCTOBER 30

Our attitude after we have sinned determines if we will commit the sin again. Do we laugh off the guilt, talk ourselves into apathy, or deny the consequences? Or are we embarrassed about the way we faltered, storing a memory of what the guilt felt like deep in our minds? If we do the latter, the memory of the guilt we felt over our sin will come to the front of our minds when we ponder committing the sin again.

This proverb is discipline for our disobedience, but it is also a declaration of love. God foresees us acting foolishly. He is aware we will mess up. In fact, he granted us salvation knowing that we were going to sin even after we received it. He loves us enough to keep getting us back on track. He hates pride and he hates sin. God wants us to avoid committing the same sin twice. It's our responsibility to see that we don't.

We are not forbidden to speak about past sins and mistakes. They can often be helpful illustrations when we are teaching others. But there must be no hint of pride for those things that have been our downfall in the past.

A WORD FOR TODAY
Shame can lead to repentance.

Today, Lord, I won't be cocky about my sin. I will keep my attitude humble.

Read
Proverbs 30

EMBARRASSED
BY SIN
If you have been a
fool by being proud
or plotting evil,
cover your mouth
in shame.
Proverbs 30:32

OCTOBER 31

**Read
Proverbs 31**

❦

THE PERFECT WOMAN

*Her children stand
and bless her. Her
husband praises
her: "There are
many virtuous and
capable women
in the world,
but you surpass
them all!"*
Proverbs 31:28-29

The woman who receives the praises in Proverbs 31:28-29 has obviously been doing something right. She's an extraordinary wife and mother who touched the lives of her children and husband in an extra-special way. Reading the entire passage, we understand the reasons why her family rises to praise her.

The husband says that his wife is doing something noteworthy among other moral, skillful women. The question is, what makes her so different? It is most likely her spirit and attitude that are leaving marks on her family. Proverbs 31 runs through a list of duties she handles. The text conveys that it is her heart that makes her stand out from the rest. Her family is delighted that she brings such richness into their home!

Not only is this a woman whom we can aspire to be like, but she is also an example of the type of woman that makes a good life mate. When a marriage is formed between a man and a woman with these qualities, the result is a healthy, loving home.

A WORD FOR TODAY
Those close to us can confirm our wise choices.

Today, Lord, I recognize my need for your help if I am to emulate any of the qualities of the virtuous woman described in Proverbs 31. Build these character traits into my life.

NOVEMBER 1

Many nonbelievers accuse the spiritually inclined of being mindless. They simply cannot accept the leap of faith as anything other than abandoning one's intelligence. However, God warns that those who abandon his ways in deference to their own are the real fools.

For example, consider a nonbelieving executive who climbs to the top, working eighty-hour weeks. This person would hardly be described as unintelligent. The word *lazy* is likely absent from his or her vocabulary. Yet, the Bible refers to such a spiritually independent soul as a complacent simpleton. The issue is not effort itself, for many people work hard at unbelief. Rather, the baseline for a fool is *misguided* effort. The thesaurus describes fools this way: ill-advised. They determine their life's priorities by working hard at earthly things to the neglect of spiritual things. A fool can be a corporate dynamo and a spiritual loafer wrapped up in one person. He or she can achieve temporary earthly success and yet be destined for eternal failure all at the same time.

Read
Proverbs 1

FRUITLESS
EFFORT
Simpletons turn away from me—to death. Fools are destroyed by their own complacency.
Proverbs 1:32

A WORD FOR TODAY
Even smart people can miss wisdom.

Dear Lord, I can't afford to play the fool, relying on my own ways. Help me to look to you for guidance today.

NOVEMBER 2

Read
Proverbs 2

THE RIGHT
LEADER

Follow the steps of
good men instead,
and stay on the
paths of the
righteous. For only
the godly will live
in the land, and
those with integrity
will remain in it.
Proverbs 2:20-21

"Follow the leader" is perhaps one of the more popular playground pastimes in childhood. The phrase has the power to spontaneously motivate children to line up in succession behind their lead adventurer, anxious to follow one child's whims across the playground. Up the slide. Down the slide. Across the monkey bars. And around the basketball goal. The display of trust is enormous. The crowd unquestioningly follows the path's surprising twists and turns, finding joy in the journey. Fortunately, good leaders can be trusted to avoid pitfalls and lead the group in safe passage.

In the same way, we must follow the example of godly men and women—our lead adventurers in life. The mere mention of this proverb should call to mind the image of trusting children who are committed to following the one in front. If we stay on the path of the righteous, we will experience the adventure of faith walking. We may not know for ourselves what lies ahead, but we simply trust in the footsteps of the godly one who goes before us.

A WORD FOR TODAY
Follow the right leader.

Today, Lord, I thank you for those who live a godly life
for me to follow. Help me see the path of righteousness
and stay on it.

NOVEMBER 3

A well-manicured lawn is not necessarily the sign of a blessed home. Nor does a godly residence imply faultless inhabitants. Both Christian and godless homes can be prone to problems. In truth, the homes of the upright are not perfect—only perfectly blessed.

The blessing referred to by this proverb comes in the form of God's presence and power. A godly home can experience tragedy and yet endure in spite of it. A godly home can have a rebellious child. The home of the upright can be cramped, yet still be full of love. All this is due to God's presence and power within that imperfect home. However, what hope is there for a family apart from God's blessing? That family can experience only God's curse—the very opposite of his blessing. The house of the wicked is simply that—a house. God's blessing transforms a house into a home.

A WORD FOR TODAY
God blesses a godly home.

Today, Lord, I am thankful for your blessings, your presence, and your power in my life.

**Read
Proverbs 3**

HOME
INTERIORS
*The LORD curses
the house of the
wicked, but he
blesses the home
of the upright.*
Proverbs 3:33

NOVEMBER 4

Read
Proverbs 4

ACCOUNTABLE
EXAMPLES

What sorrow awaits
the world, because
it tempts people
to sin. Temptations
are inevitable, but
what sorrow awaits
the person who does
the tempting.
Matthew 18:7

The last thing a person in today's society wants is to be responsible for someone else. Those in the public eye, from sports figures to movie stars, shrug off the idea of being role models for young people.

Most people—the famous as well as the not so famous—have enough trouble handling responsibility for their own lives, much less the lives of others. The invention of the no-fault divorce represents just how far we've come with this idea. We don't want to take responsibility for our own actions—and by default, we can't bring ourselves to assign blame to others either. We cower as a culture behind the motto "To each his own." However, Jesus peers over our shabbily constructed defenses to deliver the news: We *are* responsible for our influence on others. What a terrible and terrifying proposition for a culture that would rather look the other way.

A WORD FOR TODAY
Influence implies responsibility.

Today, Lord, I know others are watching me as I try to
live for you. Help me be conscious of my character and
not tempt others to sin.

NOVEMBER 5

This proverb pictures a person who, spiritually speaking, trips over his own feet. Although we rarely enjoy accepting responsibility for our mistakes, we have to admit they are *our* mistakes. Though we live in an adversarial culture, we cannot blame our sinfulness on it. Though we may be bombarded with temptation in everyday circumstances, we are not so easily let off the hook.

We are like a deep-sea tuna following its instincts toward bait, only to be ensnared by a fisherman's net. Likewise, in our natural habitat—the world—we follow our natural instincts toward the things we want: money, power, sex. Yet we soon find ourselves ensnared by such vices. We are roped in, caught, and held tightly in sin's grip. Ironically, we find ourselves in such a predicament because of personal choice. We are our own captors. This proverb reminds us that everyone sins by nature and by choice.

A WORD FOR TODAY
Sin ensnares.

Today, Lord, free me from my sin and the temptations that ensnare me.

**Read
Proverbs 5**

TRAPPED!
An evil man is held captive by his own sins; they are ropes that catch and hold him.
Proverbs 5:22

NOVEMBER 6

Read
Proverbs 6

CAUSE AND EFFECT

So it is with the man who sleeps with another man's wife. He who embraces her will not go unpunished.
Proverbs 6:29

One of the distinctive features of a proverb is its ability to put a new spin on an old truth. Common sense appears uncommonly wise when phrased in the form of a proverb. So it is with this particular truth concerning the inevitability of punishment for sin. Certainly, the context of sexual promiscuity is particularly relevant, although the principle can apply to any wrongdoing. Sin brings consequences—plain and simple.

The proverb details a "what goes up must come down" common-sense philosophy. Yet, consider the lengths many people will go to to defy common sense. We rationalize wrongdoing. We believe we are the exception to the rule. Like a driver racing under a lowered railroad crossing guard, we interpret the odds in our favor. We routinely practice the fool's philosophy of "just this once." Why else would we continue to stoop to sin unless we somehow believed we wouldn't be punished? This proverb reminds us of the certainty of consequences, despite our best arguments against it.

A WORD FOR TODAY
Adultery has consequences.

Today, Lord, I need to be reminded of the seriousness of sin and not rationalize wrongdoing.

NOVEMBER 7

Subtlety is one of nature's more powerful forces. For example, single drops of water, steadily spread over millions of years, combine to form wondrous limestone creations, housed like sculptures within cavernous museums. These creations provide convincing evidence of the power of subtlety.

Likewise, perhaps one of the greater forces at work in a person's life is subtle moral drift. It is defined by straying choices and wayward reckonings (which, like water droplets, don't seem to amount to much). Yet, multiplied together over a lifetime, these little compromises result in large consequences. This proverb accurately pinpoints a *straying* heart and a *wandering* mind as the most likely beginning point of a ruined character. Most people who come to ruin do so at a gradual pace. They don't race down sin's streets; they simply wander off the righteous path. Take a lesson from nature—little missteps have the potential to create gargantuan compromises in our character.

A WORD FOR TODAY
Temptation's horizon is ruination.

Today, Lord, I need your help to stay on the righteous path. Guard my character against little compromises.

**Read
Proverbs 7**

MORAL DRIFT
*Don't let your
hearts stray away
toward her. Don't
wander down her
wayward path. For
she has been the
ruin of many; many
men have been her
victims.*
Proverbs 7:25-26

NOVEMBER 8

Read
Proverbs 8

WISDOM
CHEERS

How happy I was
with the world he
created; how I
rejoiced with the
human family!
Proverbs 8:31

This proverb presents wisdom come to life—a personality filled with emotion and self-will. Scholars believe personifying wisdom in this way provides a unique background for understanding Christ himself as the very wisdom of God.

Though not necessarily a direct description of Christ, the point of this proverb is to show wisdom rejoicing in our favored status with God as his creation. Wisdom is on our side. Sadly, many people are convinced that practicing God's laws and adhering to wisdom is just the opposite. They believe wisdom takes all the fun out of life. They say wisdom is reserved for stone-faced monks and mountaintop monasteries; it certainly is not practical for life in the real world. Yet Scripture reminds us that wisdom was an integral part of this real world's very beginnings. In this sense, wisdom was created for human happiness and is the creator of happiness itself. The entire human family and the world in which we live spring forth from this truth.

A WORD FOR TODAY
Joy is a trait of wisdom.

Today, Lord, I realize you have given me wisdom for
my own happiness. Help me to practice wisdom today.

NOVEMBER 9

There are those who find delight in taking culinary risks and those who prefer to find their thrills elsewhere. Daredevil eaters crave the delicacies of a hole-in-the-wall eatery or a dive cafe, notwithstanding that there are certain inherent risks one must recognize—for salmonella is no respecter of persons. This proverb employs a similar backdrop whereby people frequent a promising cafe filled with tempting fare. However, the dining area is strangely empty—eerie evidence that something is wrong.

Sin's "menu" is always tempting—refreshing and secretly delightful. In the world of food, presentation is everything. Compromise is served in bite-sized pieces—no one can stop with just one bite. Adultery is garnished with petite lies carved to look like roses. And greed is served on tap. However, what is *not* on the menu is what one must beware of. Former guests have died from their naivete. Take note of those whose sinful indulgences have led to ruin.

A WORD FOR TODAY
Sin is a delicious but deadly poison.

Today, Lord, I thirst for your truth and hunger for your ways. Feed my soul with what is right and good for me.

**Read
Proverbs 9**

SIN'S MENU
"Stolen water is refreshing; food eaten in secret tastes the best!" But little do they know that the dead are there. Her guests are in the depths of the grave.
Proverbs 9:17-18

NOVEMBER 10

Read
Proverbs 10

🦅

STORMY WEATHER

When the storms of life come, the wicked are whirled away, but the godly have a lasting foundation.
Proverbs 10:25

Storm trackers are usually the first to sight storm activity. However, even with their advanced equipment to measure air pressure and wind, they can provide no more than a few minutes' warning for those in a storm's path to seek shelter. In the same way, stormy trials can drop in unexpectedly in all of our lives.

The distinction in this proverb is not *who* goes through a storm—the wicked or the godly. Both are thrust into the middle of the storm. However, the dramatic difference is the outcome. Everything the wicked owns and even the wicked themselves are whirled away in the storm's fury. However, the godly withstand the trial. The difference is in their foundation.

The image in this proverb is similar to a commonly televised aerial shot panned early the next morning after a destructive storm. Some houses remain unscathed, while the homes of next-door neighbors have hardly a stacked brick remaining. The godly will survive life's storms because of their Christ-centered foundation.

A WORD FOR TODAY
The godly experience, but survive, disasters.

Today, Lord, I need your strength to get through life's storms. Teach me what it means to have you as my strong foundation.

NOVEMBER 11

Jesus didn't think it was enough to be kind or nice to our neighbor. He insisted on repeating his Father's standard (Leviticus 19:18)—love your neighbor as you love yourself.

The second part of the great commandment completes a triangle of love that challenges each person: love for God, love for neighbor, love for self. Each one affects the other two. None of the three is optional. All of them must be present for healthy living. Without love for God, love of self and neighbor is reduced to human effort. Without love for neighbor, love for self and for God becomes suspect (see 1 John 4:20). And without love for self, love for God and neighbor becomes impossible. All these exist for one reason—because God loved us first. God's love invites our direct response. God's love directs our response to include our neighbor. And God's love demonstrates that we are lovable (see 1 John 4:9-10).

A WORD FOR TODAY
The greatest proverb—"Love God."

Lord, teach me that I can learn a lot about loving my neighbor by letting you help me love myself the right way.

Read
Proverbs 11

AS YOURSELF
Jesus replied, "The most important commandment is this: 'Listen, O Israel! The LORD our God is the one and only LORD. And you must love the LORD your God with all your heart, all your soul, all your mind, and all your strength.' The second is equally important: 'Love your neighbor as yourself.' No other commandment is greater than these."
Mark 12:29-31

NOVEMBER 12

Read
Proverbs 12

TIMELY RELIEF
Worry weighs
a person down;
an encouraging
word cheers a
person up.
Proverbs 12:25

Proverbs' consistent message revolves around recognizing the power of our words. For example, encouragement can make a difference in the lives of those around us. Oftentimes, we meet needy people consumed with troubles. We feel we can do nothing to lift their burdens—we may say a prayer, if that, and go on our way. However, Scripture exhorts us to a ministry of encouragement.

Our words of hope and support may be the very balm a worrier needs to get through a particular problem. From strangers on the street, to store clerks, to good friends and family members, encouragement should be the theme of all our conversation and interaction. Compliment strangers. Find something good to say. When you notice trainees in a store, affirm them. If a friend is struggling, offer your prayers. There is enough worry weighing down the world for everyone to have a share. Believers can make it their mission to make sure encouragement is as equally abundant.

A WORD FOR TODAY
Worry is an unnecessary weight.

Today, Lord, help me be sensitive to what I say. Let
my words be encouraging to those around me.

NOVEMBER 13

Laughter helps learning. Studies show that motivational speakers who use humor in their presentations have a more attentive audience. Accordingly, Proverbs often uses humor in its teachings. Here, we see an exaggerated portrayal of how God uses persistency to make his point. "Trouble" is like a guard dog, nipping at the heels of the sinful. However, blessing is a faithful companion who follows after the godly.

God overwhelms the righteous with his favor—so much so that it appears as if they can't get away from his goodness even if they tried! Blessings and curses are God's means for teaching us lessons. Curses pursue those who are sinful—they can't get away with their crimes. However, blessings are always on the heels of the righteous person. So, if we are having a hard time discerning the wicked from the righteous, look around. Is a person constantly surrounded by troubles? Or hardly able to keep up with the outpouring of God's blessings?

A WORD FOR TODAY
Laugh in the face of trouble.

Today, Lord, I am grateful that your blessings are my faithful companion. Thank you for all you have done for me.

**Read
Proverbs 13**

HOT PURSUIT!
Trouble chases sinners, while blessings reward the righteous.
Proverbs 13:21

NOVEMBER 14

RELIEF
*People with
understanding
control their anger;
a hot temper shows
great foolishness.*
Proverbs 14:29

At any given time, hundreds of thousands of people in our society are teetering on the edge of rage. And it's not whom you might expect. They are young mothers who grow impatient on the freeway. They are wallflower employees who silently grow disgruntled, and quiet back-row students plotting revenge. They are apparently religious people who suddenly snap. News reports frequently detail how otherwise ordinary people in otherwise ordinary circumstances suddenly explode into extraordinary rage. And the mistakes they make are legion—verbal abuse, physical abuse, even murder. Anger can be deadly.

The Bible recognizes anger's lethal potential and says we must control it. "Understanding" is the by-product of someone who has learned to control his or her temper. We begin to understand that we actually never "lose" our temper; we "choose" it. No one can "make" us mad. We choose our response of our own accord. Asking God for great understanding will help us think about our course of action.

A WORD FOR TODAY
Slow anger avoids mistakes.

Today, Lord, forgive me for "choosing" to lose my temper. Give me great understanding for how to control anger.

NOVEMBER 15

Ann Landers, a popular advice columnist until her death in 2002, had nothing on Proverbs—the ultimate daily column. Her millions of readers, however, proved this truth: Everyone loves to give advice. By her own testimony, she received a sizable volume of letters from people who were not seeking advice. They were giving it, and doing so in abundance. Apparently for every printed reply to a problem, her readers offered their own version. Even so, her daily task was to attempt to say the right thing at the right time.

Though it is unlikely that we will ever see our words read by millions, this proverb reminds us of the value of a well-said word. We must ask God's help in choosing our timing as well as our words. Many people feel they often don't know what to say when a friend is hurting or in need of advice. However, God extols us to say the right thing at the right time—and promises his help in doing so. We won't do it perfectly every time, but we will get better the more we do it.

A WORD FOR TODAY
There is pleasure in wise counsel.

Today, Lord, give me the right things to say at the right times. May you be pleased in all I say.

Read
Proverbs 15

PRECISION
Everyone enjoys
a fitting reply;
it is wonderful to
say the right thing
at the right time!
Proverbs 15:23

NOVEMBER 16

Read
Proverbs 16

STRATEGIC VICTORY

Better to be patient than powerful; better to have self-control than to conquer a city.
Proverbs 16:32

The mission of the believer is not too different from that of history's most noted conquerors. We must be determined. Forceful. Inspired. Yet we do not set our sights on triumphing over nations. Our foe is our nature—the sinful nature that is used to getting what it wants. Our weapons of war are patience and self-control. Learning to be patient is the mark of maturity. For example, a baby cries until it gets what is needed. It is impossible for a baby to understand or appreciate the principle of delayed gratification. However, a mature adult learns to control his or her desires and practice patience.

Self-control allows us to disarm natural urges. Delayed gratification means waiting for sex until marriage. Patience allows us to discipline our children in love, never in anger. Power conquers cities; patience conquers sin. We need not set sail for new horizons seeking the ultimate conquest. We can merely look into the nearest mirror. It is better to conquer oneself than to conquer an entire city.

A WORD FOR TODAY
Power is revealed in self-control.

Today, Lord, I will fight my greatest foe—myself. Make me victorious and self-controlled today.

NOVEMBER 17

Horse-drawn carriage rides in big cities are big business. After a delightful meal downtown, many tourists and even locals enjoy a lazy trip around the city sites. However, the setting itself is usually not so serene. Taxis screech to a halt. Buses lumber along with booming diesel engines. Pedestrians by the hundreds flood city walkways. Yet the animals seem to hardly notice the thoroughfare, blinded to the left and right by leather patches. Steadily they trod, centered on the road ahead.

Focus. That's the difference between a fool and a sensible person. Fools are flighty. They may set their sights on one job or relationship for a while, but then their all-consuming efforts quickly dissipate. Easily distracted, they are soon on to the next thing. The ability to focus on what is truly important is essential to success. Like the carriage horse, we must fix our eyes—on Christ, the central point of our lives. He will safely guide us to success.

A WORD FOR TODAY
Keep your eyes on the prize.

Today, Lord, bring your wisdom into focus. And guide my steps to success.

Read
Proverbs 17

ATTENTION
Sensible people keep their eyes glued on wisdom, but a fool's eyes wander to the ends of the earth.
Proverbs 17:24

NOVEMBER 18

Read
Proverbs 18

HARVEST

A good person
produces good
things from the
treasury of a good
heart, and an evil
person produces evil
things from the
treasury of an evil
heart. And I tell you
this, you must give
an account on
judgment day for
every idle word
you speak.
Matthew 12:35-36

Weeds are killers. Mowing seems like twice the chore due to the excessive number of weeds that seem to spring up almost overnight. A lovely lawn is the result of attacking this persistent plant life with a fine-grade mower . . . at least for the moment. It isn't long, however, until nature's nuisance sprouts forth from unscathed roots with a vengeance. The secret to weed killing is at the root level.

In the same way, we are often tempted to cut our bad habits at lip level—foul language, criticism. We swear off swearing and promise "not an idle word" from our lips. Soon, however, the roots of sinful behavior that are firmly implanted in our hearts sprout new growth and work their way up to become visible again. Jesus gets to the root of the issue: Evil words come from an evil heart. It is not enough to cut bad habits at lip level. We need a heart transplant—pulling up weeds of ungodliness by the roots and planting goodness in their place. Only then are we prepared to give account for our words.

A WORD FOR TODAY
Don't be ashamed of the transcript of your life.

Today, Lord, cleanse my heart and affect my speech.
May I be accountable to you for each word.

NOVEMBER 19

Role reversal is a favorite game of children who love to mimic the role of mother or father. However, fantasy sometimes has the opportunity to become reality when the children become adults with an equal or even superior position of authority. Maybe the adult children become wealthier, more educated, and/or more physically able than their parents. Many adult children find a special pleasure in mistreating parents—especially those who were raised feeling they were mistreated themselves.

At first, revenge seems sweet. Yet it comes with a price. Sure, it's embarrassing for parents to have their child disgrace them. However, this proverb says it is better to be embarrassed than to become an embarrassment. Additionally, the disgraceful behavior is a public concern because it reflects poorly on Christ himself. Supposedly Christian people who mistreat their parents demonstrate a dichotomy that is hard for others to understand. If this is the way Christians treat those who are the very closest to them, then the world wants nothing to do with their message. Their actions are much more convincing than their words.

A WORD FOR TODAY
Parental abuse is dual disrespect.

Today, Lord, don't let me be an embarrassment to you. Help me treat my family in a way that honors you.

Read
Proverbs 19

IN PUBLIC
Children who mistreat their father or chase away their mother are an embarrassment and a public disgrace.
Proverbs 19:26

NOVEMBER 20

Read
Proverbs 20

EXPOSED!
*The LORD's light
penetrates the
human spirit,
exposing every
hidden motive.*
Proverbs 20:27

There is a molecular universe that is unseen to the naked human eye. We're talking *small*. Without the benefit of scientific instruments, it would be impossible to describe the appearance of an atom. We wouldn't have a clue about the detail of a proton or neutron.

Likewise, there are components of the human spirit that have never been seen with the human eye. Does anyone other than our Creator know exactly what a motive looks like? Impossible! For motives are imbedded deep within our spirit, hidden behind good intentions and false pretenses. Only God can penetrate human defenses and expose a person's wrong motive—hidden or otherwise. The bottom line of this proverb is this—we're transparent. There's no point in keeping things from God. There's no sense in lying to him. With his penetrating gaze, he can see right through us. God has us all figured out.

A WORD FOR TODAY
God misses nothing!

Today, Lord, search my spirit freely. May my motives be pure and pleasing to you.

NOVEMBER 21

Once again, a proverb willingly plays the role of "Master of the Obvious." However, this simple piece of advice, though touted in various forms, is rarely practiced. Foot-in-mouth disease is a worldwide epidemic. We regularly spill secrets. We speak volumes about what we don't really know. We say the first thing that comes to mind with fluent precision but little forethought about its implications.

Instead of implementing the proverb's "quit while ahead" philosophy, we often open our mouths wider in an attempt to talk our way out of trouble. In short, the advice is simple, but following the advice is something else altogether. However, the whole of Scripture helps put the principle into practice. Wait on the Lord. Pray for wisdom. Meditate on God's Word. If we feel we must do something in the heat of the moment, there are many things to keep us busy as we practice keeping our mouths shut.

A WORD FOR TODAY
Don't even explain why you're biting your tongue.

Today, Lord, I am thankful for the times you have saved me from trouble by helping me stay quiet.

Read
Proverbs 21

MOUTH
CONTROL
Watch your tongue
and keep your
mouth shut, and
you will stay out
of trouble.
Proverbs 21:23

NOVEMBER 22

Read
Proverbs 22

🐟

DIVINE DEFENDER

Don't rob the poor just because you can, or exploit the needy in court. For the LORD is their defender. He will ruin anyone who ruins them.
Proverbs 22:22-23

His image cannot be found in the yellow pages or spread on the back of phone books. He will likely never tout a slogan on a billboard or bus. Don't look for him to star in his own commercial. However, he is the most powerful personal injury attorney on the planet. He is the Lord. Don't mess with him.

From cover to cover, the Bible makes it clear that God is especially interested in the poor and needy. Although biblical history is full of injustice against the afflicted, his message is still the same. He is their defender and will cause their foes to come to ruin. In contrast, our culture is generally complacent about the poor. They are often considered easy prey for robbery or exploitation in more than one sense. They are robbed of their dignity. They are exploited for their lack of resources. Yet God reserves special honor for them. How we ought to do the same!

A WORD FOR TODAY
God is offended by exploitation.

Today, Lord, make me sensitive to the poor and needy. Show me how I can share your special burden for them.

NOVEMBER 23

A piece of eraser easily serves as a missing earring back. Bubblegum can substitute for glue in a pinch. And some say duct tape can fix anything. Quick fixes do wonders for the time being, yet they rarely have anything to offer in the long run. Alcohol and drug abuse are common quick-fix solutions to life's problems. However, as this proverb points out, in the end they prove more than useless—they are deadly. People often actually wind up in greater trouble than when they first started.

Alcohol abuse is initially appealing as a means of escape—especially for people who have lost the ability to see an alternate solution. However, over time, alcohol leads a person to become progressively worse in order to feel better. The Bible calls it deception. We may try a number of ways to deal with our problems, but "in the end" they fail to provide relief. A true solution is one that both gets us through problems and makes us better people.

A WORD FOR TODAY
Some roads are not even worth starting out on.

Today, Lord, forgive me for trying to solve my problems without your help. Help me to turn to you for solutions.

Read Proverbs 23

DEAD-END SOLUTIONS
Don't gaze at the wine, seeing how red it is, how it sparkles in the cup, how smoothly it goes down. For in the end it bites like a poisonous snake; it stings like a viper.
Proverbs 23:31-32

NOVEMBER 24

Read
Proverbs 24

WISE ORDER
Do your planning
and prepare
your fields before
building your house.
Proverbs 24:27

Initially, this proverb may read like a specific message for future homeowners. However, the proverb is actually illustrating a universal principle about proper order. Just as planning and preparation are necessary before the purchase of a new home, certain things must be done in sequence for greater success.

The applications of this principle are found in more than just agricultural and business matters. For example, there must be love before marriage. And ideally marriage comes before children. Getting these steps out of order can be devastating. The Bible teaches the importance of having order to show us something about God's character. It shows us that he is a loving God—intricately involved and interested in our lives. *What* we do and *how* we do it matters to God.

A WORD FOR TODAY
Solid roots come before healthy fruit.

Today, Lord, I may be tempted to get ahead of you. Slow me down. Teach me the meaning of an orderly life.

NOVEMBER 25

In Greek, the term used here for "crown" refers to a ceremonial victory wreath in athletics or the military. Like a weary marathon runner who patiently endures muscle-testing mile upon mile, so we must commit ourselves to completing our course. In the end, the prize will be worth the effort.

Temptation and testing is part of life. However, we cannot allow them to discourage us. Like a wounded warrior battling the temptation to surrender to the enemy, we must be steadfast. For no matter how severe the trial, the outcomes that await us are far more significant: God's blessing and eternal life.

Temptation comes to us in earthly forms like materialism, sex, money, and power. They provide temporary satisfaction. In contrast, God rewards those who endure temptation with eternal benefits. He provides a winner's medal that never tarnishes and a living victory wreath that never shrivels or dies. Although earthly testing is difficult, the reward is heavenly—heaven itself!

A WORD FOR TODAY
Patience is guaranteed a long-term reward.

Today, Lord, I may be tempted and tested. Help me decide beforehand, right now, to endure and not give in.

**Read
Proverbs 25**

WORTHWHILE
REWARD
God blesses those who patiently endure testing and temptation. Afterward they will receive the crown of life that God has promised to those who love him.
James 1:12

NOVEMBER 26

BOOMERANG

*If you set a trap
for others, you will
get caught in it
yourself. If you roll a
boulder down on
others, it will crush
you instead.*
Proverbs 26:27

This proverb is not about bad luck or little-known laws of nature. Known by some as "what goes around comes around," this biblical boomerang actually describes the way God has structured natural consequences for breaking his commands. Whatever we do to harm others will ultimately harm us. Whatever we do to seek revenge against an enemy will eventually become our own downfall. For example, hatred toward others causes self-inflicted wounds.

People who are consumed with hatred stress out and worry. Sometimes their feelings are so intense that they can't sleep or eat. Hatred is a trap we set for others, yet we get hung up in it ourselves. Like a scene in a slapstick comedy, our entangled foot dangles us upside-down out on a limb. Meanwhile, our "victim" passes by unharmed. Yet it is no laughing matter. Revenge is a dangerous game, best left to the professional—God himself.

A WORD FOR TODAY
Give what you hope to get.

*Today, Lord, others may try to hurt me. Remind me
of your truth when I want revenge.*

NOVEMBER 27

Science has discovered a new way of looking at things. There is a mirror on the market that provides the most accurate reflection yet. Instead of gazing upon a reversed image seen in a typical mirror, this new technological advancement allows people to see themselves the same way the rest of the world does. People who have used it claim to prefer the new image. This "true reflection" makes a person skinnier, younger, and a number of other improvements.

The best mirror still doesn't show the real person, however. Our hearts represent the true person we are on the inside. If we want to see our whole being the way the rest of the world does, we must peer inside our hearts and face what is there. We may be startled by what we see. We may have to squint to see anything good at all. Fortunately, we are works in progress. God works in us to gradually mold and shape each heart to one day perfectly reflect the image of Jesus Christ.

A WORD FOR TODAY
Your heart can reflect Christ.

Today, Lord, mold my heart to reflect more of the character of Christ.

Read
Proverbs 27

INTERNAL
IMAGE
As a face is reflected in water, so the heart reflects the real person.
Proverbs 27:19

NOVEMBER 28

Read
Proverbs 28

VALUED
TRUTH
In the end, people
appreciate honest
criticism far more
than flattery.
Proverbs 28:23

It is possible to use flattery to gain friendships, perks, and opportunities. However, the gain may be temporary at best. At the end of a friendship paved with flattery, friends may find they really have nothing in common. At the end of a workday, puffed full of empty compliments from manipulative employees, a supervisor may feel used instead of affirmed.

This proverb is not saying that people don't appreciate flattery. In reality, they do. In general, people love to have their ego stroked. And yet the Bible teaches that people value truthfulness, couched in love, much more. Giving honest criticism is not the same as being rude. Being frank with a friend means telling a person our honest, objective evaluation of a situation or issue. Flattery means telling a person only what he or she wants to hear. According to this proverb, the bottom line is being truthful instead of insincere.

A WORD FOR TODAY
Resist giving or receiving flattery.

Today, Lord, I will follow your guidance and speak the truth in love.

NOVEMBER 29

A phobia is defined as an irrational fear that controls a person's daily life. Arachnophobia is the fear of spiders. Claustrophobia is the fear of being confined in small spaces.

The Bible describes what it is like to have an irrational fear of other people. It is a trap—a paralyzing situation where we are no longer in control of our lives. It is one thing to have appropriate concern for a person's opinion. It is quite another to cower before it. The fear of disappointing people can lead churches to abandon new visions for ministry. Leaders may compromise their own convictions due to an irrational fear of hurting someone's feelings. Believers may remain stunted in their spiritual growth, afraid of living out their faith at work or at home. Imagine an animal that deliberately runs into a trap, thinking it will find safety there. Of course, it finds the very opposite. In the same way, we cannot find safety through our attempts to please others. We must please God and trust him alone—then we find true safety.

A WORD FOR TODAY
Let your fear of God overcome your fear of people.

Today, Lord, I will trust in you. Teach me what it means to find security in you alone.

Read
Proverbs 29

TRUE SAFETY
Fearing people is a dangerous trap, but trusting the LORD means safety.
Proverbs 29:25

NOVEMBER 30

**Read
Proverbs 30**

CONNECTIONS
*As the beating of
cream yields butter
and striking the
nose causes bleeding,
so stirring up anger
causes quarrels.*
Proverbs 30:33

In the manner of "Which came first: the chicken or
the egg?" this proverb makes an important distinction about the sequence of natural causes. Beating
cream yields butter. Beaten noses yield blood. Anger
yields quarrels. Which comes first: anger or a
quarrel?

This proverb indicates that anger is the precursor
to quarrels. It is the common denominator in most
quarrelsome relationships. Fighting is a symptom of
anger. Well-intentioned parents may bring an end to
the fighting between quarreling children. Sending
them to their rooms brings temporary peace. Meanwhile, the anger remains seething just below the surface. Eventually, anger that is not properly dealt with
will give birth to more quarrels. As a result, we must
deal with anger on a deeper level to fully address our
concerns. Human relationships—marriages, friendships, and families—hinge on cause-and-effect
dynamics. We must get to the root cause of a problem in order to deal with its effects.

A WORD FOR TODAY
Keep anger in hand.

*Today, Lord, teach me how to handle my emotions so
I can enjoy the relationships I have with others.*

DECEMBER 1

Who among us would not desire a life of peace and safety, one without fear of harm? Is it true that to have that, all we must do is listen to God? Is it reasonable to conclude that if we are not experiencing peace and safety, if we are living with fear, we are not listening to God? Can it really be that simple? If so, how then should we interpret James 1:2, which says, "When troubles come your way, consider it an opportunity for great joy"? And what about 1 Peter 1:6, which says, "There is wonderful joy ahead, even though you have to endure many trials for a little while"? Trouble? Trials? Peace? Safety? How can all these come in the same package?

It is important to note that the passages in James and 1 Peter go on to say that trials produce perseverance and maturity and that suffering proves our faith. Through the eyes of a mature faith, we can begin to realize that in the midst of the temporary turmoil and strife of this life, we can know God's eternal peace and safety. We need not be concerned about harm that may come to these earthly bodies of ours, because we know what God ultimately has in store for us.

A WORD FOR TODAY
Wisdom yields good results.

Today, Lord, may I welcome with praise whatever comes my way, because I know you will use these circumstances to make me into what you want me to be.

Read
Proverbs 1

KEEP
LISTENING
All who listen to me will live in peace, untroubled by fear of harm.
Proverbs 1:33

DECEMBER 2

Read
Proverbs 2

🍂

GRATEFUL
EFFORTS

*Pure and genuine
religion in the sight
of God the Father
means caring for
orphans and widows
in their distress
and refusing to
let the world
corrupt you.*
James 1:27

One of the greatest misunderstandings of people throughout the ages is thinking that their religious efforts will make God look favorably upon them when they die and face him for judgment. Christianity is the world's only religion that doesn't make this claim. It was that very misunderstanding among the Pharisees of the New Testament that Jesus so roundly condemned. Jesus' message was that God's acceptance of us is *his* act of love and mercy, not the result of our conforming to certain standards of a religious creed. His love for us is a gift to be humbly received by coming to him through his son, Jesus.

Why, then, does this verse in James seem to say that the true religion is caring for orphans and widows? Isn't he asking us to act a certain way to obtain his favor? Certainly, God wants us to care for orphans and widows, but not in order to earn his favor. Instead, he is simply stating that if we truly love him, we will love and serve the most needy among us with selfless humility. Our good deeds will be the natural outpouring of our gratitude to God for his gift of love to us.

A WORD FOR TODAY
Caring about God leads to caring about others.

Today, Lord, may my attitude be one of humility, and may I accept and love others as you have loved me.

DECEMBER 3

The Lord mocking mockers and favoring the humble is just one variation of a theme often repeated in the Bible, namely that God's primary interest is in the attitudes of the heart. Mockers can be characterized in one of two ways, and both are the result of an improper image of self. One is blatant pride that says, "I am better than others." The other is a sense of worthlessness that says, "I try to hide by degrading others."

Pride prevents people from seeking God because it makes them think they don't need him. Feeling worthless prevents people from seeking God because it makes them think they can't measure up.

Humility, on the other hand, allows a realistic perspective. Humility recognizes that we are the pinnacle of God's creation, created by him in his image in order to worship him. But it also recognizes that we are sinners who turned our backs on God and that, except for God's grace, we would be eternally separated from him and his love. It is because of his grace that he has permitted us to reenter his presence. How can we not accept that opportunity?

A WORD FOR TODAY
Humility sees; pride is blind.

Today, Lord, may I not be a mocker separated from you, but a humble seeker of your perfect ways.

Read
Proverbs 3

HEART
CONTRAST
*The LORD mocks
the mockers but
is gracious to
the humble.*
Proverbs 3:34

DECEMBER 4

Read
Proverbs 4

☙

AVOIDING
DETOURS
*Don't get
sidetracked; keep
your feet from
following evil.*
Proverbs 4:27

Today's verse was Solomon's way of stating a very familiar principle. In 1 Corinthians 9:24 and Philippians 3:14, the apostle Paul stated it in terms of running a race, and running it with the goal of obtaining the prize. Even the well-known children's fable about a tortoise and a hare is centered around the same message: Keep focused, have a definite goal, work diligently toward that goal, and don't let yourself be distracted.

Why is that advice so often repeated? Probably because it is so difficult to follow. Diligence is work—hard work. Becoming distracted is easy; it happens when we're not looking. It is also all too easy to follow evil. It happens when we let down our guard, when we stop working toward our goal.

What should that goal be? Solomon answers that question, too. In Ecclesiastes 12:13, he says, "Fear God and obey his commands, for this is everyone's duty." The greater our focus on God and his Word, the less will be our tendency to get sidetracked.

A WORD FOR TODAY
There are two opposite destinations, but only one Way.

Today, Lord, let my mind be stayed on you. Let the words of my mouth and the meditation of my heart be acceptable in your sight.

DECEMBER 5

The primary thrust of Proverbs 5 is that a man should be faithful to his wife. But the last three verses, including verse 23, give the chapter a broader context. They speak of evil deeds ensnaring a person, the "ropes that catch and hold him" (v. 22). Verse 23 uses words we might use to describe a person's relentless addiction to drugs. We think of drug addicts as having a total lack of self-control, and of their incredible foolishness in choosing to waste their lives. In the depths of their addiction, drug addicts also like to think that they can get their fixes secretly, out of view of those who love them.

Our evil ways are like that, too. We are all addicted to sin from birth, because our mother and father were sin addicts. We were born addicted to sin, and we choose with incredible folly to continue our addiction with our evil ways. And despite our attempts to deny or hide them, our evil ways are in full view of the Lord. He knows our sin. He also knows that our addiction is beyond self-correction. That is why he gave us Jesus—to save us from our incredible foolishness and to restore us to faithfulness to him.

**Read
Proverbs 5**

BIG PICTURE
*[The evil man]
will die for lack
of self-control; he
will be lost because
of his great
foolishness.*
Proverbs 5:23

A WORD FOR TODAY
Getting what you want can be the worst outcome.

*Today, Lord, I confess my addiction to sin and accept
your extended hand to lift me from my evil ways.*

DECEMBER 6

**Read
Proverbs 6**

SELF-
DEMOLITION
*The man who
commits adultery
is an utter fool,
for he destroys
himself.*
Proverbs 6:32

If we are to believe the cultural message of the late
twentieth and early twenty-first centuries, sexual
acts of any kind are simply alternative lifestyles.
Current logic also says that the Old Testament is
not applicable to modern living, so this advice in
Proverbs can be safely ignored. Further, according
to this logic, even Jesus said in his Sermon on the
Mount, "Do not judge others, and you will not be
judged" (Matthew 7:1). So does all this mean that
we must accept these "alternatives" without con-
demnation because all choices are equally moral?
Viewed through the eyes of political correctness,
it does. But this line of thinking is just one more
example of man's attempts to rationalize behavior
that God clearly condemns.

Today's proverb says that the adulterous man is
"an utter fool." According to the descriptions in
Proverbs, a fool is not someone who lacks intellec-
tual ability, but one who chooses to rationalize
wrong behavior. The fool casts off the fear of God,
thinking and acting as if he or she could safely disregard God's righteousness. Remember this: God's
principles are eternal. They are never out of date.

A WORD FOR TODAY
Adultery is self-destructive.

*Today, Lord, may I be truly sensitive to your urgings, and
not so foolish that I ignore you. Help me to see my sin as
sin and not to rationalize it.*

DECEMBER 7

Today's verse is a familiar warning to the reader of Proverbs: Stay away from sexual sin because it is one of the mileage markers on the road to spiritual defeat. Sexual sin, like lying, never shows up alone in a person's life. You cannot participate in it without participating in many other forms of sin. Adultery is usually accompanied by lies and deceit. It is also a selfish act that involves the breaking of your marriage vows and a disregard for the well-being of your children.

But this knowledge can also lead to a misunderstanding. Because warnings against sexual sin are so frequent in Scripture, Christians often treat sex and sexuality as if they are particularly offensive to God, rather than a wonderful gift from him when used as he intended. It is only when the gift is used as God did *not* intend that it becomes sin. (That is true of all of God's gifts.) God is a generous God who bestows upon us many precious gifts, but using any of them inappropriately is sin, and "the wages of [any] sin is death" (Romans 6:23).

A WORD FOR TODAY
Sin always leads toward death.

Today, Lord, help me to confess my every sin, no matter how small, that I may be holy as you are holy.

**Read
Proverbs 7**

DANGER SIGNS
Her house is the road to the grave. Her bedroom is the den of death.
Proverbs 7:27

DECEMBER 8

Read
Proverbs 8

YOU
HAVE BEEN
APPROVED

*Whoever finds
me finds life and
receives favor from
the LORD.*
Proverbs 8:35

Confusing and incomprehensible as the Bible sometimes seems, one simple message is woven through
its pages—the message of life. In Genesis, we read
that God created the world and that he created people in his own image to walk with and worship him.
But they sinned, and at that very moment, they died
spiritually. They broke their relationship with God
and were forever separated from him. Physical death
soon followed. God could have turned his back on
his creation to let it self-destruct. But the glorious
message of the Bible is that he didn't—because he
loved us too much. That is why the Bible doesn't
end after the first few chapters of Genesis. It goes
on to record the history of God's relationship with
men and women and his offering us a restored
relationship with him.

Today's proverb speaks of this restored relationship
by saying that whoever finds God's wisdom finds life
and the Lord's favor. How do we find that wisdom?
God's wisdom is found in a person—Jesus Christ,
who is "the wonderful wisdom of God" (1 Corinthians 1:24). In Christ, we have God's wisdom. In him,
we have life!

A WORD FOR TODAY
Wisdom gets God's nod.

*Today, Lord, I acknowledge that my sin has separated me
from you, but I thank you that through Jesus, you have
provided me a second chance.*

DECEMBER 9

Our twelve encounters with this central proverb have only scratched its surface. The better we understand this great commandment, the more it challenges us. No other proverb gives us a challenge more applicable every single day.

As a thought for further meditation, consider that this proverb implies or describes ten types of love: (1) God's love for us; (2) God's love for our neighbor; (3) our heart-love for God; (4) our soul-love for God; (5) our mind-love for God; (6) our strength-love for God; (7) our love for our neighbor; (8) our love for ourselves; (9) our neighbor's love for God; and (10) our neighbor's love for us. Meditating on these will require considerable exposure to the rest of Scripture.

Consider also how this great two-part commandment exactly summarizes the Ten Commandments in Exodus 20:1-17. Remember that an increased understanding of the deep things of God will broaden your responsibility to apply them in your life.

A WORD FOR TODAY
The greatest proverb—"Love God."

Today, Lord, renew my commitment to be a doer of your Word, applying this great commandment throughout my life.

Read
Proverbs 9

❦

THE
FRAMEWORK
OF LOVE

Jesus replied, "The most important commandment is this: 'Listen, O Israel! The LORD our God is the one and only LORD. And you must love the LORD your God with all your heart, all your soul, all your mind, and all your strength.' The second is equally important: 'Love your neighbor as yourself.' No other commandment is greater than these."
Mark 12:29-31

DECEMBER 10

Read
Proverbs 10

☛

ON THE JOB
*Lazy people irritate
their employers, like
vinegar to the teeth
or smoke in the eyes.*
Proverbs 10:26

Laziness is its own self-condemnation. Laziness brings poverty (Proverbs 10:4). The homes of the lazy fall into disrepair (Ecclesiastes 10:18). But today's proverb is not directed at just the lazy. It is a warning to others. Lazy people are an aggravation to those who must deal with them, like smoke in the eyes or a fingernail scratching a chalkboard.

Employers hire workers to work. Employees who are lazy, who don't do their job, cause frustration to set in. The natural response of an employer is to fire lazy workers because they don't do what they were hired to do. If the natural and justifiable response of an employer is to fire them, how much more understandable is God's response to our sin.

Sin is living, acting, and thinking in ways not intended by God when he created us. As sinners, we should expect nothing less than expulsion from God's presence. What is surprising is that despite God's "irritation" with us, he pursues us for the purpose of bringing us back to him. That knowledge is a lesson for us. Though some people may irritate us to the point of distraction, we must still love them and work to bring them into God's presence.

A WORD FOR TODAY
Laziness invites unemployment.

Today, Lord, may I be patient with those around me and love them as you have loved me.

DECEMBER 11

Those who would argue against the truth and reli-
ability of the Bible might use this verse (and many
others in Proverbs) to support their view because
everyone knows of real situations that contradict
what the verse seems to say. We can all name people
who are greedy and stingy but also have great
wealth. And we can name very generous people
who live in or on the edge of poverty. Those who
approach the Bible with the preconceived notion
that it is unreliable deny themselves the greater
opportunity to know God and discover the deeper
meaning of these truths.

If we believe the Bible contains many historical
inaccuracies and inconsistencies, it becomes a mean-
ingless book. Then, if we read it at all, we tend to
look for shallow interpretations that support our
notion of its fallibility. But if we accept Jesus' own
testimony that the Scriptures are reliable and if we
are willing (with the help of the Holy Spirit) to
search out its deeper meanings, we will find Scripture to be utterly truthful, consistent, infallible, and
very relevant to our personal lives. To understand
that truth is to understand true wealth.

**Read
Proverbs 11**

STILL TRUE
*Give freely and
become more
wealthy; be stingy
and lose everything.*
Proverbs 11:24

A WORD FOR TODAY
Generosity preserves true capital.

*Today, Lord, as I read your Word, may I not doubt
but expect to find in it the depths of your truth.*

DECEMBER 12

Read
Proverbs 12

❦

TRUE FRIENDS
The godly give good
advice to their
friends; the wicked
lead them astray.
Proverbs 12:26

Young people, in particular, find it very difficult to distinguish between evaluating their friendships on the basis of advice those friends offer and evaluating advice on the basis of those friendships. Their desire for friendship and acceptance often overrules their awareness of bad advice. Unfortunately, those who are not true friends don't hesitate to use their "friendship" as a condition to get someone to go along with bad plans.

Conversations about friendship ought to be frequent during a child's earliest years. Culture tends to cheapen the relationship to the point where *friend* is synonymous with *acquaintance*. Young people list among their friends people whom they barely know. A child who has learned the high value of the word *friend* will be less likely to trust as friends those who have not really proven themselves trustworthy.

Both genuine friendship and good advice stand the test of time. Neither occurs instantly. Both are to be treasured.

A WORD FOR TODAY
Ask God for wisdom for your friends.

Today, Lord, I thank you for my friendships. Thank you
for being my ultimate friend. Help me be the right kind
of friend to others.

DECEMBER 13

Unfortunately, discussions about child discipline in our times have been reduced to arguments over spanking. Even more tragically, while people have debated the issue of spanking, parents have been cowed into forms of child rearing that have been as abusive by default as child rearing that has misused corporal punishment.

Parents often decide on a form of discipline long before they have actually "met" their children. However, parental concepts of discipline must take into account the character and personalities of their children. Otherwise, these parents may be poorly prepared for the differences between children who are either softhearted and respond positively to "light" discipline and children who are strong willed and require a stronger-willed set of parents. Good discipline must fit the child. Good discipline conveys love to the child. When promptly applied, good discipline produces lifelong, positive results.

A WORD FOR TODAY
Discipline demonstrates love.

Today, Lord, remind me of the benefits I have received through discipline. Help me not to withhold these benefits from my own children.

**Read
Proverbs 13**

LOVING
DISCIPLINE
*Those who spare
the rod of discipline
hate their children.
Those who love
their children
care enough to
discipline them.*
Proverbs 13:24

DECEMBER 14

Read
Proverbs 14

A KEY TO
CONTENTMENT
A peaceful heart
leads to a healthy
body; jealousy is like
cancer in the bones.
Proverbs 14:30

We're a generation of high rollers: high cholesterol, high blood pressure, high anxiety, and high levels of stress. While science pushes back the battle lines of disease, we continue to suffer devastating losses from self-inflicted illnesses. This proverb offers an unexpected insight. A "peaceful heart" does have an amazing impact on longevity, but how does *jealousy* affect life?

Jealousy implies strong feelings (some translations say "passion") about what others have, what we think they have, or what we think we deserve. If we have very narrow expectations about life, and those expectations are disappointed, what follows is the temptation to become resentful, angry, and unhappy. By way of contrast, this proverb implies a certain degree of acceptance and contentment.

The proverb doesn't argue for laziness and lack of goal setting. It simply states the fact that unhealthy desires and a jealous outlook will seriously under-mine our ability to enjoy life. We will allow what we don't have to spoil what we do have. We will shorten our lives even if we don't shorten our years.

A WORD FOR TODAY
Relax!

Today, Lord, make me aware of the differences between healthy, proper desires and those that rob and spoil my contentment.

DECEMBER 15

Throughout this year as we have sought to grow in wisdom, we have inevitably deepened our understanding of the fear of the Lord. Proverbs begins with counsel: "Let the wise listen to these proverbs and become even wiser. Let those with understanding receive guidance by exploring the meaning in these proverbs and parables, the words of the wise and their riddles. Fear of the LORD is the foundation of true knowledge, but fools despise wisdom and discipline" (1:5-7). The decision to pursue wisdom is itself a wise decision, and all true wisdom and knowledge rest on our understanding of God.

Fear of the Lord directs our use of wisdom. Fear of the Lord reminds us that understanding and knowledge are gifts to be used for the benefit of others. Fear of the Lord never allows us to forget who God is, and that *we* aren't God. Fear of the Lord fosters the right kind of humility. The finest honors we receive in life are wasted if they aren't preceded by humility and if they don't proceed from our use of wisdom to make a difference in people's lives.

A WORD FOR TODAY
Fearing God prepares us for wisdom.

Today, Lord, allow me to see ways in which I can use my skills and understanding to help others.

**Read
Proverbs 15**

GOOD FEAR
*Fear of the LORD
teaches wisdom;
humility precedes
honor.*
Proverbs 15:33

DECEMBER 16

**Read
Proverbs 16**

❧

WISE PRAYER

*The earnest prayer
of a righteous
person has great
power and produces
wonderful results.*

James 5:16

The fact that the words *prayer* and *pray* do not appear in the book of Proverbs might lead some to think that wisdom doesn't have anything to do with prayer. They would be wrong. Probably no book in the Bible describes the balance between faith and wise action like the book of James. The two go hand in hand. Faith always makes its presence known externally.

The entire book of Proverbs could be prefaced by this statement: "Once you have prayed, keep praying and do any number of the following wise actions, depending on the circumstances you face." The fear of the Lord mentioned in the first chapter of Proverbs is a fear developed and expressed in the laboratory of prayer.

A person who is growing in wisdom prays earnestly. Wisdom provides many lessons to direct and sharpen the way we pray. That is why James can confidently write that the prayer of a wise (righteous) person accomplishes results. Righteous prayer doesn't seek its own answers, but God's will.

A WORD FOR TODAY
Practice earnest prayer.

Today, Lord, I declare my renewed desire to see that your will is done in my life and in the lives of others, even as it is done in heaven.

DECEMBER 17

Much can be said with few words. A picture may express a thousand words, and a wise proverb leads to a thousand applications.

A wise person chooses his or her words carefully, and uses no more of them than necessary. As other proverbs clearly remind us, the degree of foolishness usually keeps pace with the number of words we use. The greater the quantity of words, the less likely we are to find quality.

The person with understanding can be even-tempered because he or she knows more than the immediate circumstance. Uneven temper comes from being too influenced by the moment. Even-temperedness doesn't mean that the person approaches everything the same way; rather it means that the person has an understanding that directs him to respond to each situation with the appropriate temper (response). When Jesus was angry, he was displaying a profound reaction to the dishonoring of God's house. We would do well to seek to become even-tempered people of few words!

A WORD FOR TODAY
A few well-chosen words reveal wisdom.

Today, Lord, make the few things I say really count for you.

Read
Proverbs 17

NUGGETS
A truly wise person uses few words; a person with understanding is even-tempered.
Proverbs 17:27

DECEMBER 18

**Read
Proverbs 18**

WHAT A
FRIEND
WE HAVE!
*There are "friends"
who destroy each
other, but a real
friend sticks closer
than a brother.*
Proverbs 18:24

What better meditation could we have on the meaning of this proverb than the words of Jesus? "This is my commandment: Love each other in the same way I have loved you. There is no greater love than to lay down one's life for one's friends. You are my friends if you do what I command. I no longer call you slaves, because a master doesn't confide in his slaves. Now you are my friends, since I have told you everything the Father told me" (John 15:12-15).

Jesus demonstrated the greatest love of a friend. He laid down his life for us. As wonderful and close as brothers can be, there is a place for friendship that is even closer. Part of this comes from the fact that brothers aren't chosen, but friends are. A brother (or sister) who chooses to be a friend is as close as humans can be. The only relationship closer is the one Jesus defined as his alone. His death would ransom and save his friends in a way no one else could do and which they could never do for themselves. What a friend we have in Jesus!

A WORD FOR TODAY
Friendship is proven over time and through trouble.

Today, Lord, I thank you for your sacrificial gift, for giving me the immeasurable honor of your friendship.

DECEMBER 19

Body language speaks loudly! Fingers in ears, an empty stare into space, or a turned back communicate an unwillingness to listen. Those actions are often meant to convey a rejection of the person speaking, but this proverb makes it clear that the real harm occurs to the one who turns away.

Instruction describes the means; knowledge describes the ends. Instruction lasts for a limited time; knowledge stays. If the instruction is rejected, the knowledge won't be available when it is needed.

The child in this proverb is receiving a priceless piece of counsel. Children who have been trained to listen well have been given a life skill they will use every day of their lives. The instruction may or may not be good ("friends" are always ready with "instruction"), but failure to pay attention will prevent the opportunity to reject or accept the instruction. If rejected, the young person's growth in wisdom and knowledge will be limited. There are few successful adults who don't wonder how much more they could have accomplished if they had listened to wise mentors earlier and better.

**Read
Proverbs 19**

☙

COSTLY BODY LANGUAGE

If you stop listening to instruction, my child, you will turn your back on knowledge.
Proverbs 19:27

A WORD FOR TODAY
Never stop learning.

Today, Lord, help me remember I am your child. I can't afford to stop listening to your instructions.

DECEMBER 20

Read
Proverbs 20

❧

LOOKING
BOTH WAYS
The glory of the
young is their
strength; the gray
hair of experience
is the splendor
of the old.
Proverbs 20:29

Middle age offers a unique time for reflection. This proverb sounds like someone wrote it in the central days of life. Middle-agers can look in both directions. They look back on earlier life; they look forward to their senior years. They have enough experience to realize past mistakes and can reasonably expect enough time to make important corrections.

Obviously, what amazes middle-agers about youth is the raw, seemingly unlimited energy they exude. It's tiring to even think about it. Mid-lifers also wonder when they might exhibit the kind of quiet wisdom and experience that seems so obvious in their seasoned elders.

So, what is the splendor and glory of the in-between years? As mentioned above, it is the incomplete perspective that includes two kinds of opportunity: a chance to acknowledge that the energy of youth is not inexhaustible and a chance to make significant adjustments in life as the autumn years approach. An acceptance of both these opportunities marks the wisdom and beauty of middle age.

A WORD FOR TODAY
Every passage in life has its benefits.

Today, Lord, help me live my age. Help me to be grateful
for the years you have given and hopeful of years of ser-
vice and obedience in the future. I also anticipate
heaven!

DECEMBER 21

Human will empowers us to accomplish great good or great evil. An individual or group can plan an act of terrorism that shocks the world. Meanwhile, other individuals can choose to act with such selfless abandon that the world cries with wonder and honor. Are we to conclude from such events that the world is on its own, that humanity's plans succeed or fail by chance or brilliance without God's interference?

As horrific as some acts seem, do they not create an impression of how bad things might become if all limits and all checks on human will were removed? The answer to the question, "If God loves and is all powerful, why doesn't he stop people from doing evil?" must be that God does love and is all powerful and stops acts of evil all the time. Every day. We can't see most of his work, except when he foils some evil plan.

We are eager to question God when evil breaks out but reluctant to praise God when good is done. Given the evidence from Scripture and history, is it not more amazing that good is ever done than that some people succeed in expressing their sinful character?

A WORD FOR TODAY
Beyond strategy is God's sovereignty.

Today, Lord, help me to be aware of your watchfulness over the world. Help me to always submit my plans and intentions to you.

Read
Proverbs 21

LIMITED
FREE WILL
No human wisdom or understanding or plan can stand against the LORD.
Proverbs 21:30

DECEMBER 22

Read
Proverbs 22

❦

CONTAGIOUS ANGER

*Don't befriend
angry people or
associate with hot-
tempered people, or
you will learn to be
like them and
endanger your soul.*
Proverbs 22:24-25

What is the distinguishing characteristic of the people this proverb describes as angry, hot-tempered people? They live in a constant state of anger that is capable of almost instant and unexpected escalation to rage. Two types of people stay away from this kind of person: those who are under attack by them and those who are wise.

So, why is the warning necessary? Because angry, hot-tempered people work hard to recruit allies. There often occurs an almost eerie process in which friends of angry, short-tempered people take on the same characteristics out of an instinct for self-preservation. The old "If you can't beat them you might as well join them" principle seems to take over. The results, this proverb points out, can endanger the soul.

Because attraction and attachment to angry, short-tempered people are difficult to understand or figure out, this word of wisdom usually has to be practiced before its value is recognized. Keeping a distance allows for better perspective.

A WORD FOR TODAY
Don't enable angry people.

Today, Lord, help me be aware of the clues I get from my surroundings. Don't let me pick up bad habits from those I'm with, and keep me from influencing them badly.

DECEMBER 23

Two blessings and three conditions are included in this proverb. God promises to bless those who read the prophecy to the church. God also promises to bless those who listen and obey what it says. The conditions are clear and the blessings are worth pursuing.

Particularly when it comes to the book of Revelation, Christians seem far more interested in listening to others offer their interpretation of John's great vision than in actually reading the book themselves. But no blessing is offered in this proverb for those who interpret the vision. The listening seems to refer to an attitude of attentiveness to commands that will then be obeyed. Our overattention to *descriptions* in Revelation often blunt our interest in the *prescriptions* of Revelation.

The final phrase of this proverb, written nineteen hundred years ago, points to Jesus' towering words: "You also must be ready all the time. For the Son of Man will come when least expected" (Matthew 24:44). Listen and obey—be ready.

A WORD FOR TODAY
Live prophetically expectant!

If you come today, Lord, I'm ready! I know I don't expect it, but I'm ready to be surprised!

**Read
Proverbs 23**

JUST LISTEN
God blesses the one who reads the words of this prophecy to the church, and he blesses all who listen to its message and obey what it says, for the time is near.
Revelation 1:3

DECEMBER 24

**Read
Proverbs 24**

YOU SNOOZE, YOU LOSE

*A little extra sleep,
a little more
slumber, a little
folding of the
hands to rest—
then poverty will
pounce on you like
a bandit; scarcity
will attack you like
an armed robber.*
Proverbs 24:33-34

Long before someone invented the alarm, people invented the snooze. In fact, the snooze button is a grudging attempt to satisfy those who turn off their alarms and go back to sleep. Snooze buttons blunt the sheer effectiveness of cold-turkey wake-up buzzers.

This proverb highlights our tendency to describe laziness in diminutive terms—a little extra sleep, a little more slumber. In reality, those terms describe a bad habit. A little of this and a little of that leads to a life of inattention and poor preparation. When the alarm finally rings loud enough, the person wakes up to an overwhelming condition—poverty.

Neither scarcity nor poverty is an armed robber. There's nothing left to steal. But these experiences tend to demoralize people and rob them of the desire to reverse their habit. The warning of this proverb comes early in the process. The best time to break the tendency to be lazy occurs when it's still "a little" laziness. Fill your life with reasons to get up. Anticipate using tomorrow well. When the alarm goes off, get up! God has given you another day!

A WORD FOR TODAY
Don't sleep at the wheel.

Today, Lord, allow me to plan tomorrow in such a way that I will be eager to get up and be useful for you in the morning.

DECEMBER 25

Ancient cities depended on their walls. Tall parapets and towers, built from massive blocks of stone, provided a measure of security. Those inside the city controlled access by means of narrow, fortified gates. Once the walls were breached, attacks could come from any direction. The terror of defenselessness that underlies this proverb is difficult for us to feel; it's ancient history. Perhaps a current concern like disease would give us a better sense of the crucial insight of this wise saying. A person without self-control is as helpless as a body whose autoimmune system has completely collapsed.

Self-control, like strong walls and healthy immune systems, doesn't mean that challenges or attacks won't come. It does mean that a person has established a thoughtful way to respond to pressure or attack. Without self-control, every challenge (even unintended ones) tends to be seen as a life-threatening attack. A person without self-control becomes exhausted from battling in all directions, often against imagined opposition.

A WORD FOR TODAY
Self-control begins with asking God for help.

Today, Lord, I too need self-control. I invite your Holy Spirit to create in me the kind of self-control that pleases you.

Read
Proverbs 25

EASY TARGET
A person without self-control is like a city with broken-down walls.
Proverbs 25:28

DECEMBER 26

Read
Proverbs 26

DEADLY LIES
A lying tongue hates
its victims, and
flattering words
cause ruin.
Proverbs 26:28

Lying tends to be our first line of defense. The most damning evidence presented by our original ancestors that they had accepted their fallen condition was their attempt to lie to God. The shame they felt after eating the forbidden fruit indicated that their consciences had been awakened. They hid from God for the same reason. Up until God asked his questions, Adam and Eve could have repented. Instead, they lied. Every time we lie, we confirm that ancient family trait.

This proverb points out that lying fosters or reveals that we hate those to whom we lie. When we lie to people we love, we are treating them with hatred. Because successful lying creates powerful guilt, and because we want to avoid guilt, we tend to develop hatred toward those who accept our lies under the false excuse that they are gullible. Hatred toward a victim of our lies indicates that we have seriously succumbed to our own lies. To adapt an old saying, "We have lied to the enemy, and he is us."

A WORD FOR TODAY
Dishonesty is a form of hatred.

Today, Lord, help me remember that lying includes an
expression of hatred toward you. Help me abhor and
resist it for that reason.

DECEMBER 27

How do we respond to praise? Do we say, "It was really nothing," or, "Anyone could have done that"? What if we feel like saying, "You know? You're right. I am the best!" Praise does turn out to be a significant test.

God designed us to respond positively to praise. We enjoy being encouraged. We relish affirmation. In fact, a central motivation for Christians is the hope that we will one day hear God say to us, "Well done, my good and faithful servant" (Matthew 25:23).

This proverb offers a hint on how to respond to praise. Like fire, praise melts and purifies what is valuable while burning up what is impure. It can bring to the surface things that aren't good. For example, "Great job with that presentation! It made me rethink some assumptions I was making. But one illustration you used distracted me from your main point. Why not come up with a different one that drives home your helpful idea?" Wise praise includes a little heat.

Those receiving it shouldn't take superficial praise or flattery too seriously. It's a fire that hasn't gotten hot enough to purify.

A WORD FOR TODAY
Receive compliments thoughtfully.

Today, Lord, help me to express gratitude to those who make it a point to give me helpful praise.

Read
Proverbs 27

PRAISE
GAUNTLET
Fire tests the purity of silver and gold, but a person is tested by being praised.
Proverbs 27:21

DECEMBER 28

Read
Proverbs 28

TRUST
INVESTMENT

*Greed causes
fighting; trusting
the LORD leads
to prosperity.*
Proverbs 28:25

The contrasts included in many proverbs offer startling insights about life. They are not mathematical equations about life, but truthful observations that guide life. More often than not, these proverbs help us look at practical issues from God's perspective.

Greed might be defined as the human tendency to create a god out of our desires. Untamed greed is an idol that must be served and satisfied. Greed abhors humility, generosity, and compassion. Greed tends to attack anything or anyone that dares to come between it and possible satisfaction. Greed leads to fighting. And it is never satisfied.

Trusting God turns greed on its head, however. It replaces our desires with God's desires. We are trusting God when we say, "I desire to see your will done, Lord, more than my will." Trusting God does lead to prosperity. It leads to confident living. It results in a full life, measured not against what everyone else has, but by the contentment that God has supplied what we need and will continue to do so. Eventually, trusting God leads to the ultimate prosperity—eternal life.

A WORD FOR TODAY
Trusting God destroys greed.

Lord, allow me at least one very clear opportunity to practice trusting you as I go about my routine today.

DECEMBER 29

The system of justice in our fallen world often operates on the principle of the highest clout. To paraphrase this proverb, "If you have the king's favor, you've got nothing to worry about." In a sense, people understand an underlying principle in the universe: There is someone at the top. There is someone beyond whom there is no further appeal. The problem isn't so much that people want to appeal to a higher power to settle the issues of life. The problem is that people don't go high enough!

This proverb does not say that lower forms of authority and justice never operate. Nor does this proverb attempt to dissuade people from seeking the king's favor. It does, however, remind us that even the ruler receives his authority from God. This truth reminds us that depending on anyone other than God for ultimate justice is a hopeless effort. Eventually, we must trust that an all-wise, all-knowing, and absolutely just and holy God will settle the loose ends that keep tripping us up in life.

**Read
Proverbs 29**

SUPREME COURT

Many seek the ruler's favor, but justice comes from the LORD.
Proverbs 29:26

A WORD FOR TODAY
God's got ultimate clout.

Today, Lord, as this year winds down, I trust that you have been pleased with my efforts to grow in wisdom. Thank you for all the lessons along the way.

DECEMBER 30

Read
Proverbs 30

WISE
DETERGENT
Blessed are those
who wash their
robes. They will
be permitted to
enter through the
gates of the city
and eat the fruit
from the tree of life.
Revelation 22:14

One of the most popular and least expensive forms of advertising is the practice of announcing that a product is "new and improved!" Detergents promise to clean cleaner, brighten brighter, and whiten whiter. The enthusiasm of the claims is rarely proven by the results in the laundry.

How appropriate to bring the year to a close with this last blessing from Scripture! The washing to which this proverb refers cannot be improved, and it is ever new. It is described more specifically in Revelation 7:14: "Then he said to me, 'These are the ones who died in the great tribulation. They have washed their robes in the blood of the Lamb and made them white.'" Jesus is God's detergent, the only one capable of washing us clean from our sin. Jesus used three single-word titles to describe how he provides a spiritual cleansing to our lives. "Jesus told him, 'I am the way, the truth, and the life. No one can come to the Father except through me'" (John 14:6). The Way, Truth, Life—now there is a detergent that can wash you whiter than snow!

A WORD FOR TODAY
Eternity will make everything clear.

Today, heavenly Father, allow me to live as someone
trusting fully in the one who washed me of my sin
and gave me a new life—Jesus, my Lord.

DECEMBER 31

The last day of the year marks a turning point in time. It counts down earthly life. It reminds us, like a birthday, that we have accumulated another year of experiences and memories in exchange for 365 precious days that cannot be retrieved. We often use the last day of the year for reflection, resolutions, and reaffirmation of our purposes in life.

The book of Proverbs ends the same way the king ended Ecclesiastes. Solomon's closing thoughts in that book were, "Here now is my final conclusion: Fear God and obey his commands, for this is everyone's duty. God will judge us for everything we do, including every secret thing, whether good or bad" (Ecclesiastes 12:13-14). The woman in today's proverb represents everyone. Like her, we are challenged to fear the Lord.

The fear of the Lord begins and ends the book of Proverbs. It is that state of humble awe in which we remind ourselves every day of God's greatness, grace, and holiness. It is that state of mind in which we passionately pursue wisdom. The outcome will be God's praise.

A WORD FOR TODAY
Character will outimpress beauty.

Today, Lord, thank you again for the taste and texture of wisdom that has been such a healthy spiritual diet for me this year.

Read
Proverbs 31

WHAT
DOES LAST
Charm is deceptive, and beauty does not last; but a woman who fears the LORD will be greatly praised.
Proverbs 31:30

SCRIPTURE INDEX

Keep your
Devotional Time

fresh

with these
popular

For Youth

The One Year® Book of Devotions for Kids

The One Year® Book of Devotions for Boys

The One Year® Book of Devotions for Girls

The One Year® Devos for Teens by Susie Shellenberger

For Family

The One Year® Book of Family Devotions

The One Year® Book of Josh McDowell's Family Devotions

For Couples

The One Year® Book of Devotions for Couples by David and Teresa Ferguson

General

The One Year® Great Songs of Faith

One Year® through the Bible

The One Year® Book of Praying through the Bible by Cheri Fuller

If You Need a
Quick Moment of
refreshment
during Your **Busy Day,**
Try These

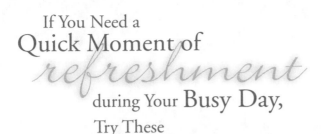

The **ONE YEAR**® MINI Gift Devotionals.

The One Year Mini for Women
helps women connect with God through several
Scripture verses and a devotional thought.
Perfect for use anytime and anywhere between
regular devotion times. Hardcover

The One Year Mini for Men
helps men connect with God anytime,
anywhere, between their regular devotion
times, through Scripture quotations and a
related devotional thought. Hardcover

The One Year Mini for Students offers
students from high school through college
a quick devotional connection with God,
anytime and anywhere. Stay grounded
through the ups and downs of a busy student
lifestyle. Hardcover

The One Year Mini for Moms
provides moms with encouragement and
affirmation for those moments during a
mom's busy day when she needs to be
reminded of the high value of her role.
Hardcover